Praise for *ORGANIZED TO BE THE BEST!* and SUSAN SILVER

Every present and future leader who aspires to excellence should read *Organized to be the Best!* It is truly a hands-on masterpiece."

–Joe Batten
Author of *Tough-Minded Leadership*

Two hours with Susan changed my life. I turned a wasted room into a wonderful working environment. I had thought I should be able to do it myself. Wrong! Her guidance was what I needed.

–Sharon Bloom, Ph.D.
Psychotherapist

I really enjoyed your book. It was inspiring. I was able to read the required chapters, do the exercises and focus on several other interesting topics–in less than two hours!

–Becky Shelton
Vice President and Area Manager, Union Bank

We all felt the opportunities presented by you for organizing our daily life in the office were without equal. Thank you for increasing our office's efficiency, positively! Your sessions were a catalyst in which our entire staff responded so enthusiastically that we are still buzzing over your presentation, discussions and the projects you inspired.

–Robert Aronoff
Controller, Weight Watchers of Los Angeles County

Thanks for a terrific job on your mini seminar at our annual management conference.

–Barbara Klemm
Director of Conferences
Credit Union Executives Society

more...

Susan has a remarkable talent for identifying habits and work conditions which are unnecessary complications and prevent you from becoming more productive. She has a first-rate ability for selecting the tools or ideas that are best-suited to your style and needs. Add to this the fact that she is a delight to work with and you have an invaluable consultant who can make a real difference in your productivity.

–Waltona Manion
The Manion Firm, Public Relations

My newly acquired organizational skills have paid off. A co-worker who shares my work area commented that I seem to always have a neat and orderly desk and miraculously my daily assignments get accomplished. Thank you for your great ideas.

–Ramona Carey

Author **Susan Silver** is a nationally recognized speaker, writer and consultant on organization who directs the Santa Monica, California, firm **Positively Organized!** Featured in *Who's Who in America*, Ms. Silver helps clients enhance personal productivity, improve office management and streamline day-to-day business operations.

Ms. Silver designs and conducts training programs for corporations, professional associations and universities around the country. Her private practice includes individuals who work in a variety of fields and professions.

Ms. Silver blends more than a decade of experience as a management consultant, manager, educator, writer and entrepreneur. A recognized expert on organization, she frequently appears in the media. She is president of the Los Angeles Chapter of NAPO–the National Association of Professional Organizers.

Using organization as an indispensable tool for achievement and teamwork, Ms. Silver shows professionals easy, effective ways to manage time, track projects and activities, use personal computers, organize work space, simplify paperwork, maximize filing and information systems and achieve personal goals.

ORGANIZED to be the BEST!

Winning Solutions To Simplify How You Work

Susan Silver

ADAMS-HALL PUBLISHING
Los Angeles

Adams-Hall Publishing
PO Box 491002
Los Angeles, CA 90049

Library of Congress Cataloging-in-Publication Data

Silver, Susan
Organized to be the best! : winning solutions to simplify how you work.

Bibliography: p.
Includes index.
ISBN 0-944708-15-3
1. Business records–Management–Data processing. 2. Information resources management. I. Title.
HF5736.S54 1989
651.8--dc19 88-38456

Adams-Hall books are available at special, quantity discounts for bulk purchases for sales promotions, premiums, fund-raising or educational use. For details, contact:

Special Sales Director
Adams-Hall Publishing
PO Box 491002
Los Angeles, CA 90049
213/399-7137

Printed in the United States of America
10 9 8 7 6 5 4 3 2 1

First printing 1989
First edition

Striving for the best
will bring you closer to the best.

– Chinese fortune cookie

CONTENTS

ACKNOWLEDGEMENTS xi

TRADEMARKS xiv

INTRODUCTION:
HOW TO BENEFIT FROM THIS BOOK 1

1 HOW TO BE POSITIVELY ORGANIZED! 5
Quick Scan 5
Targeting Challenging, Achievable Goals 5
Designing a Personal System That Works For You 9
Where Are You Now? 10

2 TIME MANAGEMENT:
WHAT YOU REALLY NEED TO KNOW 13
Quick Scan 13
Getting the Most Important Things Done 14
Handling Too Much to Do in Too Little Time 28
The Best Time Management Tools 38
Resource Guide 40

3 MASTERING YOUR DESK AND THE PAPER JUNGLE 47
Quick Scan 47
The Myth of the Messy Desk 48
Clearing a Path 49
Paper and Work Flow Solutions 52
Resource Guide 59

4 A PRICELESS RESOURCE: CAPITALIZING ON UP-TO-DATE FILES 81
Quick Scan 81
How Do Your Files Stack Up? 81
Filing Phobias 82
Creating a System in Five Easy Steps 83
Resource Guide 98

5 POWERFUL COMPUTING: ORGANIZING YOUR IBM PERSONAL COMPUTER FILES 111
Quick Scan 111
Starting at the Root of the Matter 112
Organizing Your Subdirectories 114
It's All in a Name–a Path Name, That is 116
May I See a Menu, Please? 119
DOS is Not a Dirty Word 120
Resource Guide 123

6 MAKING THE MOST OF YOUR MACINTOSH FILES 129
Quick Scan 129
HFS and How to Use It 129
Desktop Management 141
Resource Guide 150

7 THE BEST OF BOTH WORLDS: SPECIAL ORGANIZATION TIPS AND TOOLS FOR THE IBM AND THE MAC 155
Quick Scan 155
The Rewards of Computer File Maintenance 156
Keep It Clean 157
Back It Up! 160
Resource Guide 166

8 DETAILS, DETAILS: GETTING THEM UNDER CONTROL 177
Quick Scan 177
Work and Project Management Shortcuts 178
Top Tools and Systems to Manage Information Resources and Records 213
Resource Guide 225

9 FOR COLLECTORS ONLY: HOW, WHEN AND WHAT TO SAVE 249
Quick Scan 249
Types of Collectors 250
To Save or Not to Save—That is the Question 251
How to Prevent Long-term Buildup 255
Resource Guide 256

10 WORK SPACE BASICS: ENHANCING YOUR PHYSICAL WORKING ENVIRONMENT 269
Quick Scan 269
Maximizing Your Physical Space 270
Furnishings That Fit 280
Your Total Environment 291
Resource Guide 295

11 THE TRAVELING OFFICE: HOW TO TRAVEL SMOOTHLY AND GET THINGS DONE 301
Quick Scan 301
Working on the Road 302
Handling Paperwork on the Road 303
The Traveling Telephone 307
Special Travel Tips 309
Resource Guide 320

12 POSITIVELY ORGANIZED! IN ACTION 327
Quick Scan 327
An Action Orientation 328

ONLY THE BEGINNING: A NOTE FROM THE AUTHOR 333

APPENDIX: RESOURCE GUIDE SUMMARY 335

BIBLIOGRAPHY 339

INDEX 349

ACKNOWLEDGEMENTS

Now I know why Oscar winners thank everyone they've ever known and authors write endless acknowledgements. A book, like a movie, is a monumental accomplishment that is the blending of countless contributions, insights and talents.

And in *my* book, I'm not Organized to be the Best unless I stop a moment and recognize all of you who have given so much to me personally and professionally and have contributed directly or indirectly to the creation of this book.

Let me begin by thanking those who reviewed the manuscript. My deepest appreciation goes to Joe Batten, Lee Gardenswartz, Michael LeBoeuf, Buck Rodgers, Anita Rowe, Becky Shelton and Sanford Sigoloff for making time in their busy schedules to read the manuscript and offer praiseworthy comments.

Thank you Lin Conger, Michael Eusey, Lloyd Pentecost, Nicki Riedel, Dan Shoff and Carol Weiss for sharing your Macintosh expertise. Thank you, additionally, Lin, for doing all the wonderful illustrations in Chapter 6.

Speaking of illustrations, I want to thank all of the office supply firms featured in the book who supplied line art, halftones or photographs. I especially appreciate the following individuals who "went back to the drawing board" to provide custom art for the book: Sunny Banfield and Felice Willat, Day Runner, Inc.; Sharon Schulberg, Law Publications, Inc.; Nancy Valeska-Pennell, Light Impressions; Rich Covyeau, Moore Business Products; Doug Smith and Don Lederach, Safeguard Business Systems; Scott Leonard, Marketing Arts, Inc. (for Smead); and Richard Danielson and Richard Harney, SYCOM.

I'm grateful also to all the organized professionals I've interviewed for articles or in preparation for Positively Organized! seminars, as well as seminar participants who have shared their successes. I'm delighted to include you in this book: Duane Berger, Bill Butler, Derrick Crandall, Greg Jarrells, Kathryn Johnson, Betsy Kovacs, Sharon Lawrence, Coleen Melton, Kathy Meyer-Poppe, Judy Nowak, Jeanne Robertson, Nancy Schlegel, Barbara Suitor, Jim Suitor, Ben Tyler and Mike Welch.

I'm proud to acknowledge fellow members of the National Association of Professional Organizers (NAPO) and other colleagues contributing to the burgeoning profession of "organizing"–in particular, Beverly Clower, C. C. Crawford, Stuart Crump, Stephanie Culp, Paul Edwards, Sarah Edwards, Ronni Eisenberg, Paulette Ensign, Ann Gambrell, Andrew Gross, Barbara Hemphill, Linda Henry, Nadia Holland, Kay Kleifgen, Joyce Klenner, Sharon Kristensen, Susanne McGraham-Paisley, Maxine Ordesky, Toni Pighetti, Mary Rossow, Jill Rothstein, Harriet Schechter, Sunny Schlenger, Jeanne Shorr, Sally Westwood and Stephanie Winston.

Smooth book production was made possible by several very talented pros. My heartfelt thanks to Blair Coburn Randall, my editor at Adams-Hall, who not only believed completely in my book right from the start but has maintained a special caring attention to detail throughout the project. Thank you to Dennis Kugizaki and his staff at Kugizaki Design for the wonderful book cover. June Winson did a fine job on paste-up, especially with the numerous illustrations. Thank you to Chris Shore at Thomson-Shore who patiently answered all my printing questions and to Christopher Meeks for his computer expertise.

Thank you to my writing and publishing contacts, colleagues and gurus from whom I have learned so much: Julie Bennett, Bonnie Beren, Nat Bodian, Gordon Burgett, Cheryl Crooks, Dorothy Elchoness, Monty Elchoness, Peggy Glenn, Jonathan Kirsch, Maggie Kleinman, John Kremer, Jeffrey Lant, Ben Martin, Eileen McDargh, Gary Moselle, Jan Nathan, Polly Pattison, Dan Poynter, Susan Quinn, Marilyn Ross, Tom Ross, Kathryn Leigh Scott, Charlie Winton and Marvin Wolf.

And for those of you who continue to teach me the value of balance, of keeping things in perspective, of remembering the big picture, I thank you for your support and inspiration. To Elie Wiesel, Dennis Prager, Neil Comess-Daniels, Ellen Rabin and the Shostakovsky family, thank you for reminding me of the important work to be done in the world and that organization is a vital tool for that work.

To my dear friends and family, your nurturing support and understanding, especially during this book project, means everything to me. Special thanks to Tim, Kim and Jordan Villeneuve; Ron and Sylvia Richardson; Harry, Minki, Larry, Gail, Amy, Eric, Ron and Beverly Becker; Ilene Doernberg; Diane Engstrom; Bee Epstein; Ed Fine; Marc and Sema Gamson; Tessie, Bill and Kevin Goddard; Larry, Ginny, Shana and Kenny Gotlieb; Sylvia Greer; Stan, Linda, Ilana and John Hoffman; Jon and Carol Karp; Jim Kleckner; Larry Lipsman; Al Macdonald; Elaine and Bernie Mendes; Janice Millar; Anne Miller; Don and Debbie Mink; Harold Oaklander; John O'Connor; Robyn, Larry, Scott and David Paletz; Caroline and Chris Reid; Joan Reighley; Don and Peggy Richardson; Ken Ross; Pat and Dianna Ryan; Estherae Sanford; Howard and Michele Serbin; Mike and Linda Siegel; Betsy, Lisa, Lora and Richard Silver; Steve and Virginia Skolnik; Leo and Elaine Winer Smith; Bill and Stephanie Sarnoff; Bill, Marian, Jeff, Rachel, Adam and Paula Sornoff; Ralph, Marcia, David and Debbie Uri; Marilyn Ziemann; and the Volleyball Group. Most of all, I want to thank Emily and Charles Silver and my parents, Marilyn and Ralph Marks.

No words can express the depth of gratitude and love I have for my husband, Don–who brings out the best in me.

Susan Silver
Santa Monica, California

Trademarks

All terms mentioned in this book that are known or believed to be trademarks or service marks are listed below and/or capitalized in the book. Adams-Hall Publishing cannot attest to the accuracy of this information. Use of a term in this book should not be regarded as affecting the validity of any trademark or service mark.

Add-A-File, Catch'all, Mini Catch'll, Eldon, The Folder, The Holder, Hot Files and Pockets, Hot Rack, Image 1500, Reflection 2000, Stackable CRT Tray, Step-Up Step Rack, Versatilt, 71-72 are registered trademarks of Eldon Office Products.
Agenda is a trademark of Lotus Development Corp.
Apple, Font/DA Mover, HyperCard, Macintosh, MultiFinder, Switcher Construction Kit are registered trademarks of Apple Computer, Inc.
Arrow Klips and Plastiklips are registered trademarks of Baumgarten.
ArtFile is a registered trademark.
Art-Folio, Bankers Boxes, Econo/Stor 40 Diskette Filing Tray, Neat Ideas Active Files, Neat Ideas Folder Files, Neat Ideas Desk Top Sorter, Neat Ideas Folder Holder, Neat Ideas Personal File, Neat Ideas Portable File, Portable Storage Case, Premier Line Mail/Literature Center, Premier Line Visible Folder Files, Roll/Stor Files, Roll/Stor Stands are registered trademarks of Fellowes Manufacturing.
ASAP-10 Call Director is a trademark of Command Communications.
Back-It is a trademark of Gazelle Systems.
Bernoulli Box is a trademark of Iomega Corp.
Biotec is a trademark of BIOTEC SYSTEMS, a division of Hamilton Sorter Co., Inc.
Boorum Prizm Desktop File Organizer, Boorum Wireworks Catalog Rack, Boorum Wireworks FileAll, Boorum Wireworks Sort-R-Rack, Boorum Wireworks Steprack, Oxford, Oxford DecoFile, Oxford DecoFlex, Oxford DecoRack, Oxford File-It Portable File Box, Oxford Tote-File and Pendaflex are registered trademarks of Esselte Pendaflex Corporation.
Business Filevision is a trademark of Marvelin Crop.
Cardwear Hardware is a trademark of Izer International.
CarFinder is a trademark of Design Tech.
CaseGuard is a trademark of Law Publications Inc.
C.A.T. is a trademark of Chang Laboratories, Inc.
Cat-Mac is a trademark of Phoenix Specialties, Inc.
Cellugraf Plastic Signals, Graffco Nu-Vise Metal Signals, Owl Clips and Triumph Clamps are registered trademarks of Labelon.
CMS Software is a trademark of CMS Software Systems.
Code-A-Phone is a trademark.
Color-Life is a trademark of WilsonJones.
Comcor is a trademark of Communications Corner.
Communitech is a trademark of Communitech.
Concurrent DOS is a trademark of Digital Research, Inc.
Congressional Toolkit is a trademark of BJ Toolkit.
Copy II is a trademark of Central Point Software, Inc.
CPA Tickler is a trademark of Front Row Systems.
CPM is a trademark.
Cubit, Disk Optimizer, DoubleDOS and SoftwareCarousel are registered trademarks of SoftLogic Solutions Inc..
Cue Pager is a trademark.
Dac-Easy Base is a trademark of Dac-Easy.
Danish Bookbag is a trademark.
DataCare is a trademark of Ellicott Software Inc.
Day Runner, Cardfiler Plus, Express-it are registered trademarks of Day Runner.

Day-Timers is a trademark of Day-Timers, Inc.
Design-a-Space and Quicksnap Vertical Filing System are registered trademarks of Rubbermaid.
Deskview is a trademark of Quarterdeck Office Systems Inc.
Dictaphone Travel Master LX is a trademark of Dictaphone Corp., a Pitney Bowes Company.
Direct Access is a trademark of Delta Technology International.
Diskette Manager II is a trademark of Lassen Software, Inc.
Disk Express is a trademark of Alsoft Inc.
DiskFit is a trademark of SuperMac Software.
DiskQuick is a trademark of Ideaform, Inc.
Disk Ranger is a trademark of Graham Software Co.
Disk Technician is a trademark of Prime Solutions Inc.
DiskTools Plus is a trademark of Electronic Arts.
Disktop is a trademark of CE Software.
DOS2ools is a trademark of E-X-E Software Systems.
DS Backup + is a trademark of Design Software, Inc.
Eureka! is a trademark of Personal Computer Peripherals Corp.
Executive Scan Card Organizer is a trademark.
Fastback Mac and Fastback Plus are trademarks of Fifth Generations Systems.
FIDO and File Facility (Filefac) are trademarks of International Business Machines Corp.
FileMaker Plus is a trademark of Nashoba Systems, Inc.
File-N-Shuttle is a trademark.
File Pal II is a trademark of Remarkable Products.
Filofax is a trademark of Filofax.
For Comment is a trademark of Broderbund Software, Inc.
FormsFile is a trademark.
FormWorx is a trademark of FormWorx Corp.
Genoa's Galaxy 3260 is a trademark of Genoa Systems Corp.
Gofer is a trademark of Microlytics.
GrandView is a trademark of Symantec Corporation.
Hard Disk Backup is a trademark of FWB Software, Inc.
HFS Backup is a trademark of Personal Computer Peripherals Corp.
HFS Locator Plus is a trademark of PBI Software, Inc.
Hold Everything is a trademark of WILLIAMS-SONOMA.
Homebase is a trademark of Brown Bag Software.
HyperEASY is a trademark of Personal Training Systems.
IBM and IBM PC are registered trademarks of International Business Machines Corporation.
Idealiner is a trademark of Jimmy Mac Software.
IN.SIGHT is a trademark of Pearlsoft Inc.
Instaplan is a trademark of Instaplan Corp.
Intelligent Backup is a trademark of Software Laboratories, Inc.
IZE is a trademark of Persoft, Inc.
KeepTrack Plus is a trademark of The Finot Group.
LIST is a trademark of Vernon D. Buerg.
Little Black Book is a trademark of Cignet Technologies.
Mace Utilities is a trademark of Pace Mace Software.
MacInUse is a trademark of Softview, Inc.
Magic Mirror is a trademark of SoftLogic Solutions.
Magna Chart is a trademark of Magna Visual, Inc.
Market Master is a trademark of Breakthrough Productions.
Maximizer is a trademark of Pinetree Software, Inc.
Maynard's Maynstream 20 is a trademark of Maynard Electronics.
Media-Flex Workstations is a trademark of Acme Visible Records, Inc.

Memofile is a trademark of Memindex.
Memogenda and Zipagenda are registered trademarks of Norwood Products.
Memory Lane is a trademark of Group L Corp.
Metro is a trademark of Lotus Development Corp.
Microsoft Project is a trademark of Microsoft Corp.
MORE is a trademark of Symantec Corporation.
Motorola Spirit is a trademark.
Mountain Computer Drive Cards is a trademark of Mountain Computer, Inc.
Mountain FileSafe Series 7120 is a trademark of Mountain Computer, Inc.
myDiskLabeler is a trademark of Williams & Macias, Inc.
NCR is a trademark of of NCR Corporation.
Nega*Guard System is a trademark.
Norton Commander and Norton Utilities are registered trademarks of Peter Norton Computing, Inc.
The #1 Personal Management System is a trademark of American Leadership Institute.
Overdrive is a trademark of TurboSoft.
Passport is a trademark of Plus Development Corp.
PC-File:db is a trademark of ButtonWare, Inc.
PC Manager is a trademark of Sterling Castle.
PC-MOS is a trademark of The Software Link Inc.
Perma Pak is a trademark of Perma Products.
Personal Resource System is a trademark of Personal Resource Systems, Inc.
PLAN-A-FLEX OFFICE DESIGNER is a trademark of Stanley Tools.
Planner Pad is a trademark of Planner Pads, Inc.
Planning Guide is a trademark.
The Pocket Secretary is a trademark.
Pop-Up DeskSet Plus is a trademark.
Post-it and Scotch are registered trademarks of 3M.
PreCursor is a trademark of The Aldridge Co, Inc.
PrimeTime is a trademark of Wiseware, Inc.
PrintFile is a trademark.
Pro-8 Client Timekeeping System is a trademark of Time Mark Corp.
Project Billing is a trademark of Satori Software.
Q&A is a trademark of Symantec Corporation.
Q-DOSII is a trademark of Gazelle Systems.
QuickDEX is a trademark of Greene, Inc.
QuickKeys and DialogKeys is a trademark of CE Software.
RecordHolderPlus is a trademark of Software Discoveries, Inc.
Redi-Tags is a trademark of Barbara Thomas Enterprises Inc.
Re-Markable is a trademark of Remarkable Products.
Reminder System and Reminder System Plus are registered trademarks of Campbell Services, Inc.
Rolodex is a trademark of Rolodex.
RPMS (Rep Profit Management System) is a trademark of Creative Software Systems, Inc.
Safco and E-Z Stor are registered trademarks of Safco.
SaleMaker is a trademark of Software of the Future.
Sentinel is a trademark.
Sharp Dial Master Pocket Auto Phone Dialer is a trademark.
The Sharper Image is a trademark.
Shoebox is a trademark of Techland Systems, Inc.
Shopkeeper is a trademark of ShopKeeper Software, Inc.
Sidekick, SideKick Plus and Traveling SideKick are registered trademarks of Borland International.

Smart Alarms/Appointment Diary is a trademark of Imagine Software.
SmartNotes is a trademark of Personics Corp.
SmartScrap & The Clipper is a trademark of Solutions International.
Smead, Chan-L-Slide Follow-Up Folder, Flex-I-Vision, Seal & View Label Protectors are registered trademarks of Smead Manufacturing.
SoftBackup is a trademark of Diversified I/O, Inc.
Sonar is a trademark of Virginia Systems Software Services, Inc.
SpaceBase is a trademark of Stadis Corp.
SpinRite is a trademark of Gibson Research Corp.
Sterling Step-Rack is a trademark of Sterling Plastics.
Suitcase is a trademark of Software Supply.
Superproject Plus is a trademark of Computer Associates International, Inc.
Swap is a trademark of Wiley Professional Software.
Sysgen QIC-File is a trademark of Sysgen, Inc.
Take Two is a trademark of United Software Security, Inc.
Tecmar QIC-60H and Tecmar QT-Mac40 are trademarks of Tecmar, Inc.
TeleMagic is a trademark of RemoteControl.
That Reminds Me is a trademark of SYCOM, Inc.
TIC-LA-DEX is a trademark of Tic-La-Dex Business Systems.
Time Line is a trademark of Breakthrough Software.
Time Manager is a trademark.
Timeslips III is a trademark of North Edge Software Corporation.
Tornado is a trademark of Micro Logic Corp.
ViewPoint is a trademark of Computer Aided Management.
Windows 386 is a trademark of Microsoft Corp.
Word Guide is a trademark.
The WorkManager System is a trademark of MicroComputer Accessories, Inc.
WordPerfect is a trademark of WordPerfect Corp.
XTreePro is a trademark of Executive Systems.
Zoo Keeper is a trademark of Polaris Software.
ZyINDEX Professional is a trademark of ZyLAB Corp.

INTRODUCTION: HOW TO BENEFIT FROM THIS BOOK

Nearly everyone says, "Boy, could I use *you!*" when they hear of my business called Positively Organized!

Most people will go on to joke about the sorry state of their desk and office and how they've simply got to get more organized.

But like many people, you, too, may have kidded yourself into thinking all you need to get organized are some good intentions, a little willpower and a free Saturday. All common sense, right? But if all it took were common sense, it would be common practice.

The secret to organizing your desk, your work space and yourself is much more than common sense. It's *learning and applying specific skills, systems and shortcuts.*

This book is the answer for you if you're often:

- swamped with paperwork
- struggling with too many priorities
- working in a chaotic or cluttered environment
- projecting a less than successful, competent, professional image to your clientele, your colleagues or yourself.

THE POSITIVELY ORGANIZED! PROGRAM FOR ACTION

This book is different from all others because it is *interactive.* This book is as close as possible to having a personal consultation with me right now. Together we will use the Positively Organized! Program for Action. Tried and tested over the years, this is a proven program designed for professionals who already possess strong determination and clear goals. The Positively Organized! Program recognizes the level of success you have already achieved and keeps on building and refining.

WE'RE A TEAM

In the Positively Organized! Program, you are the player and I am the coach. As a coach I require your full attention and commitment and I, in turn, will help you see what could be working better for you. I will point out the best strategies around so that you won't have to waste your precious time and energy reinventing the organization wheel.

You're not alone if you're always putting organization on the back burner. ("Someday, when I have some time, I'll clean out these drawers.") The problem is "someday never comes" and paper builds and builds until you've created a mountain out of a molehill.

ACHIEVE YOUR GOALS

This book will help you do what you've always wanted to do. You'll reduce your stress, find extra hours in the day and achieve more of your goals. You'll accelerate your performance, productivity and your own personal sense of achievement.

You'll take what you *read* and translate it into *action.* You'll create a simple plan of action for tackling your desk, work surfaces, drawers (never again will you have to use them to clear your desk when you're expecting visitors!), paperwork, projects, filing cabinet and storage areas.

You'll also discover handy desk accessories and helpful office products, including many for your personal computer.

And you'll learn that just as important as having the right equipment and tools is having the right *habits* to use the tools. You'll create your *own* personal organization system--because there's *no one right way to get organized.* We're all different and this book recognizes and appreciates those differences.

HOW THIS BOOK IS DESIGNED TO MAXIMIZE YOUR TIME

This book is easy to use and will save you time because it has been specially designed for you, the busy professional. Special features make this book instantly accessible and usable. There is a complete table of contents and a useful index for easy reference. Also there are brief "Quick Scan" summaries at the beginning of each chapter, distinct subheads in the chapters to help you read more quickly and plentiful resource guides at the end of each chapter.

And what's more, **you don't have to read the whole book!** Outside of Chapters 1, 2 and 12 (which are "required reading"), read only those chapters that apply to you.

The "Quick Survey" in Chapter 1 will let you see immediately where to fine tune and where to do a complete overhaul. After the survey, go to the table of contents and mark those chapters that relate most directly to the items you marked that need improvement. The "Quick Scan" summary at the beginning of a chapter will help confirm whether you should read the chapter. Whichever chapters you select, *be sure to read Chapter 12* to actually put the ideas from this book into action.

All you need right now is a pen or pencil for marking key points and the eagerness to get started. Getting started, as you probably know, is the hardest part. On your mark, get set, get organized!

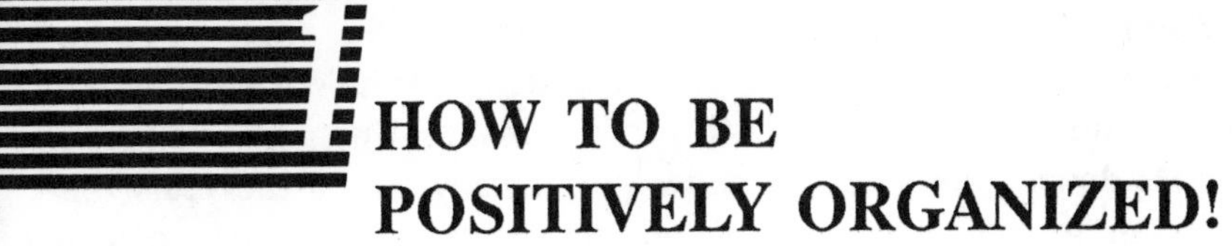

1 HOW TO BE POSITIVELY ORGANIZED!

Quick Scan: This chapter is "required reading" because it helps pinpoint where you are now in terms of your goals and where you are going. You'll see how to begin designing your own personal organizational system--one that's right for you. Through the Quick Survey, you'll assess your organizational strengths and weaknesses.

Yogi Berra once said, "If you don't know where you're going, you'll end up some place else."

This is the first secret of being organized--Positively Organized! All the organizational tools and techniques in the world and this book are useless if you don't know where you're headed, that is, what you want to accomplish.

TARGETING CHALLENGING, ACHIEVABLE GOALS

Start with an up-to-date list of goals. Not having this list is like taking a trip without a map. Goals give you focus, purpose and direction. Goals help you *attain* something you don't have or *maintain* something you do. Effective goals are simple, clear-cut and direct. They should reflect both professional and personal values.

Write down your goals on paper periodically during the year (this means more than once!). Make appointments with yourself to plan your goals on paper. Twice a year may be sufficient–in January and then again in July. Others (Lee Iacocca included) prefer quarterly goals.

THE THREE BIG QUESTIONS

For each goal, answer these three questions: *What? Why? and How*?

WHAT?

Begin by listing "what" you want to attain or maintain and the extent or degree of accomplishment. In describing your goal, ask yourself what you want to **do**, **be** or **have**. Be as specific as you can. Write your goal in the present tense, whether or not it is something in the future or is a part of your life right now. Here are three "do, be, have" examples of goals:

> Do: I exercise three times a week; I play volleyball on Sunday, tennis on Tuesday and racquetball on Thursday.
>
> Be: I am a peaceful person who greets problems as challenges and opportunities.
>
> Have: I have a meaningful relationship with a significant other who shares my passion for life and my value system.

WHY?

Answer "why" by listing any benefits and results you expect from accomplishing your goal. The "why" should also state the *value* this goal has for you in your life as a whole. If you choose goals that conflict with your life values, you'll be setting yourself up for sabotage and failure. Your goals need to be in harmony with your most important life values. For example, let's take one of the previous examples of goals, the "do" goal. Here are some benefits or results to be derived:

feeling fit
increased energy and vitality
to get those endorphins flowing
less stress
feeling more relaxed (exercise is one of the four natural tranquilizers–laughter, music and sex being the other three)
to have fun
to socialize
to balance a hectic lifestyle

HOW?

Answer "how" by listing all the specific ways you plan to achieve your goal–any strategies, action steps or tasks, in addition to the amount of time required (per day, week, month or year). Assigning deadlines–or "lifelines" as one person I know prefers to call them–will make your "hows" much more specific and helpful. Some specific "hows" for the "do" goal could include:

calling to make reservations
confirming tennis and racquetball times with partner
writing down activities and times in a calendar
putting out sports clothes the night before by the door

Now take five to ten minutes to complete the Goals Work Sheet in Figure 1-1 to quickly jot down three or more of your goals, including the "what," the "why" and the "how" for each one.

Figure 1-1. GOALS WORK SHEET

Date:__________

WHAT is your goal?	WHY do you want this goal?	HOW will you proceed?

THE POWER OF THE PEN

Don't be afraid you won't accomplish your goals. First of all, your chances of accomplishment are greater when you write them down. Putting your goals in writing helps affirm your *commitment.* It makes your goals more real. It also helps plant them into your subconscious. One professional woman I know writes down her goals each year in January, seals them in an envelope, opens the envelope at the end of the year and discovers she has accomplished almost all of them.

AIM HIGH

Second, who says you have to accomplish them all? There's a saying that goes like this, "If you accomplish everything you planned, then you haven't planned well enough." You *should* plan a little more than you may actually do; practice aiming high because you'll probably accomplish more than if you lower your expectations and make them "realistic." There's an Indian parable that explains why. The parable asks, "Is it not better to aim for the moon and hit an eagle than to aim for an eagle and hit a rock?"

TECHNIQUES TO ENSURE SUCCESS

So aim high and use these eight ways to increase your chances of reaching your goals:

1. Put your goals in writing.
2. Take some action on your goals every day or at least every week.
3. Share them with one other person (and listen to theirs). But only share them with other people who also set goals of their own and reach them. Those are the kind of people who'll be most supportive.
4. Read them daily before you do your planning and before you go to sleep.

5. Every week write down and accomplish smaller goals that relate to your long-term goals. List these weekly goals where you will see them every day.
6. Review and revise your goals at least twice a year, always making sure they reflect your deepest values.
7. Let them *inspire* not haunt you.
8. Include both professional and *personal* goals to increase the balance of your life. Make sure, too, that your goals harmonize with those of your career, position or company–if they don't, you could experience some conflict in your life.

DESIGNING A PERSONAL SYSTEM THAT WORKS FOR YOU

Once you've isolated your goals, you're ready to focus on developing your own **personal organization system**–the tools and habits to help you achieve your goals.

What we're talking about is a flexible set of tools and work habits for managing three essential resources:

1. **Time**–planning, scheduling, recording, completing and tracking current and future meetings, appointments, commitments, activities, projects and goals
2. **Information**–developing productive paperwork and work flow procedures; keeping manual and computerized information accessible and up-to-date
3. **Space**–creating a functional and pleasing physical working environment both in the office and on the road.

In his best-selling book, *What They Don't Teach You at Harvard Business School*, Mark McCormack devotes a whole chapter to organization and writes, "I have never met a successful person in business who didn't operate from some personal organizational system." The more successful you become and the busier your schedule, the more you need to consciously *choose and refine* the tools and habits in your personal organization system.

For many, these tools and habits have evolved quite by chance over the years. This book will help you make choices about the best organizational solutions for you and how to *apply* them to your situation.

Your own style and degree of organization will depend on a number of factors–your level of activity, whether you have any support staff, if you deal face to face with the public and how you like to work. It's up to you just how much organization you need.

Remember that *Positively Organized!* does not mean being *compulsively* or *perfectly organized.* **Stay only as organized as you need to be.**

WHERE ARE YOU NOW?

As a consultant, I usually begin by giving a survey to my clients. Here's yours in Figure 1-2.

Figure 1-2. QUICK SURVEY
Read and react quickly to each of the following items and check off the appropriate letter that describes how effectively the item works for you–**O** for Outstanding, **S** for Satisfactory or **N** for Needs Improvement. If an item is not applicable to you, do not respond.

	O	S	N
1. Your system for planning, prioritizing and accomplishing work and achieving your goals. [Chapters 2, 8]			
2. Your paperwork flow. [Chapters 2, 3, 4, 8, 9, 10]			
3. Dealing with interruptions. [Chapter 2]			
4. Your ability to easily access needed information. [Chapters 2-10]			
5. Your telephone time. [Chapters 2, 8]			
6. Letting go of papers and possessions. [Chapters 3, 4, 9]			
7. Your follow-ups. [Chapters 2, 8, 9]			
8. Your reading load. [Chapter 2]			
9. Your deskside filing system. [Chapters 3, 4]			
10. Your desk or table top(s). [Chapters 2, 3, 8, 9, 10]			
11. Your personal computer organization. [Chapters 5-7]			
12. Making habit changes in how you do things. [Chapter 12]			
13. Your attention to quality and/or service. [Chapters 2, 4, 8]			
14. The layout and location of your work space. [Chapter 10]			
15. Your drawers, shelves, bookcases. [Chapters 9, 10]			
16. Your furniture and equipment. [Chapter 10]			
17. Your accessibility to supplies. [Chapter 10]			
18. Your portable, on-the-go, traveling office. [Chapter 2, 11]			

HOW TO SELECT THE MOST IMPORTANT AREAS TO YOU

Rate the list of items in the Quick Survey to help pinpoint areas to improve. Look at the "N's" you've checked. Decide which three N's are most important to you right now. Star these three items. You'll be referring to them as you move through the book.

Take a moment now to reflect on what it would mean to you, your business, your career and your life to improve your top three starred items. Think about the *benefits* that you would experience. Take 60 seconds to jot down as many benefits that come to mind:

Put a star by the most important one.

BENEFITS ARE THE KEY

Just why is visualizing and listing benefits so crucial? A benefit is the reason why you do something. It's the motivation behind an action or activity and it should be connected to at least one of your major goals. You'll need a *compelling* benefit to justify spending the time and effort required to organize anything. *If there's no real payoff to getting more organized, you won't.*

Organization gets put on the back burner because it doesn't *appear* to be a top priority. Your benefit has to be strong enough to make organization a top priority and to counteract all the reasons and excuses that justify the "back burner syndrome."

Make organization a top priority. Take it off the back burner and make time for it *every day.* Get into the organization habit. It will give you the professional edge.

Great. You've got that sizzling benefit. Now what? First, keep that benefit uppermost in your mind. Second, keep reminding yourself about the benefit while you're reading this book and when you're applying what you read. You're very much like athletes in training who need to remind themselves constantly about what they want to achieve. You need to do the same.

Review your survey. Find your starred items and notice the chapter references. See which chapter numbers come up most often. Now go to the table of contents and select the most important chapters for you to read. Keep in mind, too, that you should make Chapter 2 and Chapter 12 part of your "required reading" no matter which "elective" chapters you choose to read.

And, remember, your goal isn't to be organized. It's to be organized to be the best! That means the best *you* can be.

2 TIME MANAGEMENT: WHAT YOU REALLY NEED TO KNOW

Quick Scan: The second of three "required reading" chapters, this one gives you the time management essentials every pro needs to know.

Every problem with organization is in some way a time management problem. Almost always, time constraints (those of your own as well as those of others) prevent you from handling the necessary organizational tasks in your work. But when you don't make time to do those tasks, everything usually ends up taking much longer to do and produces more stress in the process.

Time management is making choices--choices that balance the short-term and long-term, urgent and less urgent, internal and external. It's controlling what you can, when you can.

Time management is the great simplifier, putting things in focus and perspective. Time management is an awareness of time coupled with the ability to choose and control purposeful activities related to your goals.

Time management is also using the right tools and habits to improve *how* you do something. Effective time management tools and habits can improve the quality and quantity of your work, help you make better decisions and increase your performance.

In my work as an organizer, I find there are two major time management challenges that keep coming up for clients: first, getting the most important things done and second, having too much to do and too little time to do it. You'll see in this chapter how to meet these challenges in your life.

GETTING THE MOST IMPORTANT THINGS DONE

Do you often have days when it feels as if you have accomplished nothing? If so, you probably aren't doing the most important tasks and activities.

Have you considered what "most important" means? Is it something that has an urgent deadline? Is it something your boss wants? Is it something *you* want that relates to one of your goals?

It can mean all of these. But watch out if you're only making *other people's demands* the most important things you do. To be the best, make time every day to accomplish something that *you* consider important.

LEARNING THE ABCS

Learn to differentiate, also, between three kinds of priorities. Edward Bliss, in his wonderful book *Getting Things Done*, calls them "A," "B" and "C" priorities. He says A priorities are "important and urgent," as in crisis management. B priorities are "important but not urgent," as in long-term goals. You should try to spend most of your time on A's and B's. C priorities are "urgent but not important." Try to spend as little time on C's as possible.

You're probably pretty good at handling A's but how many B's do you work on each day? **Make time every day to work on your important-but-not-urgent B priorities and goals.** A good source for these priorities are the goals you listed on your Goals Work Sheet in Chapter 1. Without clear-cut goals, your time management decisions will be made in a vacuum or else will be all externally determined by outside circumstances and people. You won't be in charge. So take charge and start choosing activities that contribute to your long-term goals.

SEEING THE WHOLE PICTURE: WHAT YOU SEE IS WHAT YOU GET....ACCOMPLISHED

Get a clear picture of what you want to accomplish and when. Stay aware of all important activities, tasks, deadlines and follow-ups by grouping and seeing all major commitments easily, at a glance. But I don't mean rummaging through countless reminder notes to yourself or piles of papers on your desk. Don't get lost in the shuffle–especially the paper shuffle.

Your personal organization system should contain at least one, *concise*, visual source of *all* key ongoing activities and tasks. Seeing a listing or grouping of your activities and tasks on a regular basis will help you accomplish them.

Some people use their calendar. But a calendar isn't designed to show everything you want to do. That's the job for a **master list**.

MAKING YOUR MASTER LIST WORK FOR YOU

A master list is used to track activities that occur over a period of time, from one week to several months. Your master list serves two functions. First, it gives you an overview and some perspective. Second, you can use it to select items to put on your daily list.

To make your master list more effective, categorize and prioritize it. Some people simply flag the most important items with a red star. You may want to combine a red star with a start date or a due date.

Others prefer to have separate lists. Some of my clients create two lists, one for personal and another for professional. Some create a separate list for each project, case or type of work. Usually the fewer lists the better, but the trick is to remember to *use* them. The more lists you have, the easier it is to forget to use one of them.

Whenever possible, put your master list on *one* sheet of paper. See Figure 2-1 for an example of a simple master list in chart form that groups activities by type and priority. List your activities on the chart in pencil (to write really small and get more items on a page, use a mechanical lead pencil with 0.5mm lead). Writing in pencil lets you erase and rewrite items when your priorities change. Remember to include some kind of deadline or time frame because almost nothing gets done without one. If you carry an organizer, hole punch your list and file it under "M" for "Master List"; that way you'll always have it with you.

	ACTION	CALLS	CORRESP.
A	1. Expense report w/10-18 2. Market summary w/10-16 3. Presentation for sr. mgmt. 10-19 4. ____ 5. ____	1. Joe 293-1121 10-13 2. Chris 10-17 3. ____ 4. ____	1. Budget memo to staff w/ 10-16 2. ____ 3. ____
B	1. Annual sales mtg.—theme, location, etc. 2. Job search for temporary office mgr. going on leave 3. Set aside time to read trade journals—1 hour per week 4. ____ 5. ____ 6. ____ 7. ____ 8. ____	1. ____ 2. ____ 3. ____ 4. ____	1. ____ 2. ____ 3. ____ 4. ____ 5. ____
P	1. Paint bathroom 2. Plan surprise b/d party 3. Community dinner for homeless	1. Make plans for weekend—call friends	1. Thank you—Aunt Louise for b/d present 2. B/d card to Mom 3. ____ 4. ____ 5. ____

Figure 2-1 This master list chart groups three main types of activities in the vertical columns-"Action" or project items, "Calls" and "Correspondence." The horizontal columns group activities into "A," "B" and "P" (for Personal) priorities.

MASTER LISTS AND OTHER WHOLE PICTURE PLANNING TOOLS YOU CAN PURCHASE

Many commercial time management systems, planners and organizers provide their own master list sections or special planning forms. **Day-Timers** come with "To Be Done" sections for each month (see Figure 2-2). This kind of master list is helpful if you like to group activities by the month. If most of your items extend beyond a month, however, you may find yourself having to spend time transferring items to the next month's "To Be Done" page.

You may prefer **Personal Resource Systems**' open-ended time frame "Items to Do" form where you list and prioritize future to-do's on the front and any notes about particular items on the back. In Figure 2-3 you have a concise list that isn't cluttered with any extraneous written notes or reminders.

If you work on projects with many detailed steps, use a **project sheet** or **project planner** in addition to or instead of a master list. Make a simple list for each project, or buy project planning forms that are commercially prepared (see Caddylak Systems, Day-Timers, Day Runner and Personal Resource Systems listed in the chapter resource guide). Figure 2-4 shows one project form by Caddylak Systems and Figure 2-5 shows two by Day-Timers. See also Chapter 8 for some other examples of project forms.

If you work with others on joint projects, you may prefer large **wall charts** or **visual control boards** that display activities or specific project tasks for many people to see at one time. Different varieties include "write-on-wipe-off" boards and magnetic boards with movable strips and cards. If portability is not a factor, these boards can be just the thing. Check office supply stores and catalogs or order directly from Caddylak, Magna Chart, Abbot Office Systems or Remarkable listed in the chapter resource guide. Also see Figure 2-6 for an example of a Re-Markable board.

Memogenda is a thin, spiral bound book that is a great combination master list and project planner. You can keep an up-to-date listing of all the things you have to do in one convenient, compact, lightweight source. Particularly useful if you travel, the Memogenda (shown in Figure 2-7) is an indispensable planning tool for professional speaker **Jeanne Robertson** who is on the road much of the time.

No matter which method or product you choose, get in the habit of seeing the "whole picture," so you can operate from the total perspective, instead of by piecemeal. In this way you can spot the most important tasks without overlooking anything. Before going on, write down which sources you currently check to see your "whole picture":

Now list the sources you'd like to start using:

P AND P–YOUR BREAD AND BUTTER

Once you have the whole picture, you're ready to dig into the bread and butter of time management–daily and weekly **planning and prioritizing.**

Why take the *time* to plan and prioritize? Research indicates that for every hour of planning, you save three or four hours. Effective "P and P" will also help you get the most important things done each day and week.

Here are seven ways to maximize your P and P:

1. **Put it in writing.** Plan and prioritize on paper (or computer) where you can *see* what you need to accomplish and when. Write down your daily or weekly to-do list.
2. **Plan tomorrow, today.** Take five or ten minutes today to make up tomorrow's to-do list so you can start tomorrow fresh. (If you're an early riser, set aside some quiet time at home or at work to plan before the day really gets going.)
3. **Revise your plan–stay flexible!** Check today's list several times throughout the day and if necessary, rearrange, postpone and yes, even *procrastinate on purpose.* "Planned procrastination"–consciously choosing to put off–is what prioritizing is all about.
4. **Make at least one, screened-time appointment with yourself each day.** Give yourself at least one hour of "screened, prime time" every day to work on top priority work. "Screened time" is uninterrupted time and "prime time" is the time of the day when you're most effective. You can screen your time by doing any of the following: coming in an hour early, staying an hour later, having your calls screened by a secretary or colleague (and offering to do the same for them), working in another location (at home or a quiet, inaccessible office), closing your door, turning on your answering machine (or activating your voice mail system) and writing in a one-hour appointment with yourself on your calendar.
5. **Consolidate activities.** If you're tired of making long, laundry lists of unrelated to-do's, then shorten your lists and group like

items together. Keep scheduled appointments together. Try grouping activities by category (such as "calls" and "correspondence"). Or use priority groupings where you first list your "A" priorities–limit the number to three or four–and then your "B" priorities. As for C priorities, according to author Edward Bliss, they *seem* to be urgent but actually are not important–so guard against listing or doing them.

6. **Make time every day to work on B priorities.** These are the priorities that most closely tie in with your goals. But most people tend to put B's on the back burner, selecting only the more pressing, fire-fighting A priorities.
7. **Write down several key goals, activities or projects for the week.** Select no more than four and write them someplace where you'll see them every day as you do your daily planning.

REFINING YOUR DAILY TO-DO LIST

Use these planning and prioritizing techniques to refine your daily to-do list. But remember your to-do list is a guide. Use common sense. If something comes up during the day that bumps another item in importance, so be it. Write in pencil so you can easily erase and move items on your list.

Weigh the value of doing an item at a particular point in time. For example, it may be better to call Joe Blow at 1:00 p.m. today, even though Joe is only a "B" priority, because you're sure to reach him at 1:00; otherwise you'll be playing telephone tag with him for the next two weeks–which would be a major time waster.

A good to-do list should have two basic parts–a place for non-scheduled activities and a place for your scheduled activities. Non-scheduled activities are items on your to-do list that aren't scheduled to be done at any particular time of the day. Scheduled activities include appointments as well as blocks of time you set aside to do specific types of work–e.g., projects, paperwork and planning.

Choose forms in stationery stores and catalogs that provide these two important sections. You can buy these commercial to-do list forms separately or as part of a time management system or organizer. Figure 2-8 shows an example of Day Runner's daily planning form and Figure 2-9 shows the Personal Resource System two-page-per-day planning forms.

Figure 2-2. This handy "To Be Done" section is on the back of each tabbed monthly calendar page that comes with the loose-leaf style Day-Timers. For the front, see the next page. (Illustrations courtesy of Day-Timers, Inc., Allentown, PA 18195-1551)

1989			NOVEMBER			1989
SUN.	**MON.**	**TUES.**	**WED.**	**THURS.**	**FRI.**	**SAT.**
A.M. NOON P.M. EVE.			1	2	3	4
A.M. NOON P.M. 5 EVE.	6	7	8	9	10	11 VETERANS DAY (USA) REMEMBRANCE DAY (CANADA)
A.M. NOON P.M. 12 EVE.	13	14	15	16	17	18
A.M. NOON P.M. 19 EVE.	20	21	22	23 THANKSGIVING (USA)	24	25
A.M. NOON P.M. 26 EVE.	27	28	29	30		

NOV.

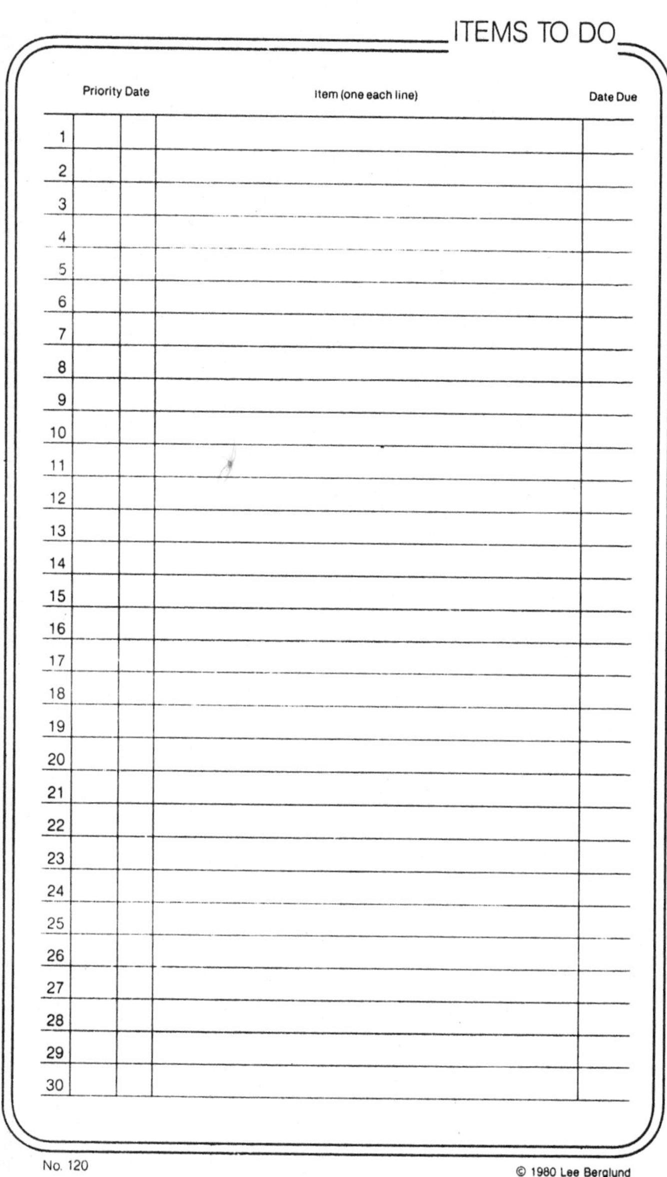

ITEMS TO DO

	Priority	Date	Item (one each line)	Date Due
1				
2				
3				
4				
5				
6				
7				
8				
9				
10				
11				
12				
13				
14				
15				
16				
17				
18				
19				
20				
21				
22				
23				
24				
25				
26				
27				
28				
29				
30				

No. 120

© 1980 Lee Berglund

Figure 2-3. The Personal Resource System Items To Do form lets you list one item per line and has you put any notes about a particular item number on the back, keeping the notes convenient but not cluttered.

DAILY/WEEKLY

PROJECT PLANNER WEEK ENDING

FROM LAST WEEK

PRIORITIES FOR WEEK

PROJECT/ACTIVITY	✓	PROJECT/ACTIVITY	✓

MONDAY ✓

TUESDAY ✓

WEDNESDAY ✓

THURSDAY ✓

FRIDAY ✓

SATURDAY/SUNDAY ✓

Figure 2-4. Caddylak Systems' Project Planner form (number AYX-3235) lets you block out projects for each day of the week.

PROJECT DESCRIPTION

Project # ________ Project Title ____________________
Description ____________________

Project # ________ Project Title ____________________
Description ____________________

Project # ________ Project Title ____________________
Description ____________________

Project # ________ Project Title ____________________
Description ____________________

Project # ________ Project Title ____________________
Description ____________________

Project # ________ Project Title ____________________
Description ____________________

Figure 2-5. Here are two project forms by Day-Timers. The form above (number 90689) gives you an overview summary of all ongoing projects. The form to the right (number 90671) lets you take a project and plan out the necessary tasks and steps. (Illustrations courtesy of Day-Timers, Inc., Allentown, PA 18195-1551)

1. PROJECT NAME ______________________ No. ______

2. ASSIGNED TO ______________ 3. RESPONSIBILITY ______________

4. COMPLETION ______________ 5. REVIEW DATES ______________ 2. 3.

BACKGROUND

PURPOSE—RESULTS TO BE ACCOMPLISHED

DETAILS

DAY-TIMERS RE-ORDER No 90671 — Printed in USA

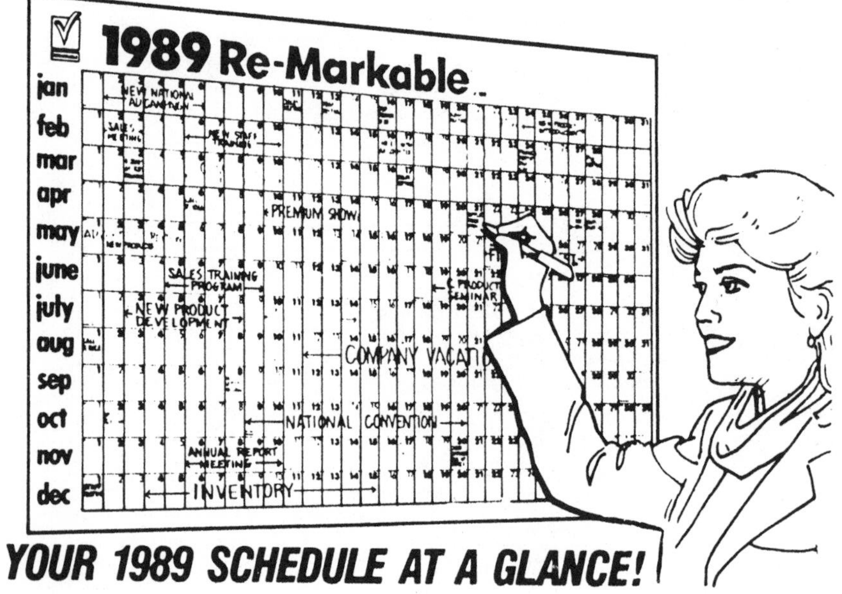

Figure 2-6. This write-on-wipe-off board by Re-Markable charts out a yearly schedule of activities.

It's important to see both your scheduled and non-scheduled activities at the same time and have them next to one another. Whenever possible or feasible, assign your non-scheduled tasks into specific time slots. When you set time aside to accomplish a task, you're more likely to do it than if it's just part of a list of to-do items. If you've set aside time to do tasks and you have trouble gauging time, use an electronic countdown timer from Radio Shack to help you stick to your schedule, whenever possible.

Parkinson's Law says that work expands to fill the time available. Sometimes the opposite is also true: work contracts to fill the time available; it's amazing how much you can get done when you have to. Of course, it's also been observed that things almost always take longer than you think they will. The lack of basic time awareness is a major culprit when it comes to scheduling problems. If you practice setting your own deadlines and time frames, and sticking to them, however, you will soon accomplish so much more.

MEMOGENDA. Typical Entries

X - Completed T - Transferred O - Abandoned

	REF	ITEM—ONE LINE TO EACH	DUE	X T O	DATE
1	P42	attorney appt 2 pm	2-16		
2		Bank Statement		X	2-12
3		Third Quarter Adv. Plans			
4		Production Meeting 2 pm	2-18		
5		Check Sales Policies *Put off a few days*		T	P28
6	LG	Dividend Meeting 10 AM	2:20		
7		Trip Expenses		X	2-10
8	CGB	Costs on Item A62 *Referred to department head.*			
9		Birthday Jim Smith *Taken care of.*	2-16	X	2-12
10	FK	How many replacements			
11		anniversary wife	3-6		
12	LC	J. P. Market 416-6241 *More information on left page.*		X	2-10
13	P46	Long term plan *Check page-46 every few days.*		T	P26
14	P42	Development notes *Special sheet.*		T	P30
15		See Marfant plant	2-20		
16	RTL	Inventory Equipment	6-30		

Figure 2-7. Here is a half page from the Memogenda system listing typical tasks and activities to remember.

If you get tired of transferring today's uncompleted to-do's to the next day's list, consider using a two-page-per-week format. You'll have a little less space to write, but you won't have to keep rewriting to-do's. You can also see your entire week, including any items that are incomplete. Consider the Day-Timers pages shown in Figure 2-10.

DISCIPLINE, DEDICATION AND DESIRE IN YOUR DAILY ROUTINE

To get the most important things done each day, set up a routine that includes not only planning and prioritizing and a to-do list but also a *commitment to yourself backed up by a daily dose of discipline.*

Build a specific time slot into your schedule every day to work on top priorities. For example, many professional writers are known to set aside certain hours every day to write.

No matter what else happens, keeping that commitment to yourself will make you feel good about the day and your accomplishments. Nothing beats out single-mindedness of purpose when it comes to getting the most important things done.

What we're talking about is real dedication to your most important priorities. **Brian Tracy** in his superb tape program, *The Psychology of Achievement,* says to ask yourself continually, **"What's the most valuable use of my time right now?"**

And take time to acknowledge your accomplishments each day. Pat yourself on the back. This is a good way to spark your desire, which in turn will fuel your dedication and discipline.

If this chapter so far seems a bit overwhelming or too structured, go back over this section and select just one or two new ideas you could implement in the next 24 hours. Just making some small time management changes can make a big difference. Also remember, I'm not suggesting you plan every minute of every day. Plan what you can, leaving enough time and flexibility in your schedule for the unexpected. (If it's *all* unexpected, good luck!)

HANDLING TOO MUCH TO DO IN TOO LITTLE TIME

Rarely, if ever, do people I meet have the luxury of working at a leisurely pace. There are always countless deadlines, shifting priorities, which all add up to mounting pressure.

The issue is not how much you have to do but rather how much you have to do that is really *important.* Once you've sorted out the important from the less important, you're ready to see if you have enough time. Unless you're well organized, however, you can't tell for sure because everything's all mixed up. So the first step is to sort work into categories and priorities. Then take a good hard look at *how* you work. Now see if there are better ways for you to get things done.

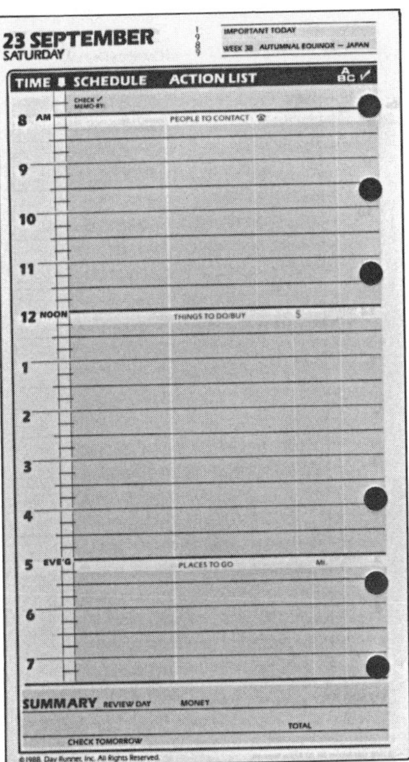

23 SEPTEMBER
SATURDAY
1989
IMPORTANT TODAY
WEEK 38 AUTUMNAL EQUINOX – JAPAN

TIME SCHEDULE ACTION LIST

8 AM
PEOPLE TO CONTACT
9
10
11
12 NOON
THINGS TO DO/BUY $
1
2
3
4
5 EVE'G
PLACES TO GO MI
6
7

SUMMARY REVIEW DAY MONEY
TOTAL
CHECK TOMORROW

©1988 Day Runner, Inc. All Rights Reserved.

Figure 2-8. Day Runner's daily planning form comes dated as shown here or undated and includes space for both your "schedule" and "action list."

The most common complaint I hear is, "There are too many interruptions." The main question to ask yourself is, "How many of these interruptions can I control, minimize or influence in some way?"

Take the telephone. You don't have to be at its beck and call, unless, of course, you're a customer service representative or a receptionist in which case telephone interruptions *are* your business. Yet even in these telephone intensive situations you can learn to maximize your telephone time so that you have more control.

SCHEDULE YOUR DAY

Today's Actions Determine Tomorrow's Results

- ☐ Review Goals
- ☐ Transfer Appointments
- ☐ Select Project Items
- ☐ Select Items To Do
- ☐ Review Other
- ☐ Prioritize Daily Activities
- ☐ Visualize Day's Results
- ☐ Review Finances

THIS WEEK'S GOAL

SCHEDULE

	3:00
	3:
8:00	4:00
8:	4:
9:00	5:00
9:	5:
10:00	6:00
10:	6:
11:00	7:00
11:	7:
12:00	8:00
12:	8:
1:00	
1:	
2:00	
2:	

COMPLETE THE DAY

- ☐ Identify Any Incomplete Items And Transfer
- ☐ Acknowledge Results Produced Today
- ☐ Schedule Tomorrow

TODAY'S NOTES

No 160

Figure 2-9. The Personal Resource System daily planning forms include sections that relate directly to goals, projects and results.

DAILY ACTIVITIES

Day/Date

THOUGHT FOR THE DAY

TODAY'S PRIORITY

DO

CALL

No. 160

OCTOBER 1989						
S	M	T	W	T	F	S
1	2	3	4	5	6	7
8	9	10	11	12	13	14
15	16	17	18	19	20	21
22	23	24	25	26	27	28
29	30	31				

NOVEMBER 1989						
S	M	T	W	T	F	S
			1	2	3	4
5	6	7	8	9	10	11
12	13	14	15	16	17	18
19	20	21	22	23	24	25
26	27	28	29	30		

DECEMBER 1989						
S	M	T	W	T	F	S
31					1	2
3	4	5	6	7	8	9
10	11	12	13	14	15	16
17	18	19	20	21	22	23
24	25	26	27	28	29	30

MONDAY • NOVEMBER 27, 1989 331st Day, 34 Days Left • 48th Week

ITEM NO.	TO BE DONE TODAY (NUMBER EACH ITEM)	APPOINTMENTS, SCHEDULED EVENTS	HOURS	DIARY, SERVICES PERFORMED, EXPENSES	$/TIME
			8 (0800)		
			9 (0900)		
			10 (1000)		
			11 (1100)		
			12 (1200)		
			1 (1300)		
			2 (1400)		
			3 (1500)		
			4 (1600)		
			5 (1700)		

TUESDAY • NOVEMBER 28, 1989 332nd Day, 33 Days Left

			HOURS		
			8 (0800)		
			9 (0900)		
			10 (1000)		
			11 (1100)		
			12 (1200)		
			1 (1300)		
			2 (1400)		
			3 (1500)		
			4 (1600)		
			5 (1700)		

WEDNESDAY • NOVEMBER 29, 1989 333rd Day, 32 Days Left

			HOURS		
			8 (0800)		
			9 (0900)		
			10 (1000)		
			11 (1100)		
			12 (1200)		
			1 (1300)		
			2 (1400)		
			3 (1500)		
			4 (1600)		
			5 (1700)		

Figure 2-10. The Day-Timers 2-Page-Per-Week Format (above and to the right) shows you the entire week. Notice there are three divided sections per day. Use the first one for to do's, the second for appointments and the third for such items as services performed, expenses incurred or telephone calls to be made. (Illustrations courtesy of Day-Timers, Inc., Allentown, PA 18195-1551)

THURSDAY • NOVEMBER 30, 1989 334th Day, 31 Days Left

	TO BE DONE TODAY (NUMBER EACH ITEM)	APPOINTMENTS, SCHEDULED EVENTS	HOURS	DIARY, SERVICES PERFORMED, EXPENSES	$/TIME
			8 0800		
			9 0900		
			10 1000		
			11 1100		
			12 1200		
			1 1300		
			2 1400		
			3 1500		
			4 1600		
			5 1700		

FRIDAY • DECEMBER 1, 1989 335th Day, 30 Days Left

			8 0800		
			9 0900		
			10 1000		
			11 1100		
			12 1200		
			1 1300		
			2 1400		
			3 1500		
			4 1600		
			5 1700		

SATURDAY • DECEMBER 2, 1989 336th Day, 29 Days Left

			8 0800		
			9 0900		
			10 1000		
			11 1100		
			12 1200		

SUNDAY • DECEMBER 3, 1989 337th Day, 28 Days Left

			8 0800		
			9 0900		
			10 1000		
			11 1100		
			12 1200		

Printed in USA

MASTERING THE TELEPHONE

The telephone can be your greatest ally or your worst foe. Here are six essential ingredients you need to make your telephone time work best for you:

1. **Phone area and equipment.** Set up a separate, *clear* phone area where you can handle calls without the distraction of other work. When you don't have to shuffle through other tasks and projects, you can really focus on each call. Your area should have enough writing surface and be close to files and other telephone information you may need. Telephone equipment should ideally include: a clock (or if necessary, several clocks in different time zones); a timer (if you have trouble keeping track of time and length of calls); a telephone answering machine or voice mail system; a telephone headset if you're on the phone at least two hours every day and/or you need your hands free for writing or typing while on the phone; and a speaker phone with on-hook dialing, automatic on-hook redialing and automatic memory dialing. Use the speaker phone when you're on hold so you can do other work while waiting. You can also use it for a conference call in your office provided that confidentiality isn't a problem and the speaker phone echo doesn't bother the person(s) on the other end.
2. **Preparation and planning.** The key to mastering the telephone is doing much of your telephone work in advance. Whenever possible, set up telephone appointments. Make more outgoing calls and take fewer incoming calls. Prioritize and consolidate all callbacks. Set up a policy on calls–e.g, how many times should the phone be allowed to ring before being answered, how long before calls are returned and when you'll make or receive calls during the day. Prepare for each outgoing call or telephone appointment by having all the necessary material in front of you and *writing down* in advance any key questions or areas to cover as well as a projected time limit for each call.
3. **PTA.** Do you have a Positive Telephone Attitude? A PTA is essential for building rapport and good working relationships.

In particular, there is nothing like the power of praise when you're trying to accomplish your goals through the telephone. Acknowledge good telephone behavior by those who assist you, be they members of your own staff, colleagues, contacts, prospects or receptionists. Besides praise, a PTA also includes helpfulness and follow-through.

4. **Concise communication.** Be specific when you communicate. Corporate communications consultant **Dr. Allen Weiner** of CDA in Sherman Oaks, California, teaches professionals "bottom line communicating," which is similar to Dragnet Sergeant Friday's, "Just the facts, ma'am." Nothing will speed up a call like getting to the point sooner. Try these two proven techniques: first, set time limits up front (e.g., "I've got five minutes to talk") and second, outline your calls (e.g., "I'd like to discuss these two questions..."). Even your telephone answering machine message should be as concise as possible. We get a lot of compliments on ours: "Thank you for calling Positively Organized! Please leave your name, number *and the best time to call you back.*"
5. **Taking notes, taking action.** Take notes anytime you may need to refer back to the call in the future. Don't rely on a good memory and don't be tempted by the thought, "I'll remember this call." I use an 8½-by-11-inch sheet of paper (as compared to slips of paper that can get lost). Always date the entry, list the party, who initiated the call, any main points to be covered and list comments *as you go.* I like to number comments. Right after the call, underline key points and take any necessary follow-up steps, such as transferring information to your calendar or listing the next action step on an index tickler card. (For more information on tickler cards, see Chapter 8.)
6. **Telephone Team.** If you're fortunate enough to have someone else in your office handling your telephone, you have an opportunity to boost your effectiveness provided you *train* that person how to screen and prioritize calls, take messages and use all of the effective telephone habits listed here. Give the person a copy of **George Walther**'s wonderful book, *Phone Power.* (You should read it first yourself.)

DELEGATE IF YOU CAN

Whether or not you're in a position to delegate, delegation is a tool to help you increase your work output and performance in the least amount of time–provided you know how to use it and you understand what delegation really means. For the delegator, it's not giving people things you don't want to do. In fact, according to **Ben Tyler**, Burlington Transportation Division president, "It's giving up things you enjoy to someone else and recognizing that not only can they do it, but sadly, they can do it better." For the delegate, delegation is an opportunity to grow and develop and to shine.

Effective delegation requires these four steps:

1. Organize.
2. Train.
3. Entrust.
4. Evaluate.

First, *organize* yourself. You need to see the whole picture in order to make delegation decisions. Think through the process. You'll also need a good personal organization system in order to follow-up later. Top designer and entrepreneur **Calvin Klein** says he organizes himself first so he can delegate effectively to others.

Second, *train* your delegate. The amount of training and direction will vary according to the delegate's abilities and the nature of the assignment. Take time to clearly teach the delegate how to do something. Helping people be the best they can be is the highest and most productive level of delegation.

Third, *entrust* your delegate with the assignment. Resist the temptation of peeking over shoulders. By the way, the dictionary definition of the verb "delegate" is "to entrust to another."

Fourth, follow-up and *evaluate.* Of course, you can't do this step if you haven't mastered step number one. So we've come full circle, back to organization.

If you find it tough getting people to follow-through and give you things on time, do what Revlon's **Kathy Meyer-Poppe** does. She tells them, "This is what I need and this is the date I need it by." Then she writes it on her calendar and her staff knows she's done so. They also know she will ask for it if it isn't done. But usually she doesn't have to ask. She says, "They know it's truly important when I say, for example, 'I need this by next Friday'–that I'm not just blowing in the wind." She stays flexible, too; if her request is unrealistic, her staff will tell her and together they'll pick a new goal and agree on it. At times she may suggest they re-prioritize their work.

REVERSE DELEGATION

When Meyer-Poppe's staff comes back to her to negotiate work assignments or deadlines, they are practicing a type of *reverse delegation*. This tool works best when you're organized and can clearly see the important things you have to do, how long they will take and how they relate to the goals of your delegator, your department and yourself.

This type of reverse delegation occurs when a person gives a delegated task back to the delegator. This type of delegation requires great tact and diplomacy and communication skills. It also requires a thorough understanding of goals and objectives for the company or office and for the delegator. There has to be a real *benefit* for the delegator whenever you reverse delegate.

When I was the communications manager for an aerospace company my boss wanted me to get involved in coordinating one of his new pet projects–the creation of a historical aviation museum. Since I had no interest in his project and saw no relation in it to either my job or career, I suggested that he involve someone else who was far more qualified than I. Coming up with the name of someone else was an easy task; the company historian worked right within our department and was a natural for this project. I didn't know it at the time, but I was practicing reverse delegation.

There's one other type of reverse delegation that you should always practice whenever you're given an assignment or project. Take each of the four steps of effective delegation–organize, train, entrust and evaluate–and make sure *you* are doing them. Organize yourself, get any necessary training or information, get the trust or authority to do a job and finally, make sure you follow-through on evaluating the job with your boss. This type of reverse delegation is a marvelous communication and self-marketing tool; it can show your boss just how well you did the job, not to mention how dependable and organized you are!

WHEN TOO MUCH IS JUST TOO MUCH

It helps to have a cooperative boss or co-worker. If you're working, however, with someone who's out to sabotage you or the company, or you truly do have too much to do and too little time, it may be best to look for a different working situation altogether. This is a last resort but consider it if you've tried the time management tools and techniques in this chapter, all to no avail.

In every seminar I give there's at least one person in one of these "impossible situations," with an autocratic boss or a highly bureaucratic structure where no amount of organization could help. If you're in such a situation, it may be better to cut your losses and bail out.

THE BEST TIME MANAGEMENT TOOLS

There is no one best time management tool. There is, however, the best tool for *you* at this point in your life and career.

One thing is certain. The more complex and demanding your life and career become, the more you need a time management tool that can help you keep track of the complex demands on your time.

CALENDARS

The most basic planning and scheduling tool is the calendar, which can track future dates, appointments, commitments, deadlines and follow-ups. Calendars come in all shapes, sizes and configurations and go by many a name: appointment books, date books, planners, diaries, desk pad calendars and wall calendars.

Don't underestimate the importance of your calendar selection. Since this is an item you use daily, you should give your selection some thought. Don't be afraid to change to a different one, even in mid-year. Ask yourself these five questions:

1. Do you have more than one calendar?
2. Is your calendar either too small or too big?
3. Is it easy to miss seeing important dates (because they're hard to spot, there isn't enough room, your calendar is too cluttered)?

4. Are you afraid of losing your calendar?
5. Is it troublesome to carry it with you when you're away from the office?

If you have one or more "yes" responses consider reevaluating your choice of calendar according to these criteria:

- You should not have more than one calendar unless you have a staff person and/or a foolproof routine to maintain the additional one. (Keep personal and professional items on the same calendar.)
- Select a calendar whose size and style are adequate for your work and appointment load. Don't force yourself to use a calendar you've outgrown even if it is the middle of the year; switch to another one.
- Maintain a reliable backup system. What would happen if you lost your calendar? Do you have xerox copies of the most important pages?
- Your calendar should be accessible to you both in and out of the office.
- Your calendar should have the right "look" for your profession and it should appeal to you in terms of appearance and ease of use.

If you're trying to cram too much information into your calendar or appointment book, consider a larger format or an organizer.

DO YOU REALLY NEED AN ORGANIZER?

Fast becoming the central core of personal organization systems, organizers in portable, notebook form help professionals manage both time and information. Organizers are more than a calendar. Organizers incorporate a variety of planning and scheduling tools, including calendars; daily to do sheets; weekly, monthly and yearly projections; master lists; and schedules for special projects and activities.

Other features usually include a phone directory, sections for "fingertip information" referred to frequently, record keeping tools, special compartments for credit cards and cash, pen and pencil holders and space for a calculator. Organizers are "Swiss army desks" equipped with all the essentials professionals need close at hand. You need never be at a loss for important resource or scheduling information–particularly vital if you're out of your office frequently.

A variety of styles and sizes adapt to many different professional needs. Some are small enough to fit in a coat or shirt pocket; others fit in a briefcase or purse; still others are self-contained mini-briefcases that can be carried on the shoulder with a strap. Many come in leather and make for professional accessories that are functional as well as attractive. (A listing of popular organizers is provided in the chapter resource guide).

TAKE THE BEST, LEAVE THE REST

What's so great about today's time management tools and systems is that many of them, especially the organizers, have interchangeable components. So you can really make your own system or at least not feel guilty if you don't want to use all of the components.

Use the resource guide as a starting point. Be thinking about these four criteria as you evaluate an existing or new system:

Size–what's the right one for you?

Portability–how much do you need?

Features and adaptability–how important are they to you?

Looks, image and appeal–what is appropriate for your position and lifestyle?

RESOURCE GUIDE

Time management is an ongoing challenge and adventure. There are no magic wands but hopefully this listing will open your eyes to the many exciting solutions that are available.

TELEPHONE TOOLS

ASAP-10 Call Director, (a call director beeps you when someone has just called your answering machine). Command Communications, 303/750-6434

Code-A-Phone 3530, telephone answering machine. 800/547-2800

Communitech telephone peripheral products–headsets, speaker phones, voice mail system, automated attendant. 455 N. York Road, Elmhurst, IL 60126, 312/941-9060

Cue Pager, nationwide pager. 800/824-9755 or 714/641-6660

National Satellite Pager. 800/443-8667 or 202/223-2780

Phone Power by George Walther (New York: Berkley Books, 1986). A great book to teach you just about everything when it comes to the telephone. Paperback, $3.50

Plantronics telephone headsets and speaker phones. Plantronics makes headsets that are compatible with every phone system. I use the $59 Spirit headset myself. 800/662-3902

TIME MANAGEMENT TOOLS AND SYSTEMS

Practically every time I turn around, I see a new time management tool or system. The following are among the best I've seen.

Caddylak Systems, wall planning systems and charts; time management forms.
62 E. 55th St.
New York, NY 10022
800/523-8060

Day Runner, notebook organizer/planners available nationally in department and stationery stores in an affordable, versatile range of styles, sizes and features. See Figure 2-11.
Day Runner, Inc.
3562 Eastham Dr., Culver City, CA 90230
800/232-9786 or 213/837-6900

Day-Timers, planners and work organizers in many different sizes and formats. Free catalog.
Day-Timers, Inc.
PO Box 2368
Allentown, PA 18001
215/395-5884

Filofax, small planners that incorporate date book, project, expense and phone/address information in compact, attractive, leather binders. Available in department and stationery stores.

Figure 2-11. The popular Day Runner Classic.

Filofax
2216 Federal Ave.
Los Angeles, CA 90064
213/312-1140 (call to get names of stores in your area)

Memindex Desk Planning Guide is a dated, color-coded, one-page per day planner with special yearly, monthly and weekly planning sections. The binder is 7 by 7½ by 1½ inches. The 500-name-address-phone insert is extra ($7.95). Ranges from $17.95 for vinyl to $34.95 for leather.

Memindex, Inc.
149 Carter Street
Rochester, NY 14601
800/828-5885; in New York: 716/342-7890

Memindex Pocket Planning Guide is a wallet style planner that lets you carry one month at a time, a yearly planner and phone/address booklet. Each day of the month is tabbed and has two pages that include space for appointments, notes, expenses. Ranges from $26.95 in vinyl to $38.95 in leather.

Memindex, Inc.
149 Carter Street
Rochester, NY 14601
800/828-5885; in New York: 716/342-7890

Memogenda, a system for keeping track of your to-do's and for getting them done. **Zipagenda** is a zippered case that contains the Memogenda system and allows you to store additional papers.
Norwood Products Co.
1012-N Thompson Lane
Nashville, TN 37211-2627
615/833-4101

The #1 Personal Management System, a compact time management system, emphasizes positive development of habits.
American Leadership Institute
PO Box 8690
Waco, TX 76714-8690
817/772-0088

The **Personal Resource System** is a cleanly designed, leather, zippered notebook organizer system that comes with an instruction booklet and tape.
Personal Resource Systems, Inc.
11588 Sorrento Valley Road, Bldg. 17
San Diego, CA 92121
800/542-8488 or in California, 800/255-9018

Planner Pad is a weekly planner in different sizes that has sections for things-to-do, appointments, expenses and space for your own categories.
Planner Pads, Inc.
PO Box 27187
Omaha, NE 68127-0187
402/592-0666

PrimeTime, time management software.
Wiseware, Inc.
3176 Pullman St., Suite 106
Costa Mesa, CA 92626
714/556-6523

Remarkable Products is a mail-order catalog featuring organizing boards, charts, forms and supplies.
245 Pegasus Avenue
Northvale, NJ 07647
201/784-0900

The Reminder System and **Reminder Plus** are versatile, easy-to-use time management software programs for the IBM.
Campbell Services Inc.
21700 Northwestern Highway, Suite 1070
Southfield, MI 48075
800/521-9314 or 313/559-5955

TIME/SELF-MANAGEMENT BOOKS AND TAPES

Time management is the process of making the most of your life in the time available. When fully understood, the concept of time management embraces self and life-management. How you manage time outside of work has a direct relationship to time management at work and vice versa. The following books and tapes will help you make the most of *all* the time in your life:

CareerTracking: 26 Success Shortcuts to the Top by Jimmy Calano and Jeff Salzman (New York: Simon and Schuster, 1988). The authors have summarized the best of what they've read, heard, seen and experienced on the subject of career success. The book is easy to read, easy to use and will save you time on your way to the top and *at* the top, as well. Hardback, $15.95

Feeling Good: The New Mood Therapy by David D. Burns, M.D. (New York: New American Library, 1980). If negativity, criticism, procrastination, perfectionism, mood swings or depression are frequent or even occasional companions, effective time management will be next to impossible. This is a breakthrough book that offers clinically tested, practical solutions presented in an inspiring, compassionate style. It's easy to read and use. Paperback, $4.95

Getting Organized: The Easy Way to Put Your Life in Order by Stephanie Winston (New York: Warner Books, 1978). Here's a great book to help you better manage personal areas of your life from financial planning to meal planning. Learn also to maximize storage space, organize your kitchen, run a household and even teach your child to organize. Paperback, $5.95

Getting Things Done by Edwin Bliss (New York: Bantam Books, 1976). Literally the ABCs of time management, Bliss takes time management and organization topics such as "Deadlines," "Goals" and "Priorities," puts them in alphabetical order and succinctly provides practical and entertaining gems of wisdom. Paperback, $3.50

How to Create Balance at Work, at Home, in Your Life by Bee Epstein, Ph.D. is a dynamic, six-cassette program for working women. Epstein herself is a model of balance and success. This is a great program to enhance your life. Available from Adams-Hall Publishing, PO Box 491002, Los Angeles, CA 90049. $49

How to Get Control of Your Time and Your Life by Alan Lakein (New York: Signet, 1973). This classic time management book is particularly useful in helping you sort out your life goals. Paperback, $2.50

How to Get Organized When You Don't Have the Time by Stephanie Culp (Cincinnati: Writer's Digest Books, 1986). Culp makes time management and getting organized *fun.* In her down-to-earth, humorous style, Culp cuts through with plenty of practical ideas to organize the time and space in your personal life. Paperback. $9.95

Newstrack Executive Tape Service, Box 1178, Englewood, CO 80150, 303/778-1692 or 800/525-8389. Weekly tape cassette series that summarizes major newspaper and magazine articles related to business.

Nightingale-Conant business and motivational audiocassettes. An excellent selection of tape programs to get and keep you inspired to and from work. 800/323-5552.

Organize Yourself! by Ronni Eisenberg (New York: Macmillan Publishing Company, 1986). Eisenberg's book is an easy-to-read, easy-to-use guide to organizing your personal life. Paperback, $7.95

The Organized Executive: New Ways to Manage Time, Paper and People by Stephanie Winston (New York: Warner Books, 1985). Not just for the executive, this classic provides nuts 'n bolts techniques to streamline your work flow and office. Paperback, $7.95

The Psychology of Achievement by Brian Tracy is a six-cassette program that distills the key ingredients of high achievement. Brian Tracy presents proven, practical methods and techniques that high achievers regularly use in their lives and careers. Available from Brian Tracy Learning Systems, 462 Stevens Avenue, Suite 202, Solana Beach, CA 92075-2065, 800/542-4252 (outside California), 619/481-2977 (inside California). $55

The Superwoman Syndrome by Marjorie Hansen Shaevitz (New York: Warner Books, 1984). This wonderful book is for women who want more balance and control in their life. Paperback. $3.95.

Taming the Paper Tiger: Organizing the Paper in Your Life by Barbara Hemphill (New York: Dodd, Mead & Company, 1988). This is a delightful, easy-to-read guide with charming illustrations and many useful tips and techniques. Available through Barbara Hemphill Associates, 2000 Pennsylvania Ave., N.W., Ste. 171, Washington, D.C. 20006, 202/387-8007. Paperback, $9.95

What It Takes: Good News From 100 of America's Top Professional and Business Women by Lee Gardenswartz and Anita Rowe (New York: Doubleday, 1987). An inspiring work, this book shows how women at the top arrange their lives to achieve their goals and how you can assess your own aptitude for success. Hardback, $16.95

Working From Home: Everything You Need to Know About Living and Working Under the Same Roof by Paul and Sarah Edwards (Los Angeles: Jeremy P. Tarcher, 1985). The Edwards put together a power-packed sourcebook that provides many time- and energy-saving shortcuts for the small entrepreneur or anyone who works at home. Paperback, $11.95

Working Smart: How to Accomplish More in Half the Time by Michael LeBoeuf (New York: Warner Books, 1980). This classic continues to sell strong and with good reason: this is a must-read book that hits the core of essential work habits you need to develop on the job. Paperback. $3.95.

MASTERING YOUR DESK AND THE PAPER JUNGLE

Quick Scan: If you're inundated with the "pile system" on your desk, if your work area is steadily shrinking into nonexistence, if desktop clutter has got you down and under, this chapter's for you. Learn why your desk represents the single most important part of your office and how to make it work for you.

Do you know where your desk is? This question is usually good for some chuckles at my seminars. The problem is most people can't even *find* their desk. It's under here somewhere...

You're not alone. You and 60 million other people in the U.S. have a desk of some kind. When I refer to a desk, I mean *any* piece of furniture that is used as your primary working surface. It may be a large executive model with many drawers in a traditional office or a simple work table at a computer work station.

Chances are good you spend many hours every day at your desk. Why not have it be the best looking, best functioning desk around?

THE MYTH OF THE MESSY DESK

No matter what you've seen on coffee cups, **a clean desk is the not the sign of an empty mind!** I know those coffee cup cliches will try to tell you otherwise. But don't be fooled. Most people think and act more clearly at a clean, well organized desk. Once you accept and embrace this basic premise, you've taken an important step.

Don't fall prey to one common myth about the "clean desk." That myth says a clean desk means you're not busy because you don't *look* busy. The reasoning is that if you don't *look* busy, you aren't productive. But being busy doesn't equate with being productive anyway, as B. W. Luscher, Jr., from the U.S. Postal Service, warns: "Don't confuse activity with productivity."

Far from indicating productivity, a messy desk signals a lack of dependability, control and focus, not to mention incomplete work, missed deadlines and lost information. One manager told me about an employee who had a ton of stuff on her desk. As the manager put it, "All those piles of paper told me she was in trouble."

While the woman was on vacation, the manager went in and saw a six-month-old check lying there with a bunch of invoices. He also discovered an important letter to 20 people that had never gone out. The letter was to announce a meeting the *manager* had planned. The manager found the 20 letters stuck in a drawer together with papers to be filed. All the letters had been typed and the envelopes addressed. All the employee had had to do was mail the letters! When the employee returned from vacation, she was devastated to learn of her mistake–she could have sworn she had mailed the letters months ago.

What was her problem? The manager says it was a combination of many things. She was very social, always wanting to know what was going on with other people and didn't take care of her own business. The manager observed, "You've got to worry first about what's on your own desk." He also said, "You've got to be a team player and let someone know if you're falling behind." In a nutshell, what she didn't have were the right organizational systems–the right tools and habits that signify a pro who is organized to be the best.

The fact is you are *not* more productive when you're working out of a cluttered desk. Besides feeling stress, you're continually distracted by all the different papers, piles and objects that keep pulling at you. It's easy to go into sensory overload as your eyes keep flitting from thing to thing and your mind keeps worrying whether you're working on the *right* task. No wonder you're exhausted at the end of each day!

CLEARING A PATH

The first step to mastering your desk is "clearing a path," as one of my clients described the process of thinning out the paper jungle and cleaning out the dead wood.

Think of yourself as an air traffic controller and your desk as the runway. You're in charge. *You* determine which papers, piles, and projects can land on your desk—and stay there.

Survey your desktop. **Do you have enough work surface?** Many people put up with a desk that is too small to begin with and becomes smaller and smaller as the paper jungle takes over. It's hard to know if you have enough work surface until you actually remove the files, the piles, the paperwork. Once you do clear a path, then try out your desktop for several days. See if you now have enough space to work.

Do not use your desktop for storage. It's a *work* surface, not a storage locker. Keep it clear, ready for action. Your desktop is *prime* work space and should contain only those items you use every day, such as your phone, calendar or planner and clock. Keep your desk as clean as possible.

But how clean is clean? That depends on a number of factors. First, consider who sees your desk. Colleagues? Clients? Customers? Patients? What kind of image do you want to create before these people? It's quite possible your desk should be spotless before the public but can be more of a workhorse before other staff members.

Incidentally, if you're concerned with image, consider this: research reveals that the cleanest desks belong to those individuals higher up in the organization. If you're on an upwardly mobile career path, have your desk look the part.

Second, consider what your level of aesthetics and function dictates. Start to become conscious of what *your* ideal level of order is and work toward it.

Some people really are more comfortable with clutter and claim they would dry up in an orderly, "sterile" environment. Neatness counts but neat isn't always organized nor necessary. If you're one of those people who prefers "organized clutter," more power to you.

Most people, though, have simply never tried working in a clutter-free setting for more than a day or so. The adage, "try it, you'll like it" certainly applies here.

ACCESSIBILITY

I once had a client who sent me a snapshot of his terribly cluttered desk and office before we began working together. The caption read, "My office...where everything in the whole damn world is at my fingertips!"

How many of those things on your desktop do you actually use every day? Every week? Every month? Every year? Make a list of the things you use every day. Of those things, which need to be sitting on your desktop? See if there isn't a better place, one that's accessible, but not on top of you.

Accessibility is the key word. Frequency of use should determine accessibility. How often are you using all of your items? Maybe you started out using an item every day in the past and at some point you stopped. But there the item remains. As a general rule, **the more often you use an item, the more accessible it should be.** Take the Accessibility Survey in Figure 3-1.

Let's suppose you have many things you use every day. Don't clutter your primary work surface by putting them all on your desktop. They can still be accessible in a drawer, on a credenza or on a table to the side.

ENOUGH WORK SPACE

Have at least two work surfaces in your office (not counting a return or table for typewriter or computer). The second surface should be accessible, placed within an easy swivel of your chair–behind you or at your side.

Don't use the extra work surface as a storage depot or junk table. This surface should only hold things that you use several times a week or daily. This surface is great for holding active, working file folders that should sit vertically in upright caddies. You might use

Figure 3-1. ACCESSIBILITY SURVEY
List in the space below the things on your desk that you use

Daily:

Several Times a Week:

Once a Week:

Once a Month:

A Few Times a Year:

Rarely or Never:

this surface for your stapler, tape and other supplies as well as reference materials, in-out boxes, mementos and index card files. Part or all of this second surface could be designated a telephone station. Maximize your work surface by also using a nearby table top, a credenza or even a two-drawer filing cabinet. If you prefer that spotless, executive, clean desk look, put items *inside* your furniture.

PAPER AND WORK FLOW SOLUTIONS

Are you suffering from a paper mill logjam? If so, you may have a tremendous amount of paperwork to process in your job and/or you probably have some *difficulty making decisions.*

If you're drowning in paperwork, chances are you tend to avoid decisions. See if one or more of the following apply to you:

1. You're insatiably curious and love to learn new things to the point of distraction.
2. Perfectionism tends to rule in your life.
3. Everything always takes longer than you thought it would.
4. You're creative.
5. You distrust structure and/or authority.
6. You're afraid of making a mistake and taking risks.
7. **You don't have a current, written list of goals that you refer to every day.**

All of these can contribute to decision-making difficulties concerning paper. But remember, number seven is the most important. Making decisions about paper shouldn't be arbitrary. They need to relate specifically to your values and goals in life.

Without goals as a guideline, as a yardstick, it is very difficult to make decisions, including decisions about those papers on your desk.

Difficult decisions about paper often signal ambivalence or conflict about what you want to do now and in the future. "I might need this someday" is such a haunting thought, especially when goals are fuzzy at best. Remind yourself frequently about your goals–every time, in fact, you pick up a paper, a piece of mail, a file folder, whatever. Remind yourself whenever you *put down a paper without making a decision.* And remember, almost always the worst decision you can make is *not* to make a decision. (See also Chapter 1 on goals and Chapter 9 on collecting.)

DAILY PAPERWORK SYSTEM

Once you've decided to keep a paper, you may then wonder, "Now where am I going to put this?" When you don't know where to put papers, they inevitably end up staying on your desk or in your in-box on your desk.

Setting up appropriate categories and containers in a **daily paperwork system** can help solve that problem. The daily paperwork system doesn't take the place of your filing system, which is discussed in detail in Chapter 4. The daily paperwork system is for *active* paperwork that you process on a *daily* basis.

The first step is to select general categories for types of papers that come your way most often. Typical categories include: Action (this week), Financial, Correspondence, Calls, Staff, Reading, Filing and Pending. You might also include specific category names for *active* projects you're using on a *daily* basis. List basic category names you could use for your everyday paperwork:

If you're having trouble thinking of ones that fit your needs, try this simple exercise. Next time you process your mail and other paperwork, have some 3-by-5 index cards handy. Go through your paperwork, making decisions about what to keep and what to toss. (For many people this is the most difficult part. Be willing to get in the habit of freely tossing–more on this in Chapter 9). On an index card, jot down the major category for each type of paper you're keeping (e.g., "Reports," "Must do today"). A broad category name will often describe the general type of activity or level of urgency. Do this for a few days or for one day if you have a lot of mail and paperwork.

Go through the cards and **select the broadest, most general categories you'll use every day.** See if some of them can be combined. A category is a good one if you'll use it just about every day. Remember the purpose of these categories is for general sorting not filing of paperwork.

Once you've decided on your basic categories, set up the tools of your daily paperwork system using existing file folders, boxes, caddies or organizers. Label these containers with your categories. Ideally, get as much off your desk as possible. Containers should be accessible but they shouldn't crowd your space.

Set up a trial paperwork system. Buy a package of assorted colored, "third cut," manila folders at your local stationery store. See what you already have on hand in terms of boxes, trays and caddies. Don't invest in a lot of equipment; remember this is just a trial system. Some people, after getting all inspired about organization, rush out and buy too many accessories without first thinking through the system. I've walked into offices of some new clients only to find five name and address files, ten letter trays and dozens of file folders–all of which had had "good intentions" but have since been abandoned. The supplies are not the system. They are *part* of the system. They are only the tools.

Start with a simple system. Select the smallest number of tools and label them with your category names. Arrange them in an easy-to-use, accessible location. A couple of pointers may be helpful. First, use *vertical* systems whenever possible, as horizontal ones tend to promote the "pile system" of stacking papers. (See Figures 3-2 and 3-3 for examples of vertical, desktop active file organizers.) Second, try the system out for two to three weeks, make refinements and *then* purchase any additional supplies you need.

Your daily paperwork system doesn't have to be visible; some of the best ones are "invisible." Use prime filing space in your desk or in an arm's-reach filing cabinet or credenza. If out of sight means out of mind, then perhaps a more visible system is indeed a good idea for you. But if you're the type of person who gets anxious just looking at paperwork, then design a more hidden, yet accessible, system and start using your time management tools to jot down things to do and remember.

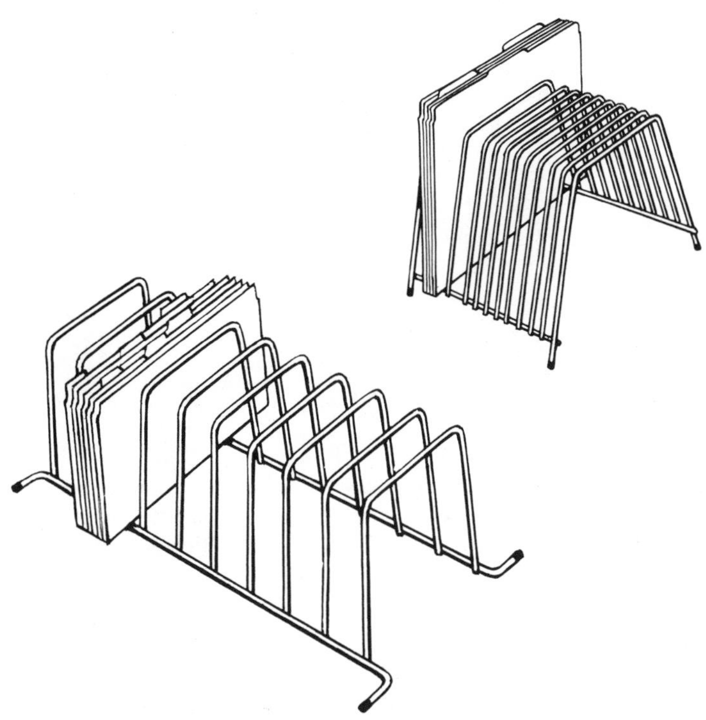

Figure 3-2. Colored manila folders for your daily paperwork system work great in a vertical wire rack such as Boorum Wireworks FileAll (top) or Sort-R-Rack.

CONQUERING DAILY PAPERWORK

Setting up the *tools* of a daily paperwork system is only half the story; setting up *regular routines and habits* is the other half. Any organizational system, by the way, consists of two components–tools and habits. I often use this simple equation in my seminars:

a system = tools + habits

The trick to making your daily paperwork system work is simply, to work the system! Here are some habits and routines that can help you work the system–circle any that you could use:

Figure 3-3. Vertical desktop file organizers for active files using colored hanging folders are great tools for your daily paperwork system. Shown here is the Oxford DecoFlex by Esselte Pendaflex, which comes with five different-colored hanging folders.

- Open and sort your mail every day you're in the office.
- Have someone else open and sort your mail.
- Make a decision about each paper that crosses your desk the *first* time it crosses your desk. For the papers you're keeping, decide if they can be handled *now* or *later*. If a paper will take only a minute or two, do it now. If you're deferring papers for a later time, resist sticking them back in the pile or the in-box. Decide *where* each should go in terms of its function and meaning to you–i.e., where's the first place you're likely to look for the item and retrieve it for action?
- Schedule appointments with yourself to process paperwork.
- Make separate reading appointments with yourself to keep up with professional reading.
- Keep it clean! At the very least, clean your desk and work area before you go. Or try the CAYGO habit–Clean As You GO–to prevent paper buildup during the day. And if filing is

a real chore use FAYGO–File As You GO or do as **Bill Butler** from BCG International does–clean a file a day.

- Use time management tools such as your calendar, master list or organizer to record key information from papers that you can then toss.
- Consolidate information. Use notebooks, charts, forms, tickler systems and a good deskside filing system. (And read chapters 4 and 8.)

STAYING IN CONTROL OF READING

Reading is a time management issue as well as a paperwork issue. It takes consistent time management habits to stay in control. You have to *make time* in your schedule to keep up with professional reading.

Here are some reading habits you could adopt. Underline each habit that involves time management:

I will keep up with my professional reading by reading the last 15 minutes of each day, which will usually be from 5:15 to 5:30. I will block out that segment of time on my planner. I will have all calls held. I will use a timer to encourage me to get through more and more of my reading pile. I will read more quickly by reading selectively–checking out headlines, subheads, first and last paragraphs and making clear decisions whether what I'm reading is *worth my time.* Whenever possible, I will separate professional from personal interest reading. I will acknowledge how reading every day helps me control my paperwork, saves me time, helps me learn more about my field and makes me feel like more of a professional.

Notice how most of these sample habits involve time management. Some of them may not work exactly for you. You may, for example, prefer to make an hour reading appointment once a week with yourself rather than trying to read 15 minutes a day. Write your own set of specific reading habits that are realistic for your work style:

PREVENTING THE DUMP-IT-ON-THE-DESK SYNDROME

Linda, an administrative assistant for a small but successful public relations firm, had a problem. Everyone would feed work to her by dumping it in the middle of her desk. They also had the habit of interrupting her from other work to explain what they wanted done.

Together Linda and I devised a special daily paperwork system that helps Linda better control interruptions and incoming paperwork. She now uses colored, two-pocket presentation folders, a different color for each person. She puts mail in the right hand pocket and they feed back work to her in the left hand pocket once a day. If a special project or deadline comes up during the day, she has a red folder on her desk to handle these top priorities.

Creating the system was only half the story since her system involved the other staff members. So I suggested she make a presentation at a staff meeting to introduce the system and ask for everyone's support in trying it out for a week. Then everyone was to get together at the following week's meeting to evaluate this new *office* system (not Linda's system). It's very important to get everyone's agreement and support whenever one person introduces a new system. Otherwise, the office staff may be resistent to a system that appears to be imposed upon them.

When introducing a system such as Linda's presentation folders, remember that good communication and training skills come into play here. First, communicate the benefits to everyone. Second, clearly train people in how you see the system functioning. Be open to reasonable modifications at this point. Encourage people to be involved in this initial discussion (which is really a training session). Give up ownership of the system–it's no longer "my" system, it's "ours."

The system is still working well several years later.

CONQUERING LONG-TERM PAPER BUILDUP

If you're suffering from this dreaded "dis-ease," (or your predecessor did), it may be difficult to fully implement the paper and work flow solutions we've just discussed.

You have several options available to handle long-term paper:

1. Trash it.
2. Quickly box and store it now and plan to sort it later as a long-term project after reading chapters 9 and 12.
3. Read chapters 9 and 12 to do something about it now.

Choose an option based on how *important* these papers are to you. Are they worth your time? If you need some specific criteria to determine the level of importance go directly to Chapter 9.

RESOURCE GUIDE

DESK AND PAPER MANAGEMENT ACCESSORIES

The selected office products here are handy, dandy items you may wish to add to your work area. Most of these accessories are available in a good office supply catalog or store (unless otherwise noted). Good office supply catalogs with hundreds of pages usually have two indexes–one listing manufacturers and the other listing general types of products. I've used general headings you're most likely to see in these catalogs.

CLIPS

Labelon Owl Clips in Figure 3-4 are rectangular clips that hold papers more securely and will not catch on other adjacent papers. This type of clip comes in three sizes.

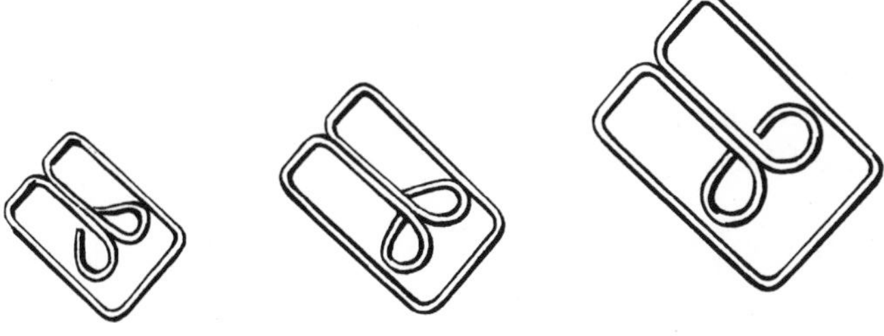

Figure 3-4. Labelon Owl Clips

Labelon Triumph Clamps hold bulky papers securely. (Figure 3-5.)

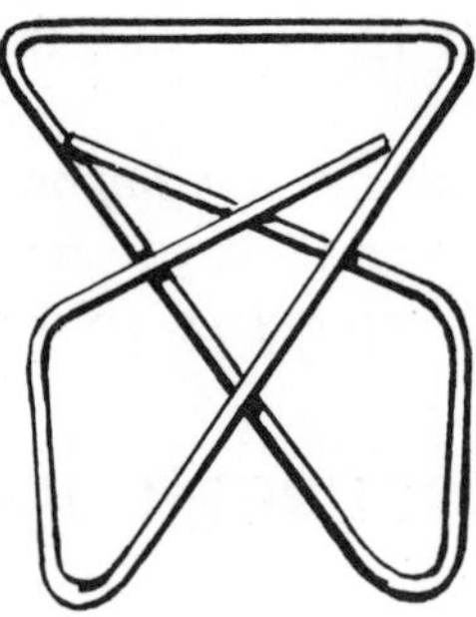

Figure 3-5. Labelon Triumph Clamp

Binder clip (Figure 3-6) is the generic name for what is probably the most secure, slip-proof clip you can buy. Use binder clips for loose bulky papers that need to be held securely.

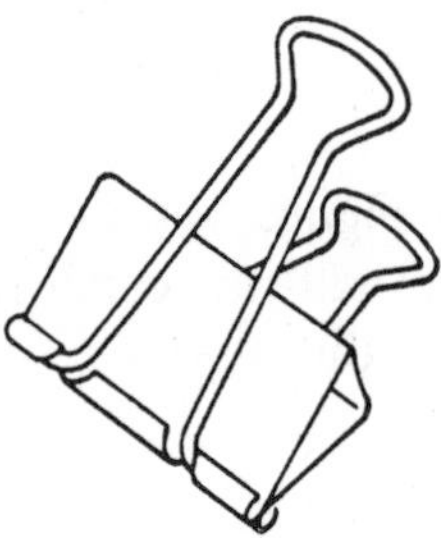

Figure 3-6. Binder clip

Baumgarten Plastiklips shown in Figure 3-7 come in a wide variety of styles and sizes. Look for the **Baumgarten Arrow Klips** for clipping as well as highlighting and color coding papers.

COLOR CODING

For color coding and drawing attention, here are several products that will help:

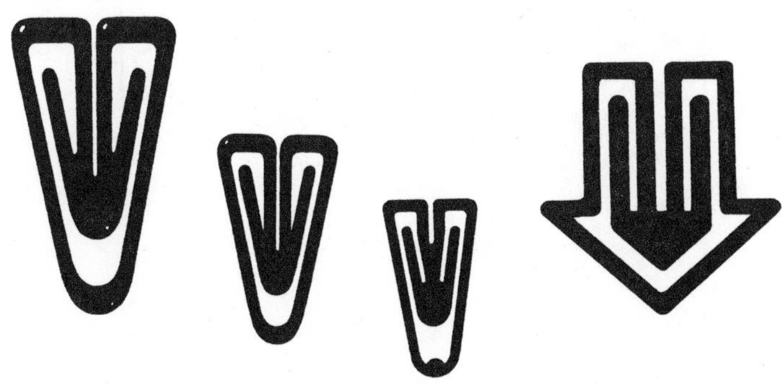

Figure 3-7. Baumgarten Plastiklips and Arrow Klip

Redi-Tags (Figure 3-8) are removable, reusable color-coded tags that have a reusable adhesive on half the tag. They come in many different colors and sizes, some with special wording such as "SIGN HERE." If your local office supply store or catalog doesn't have this item, call 714/894-4727 for a store location near you.

Post-It Brand Tape Flags by 3M (Figure 3-9) are now available with their own dispensers. Half of the tape flag is colored; the other half is a transparent surface upon which you can write with pencil or pen.

Signals, (as shown in Figure 3-10), are made of plastic or metal and clip securely to record cards, folders or papers to "signal" next action date, type of activity or level of urgency.

DESK ACCESSORIES

In the office supply world, this category includes everything from basic desk or letter trays to designer desk sets with matching components. As a general guideline, I advise clients to use the *minimal* number of accessories and those with the *smallest* capacity. It's just too easy to start stockpiling stuff.

I also urge clients to lean toward *vertical* rather than *horizontal* containers–whenever possible to put papers in files rather than piles.

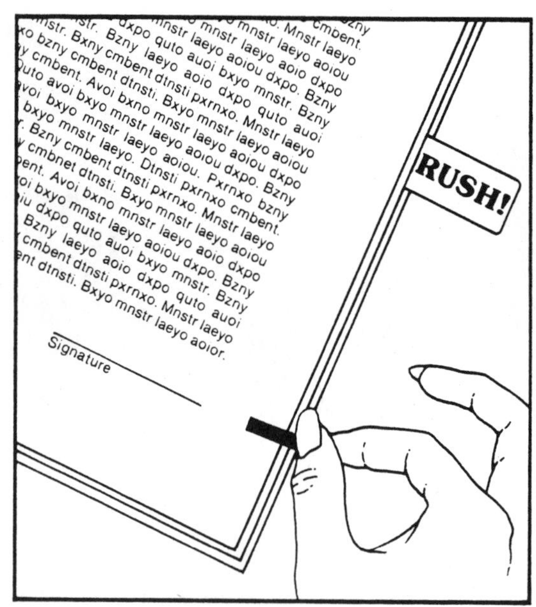

Figure 3-8. Use Redi-Tags to attract attention. Simply tag where action is needed and remove the tag when the task is finished or the reference is no longer necessary.

Of course, the type of paperwork will often determine which format you should use. A horizontal container often works best for frequently used forms, which often flop over in a vertical container.

But you'll generally want a vertical container for active files (look at the many examples in this section.)

Your in-out box or basket system will most likely be horizontal because you're probably processing different sized papers. But remember these tips: keep the depth of containers to a minimum, maintain high access and visibility (the space between the trays on the sides should be open) and clean out trays *regularly.*

Balance good function with good design. Upon getting organized, some clients reward themselves with attractive desk accessories. Check out products by **C-Line**, **Eldon** and **Rubbermaid** in office supply stores and catalogs.

Also look at **Hold Everything,** the Williams-Sonoma store and mail-order catalog. Write them at WILLIAMS-SONOMA, Mail Order Department, PO Box 7456, San Francisco, CA 94120-7456.

Figure 3-9. In six colors, these convenient, easy-to-use flags keep your paperwork organized. Use them for quick reference, easy retrieval and handy reminders. They are ideal for color coding, organizing and indexing.

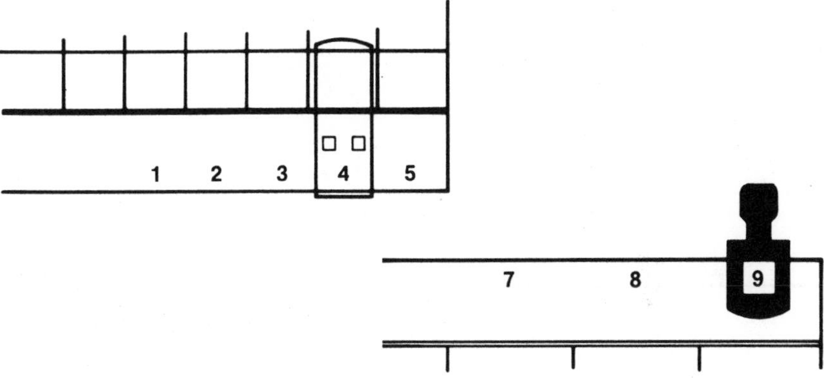

Figure 3-10. Labelon Cellugraf Plastic Signals (upper) come transparent (as shown) or opaque and in twenty-two colors. Labelon Graffco Nu-Vise Metal Signals stand above a card or folder edge, come in 18 colors and are available in numbered, alphabetical and calendar styles.

Desk Files

Take a look at some products to help you set up your daily paperwork system for your active working files and paperwork. If your work load fluctuates constantly you may prefer a modular system that expands and contracts with your work. **Eldon Add-A-File** in Figure 3-11 and **Rubbermaid Quicksnap Vertical Filing System** in Figure 3-12 are good choices.

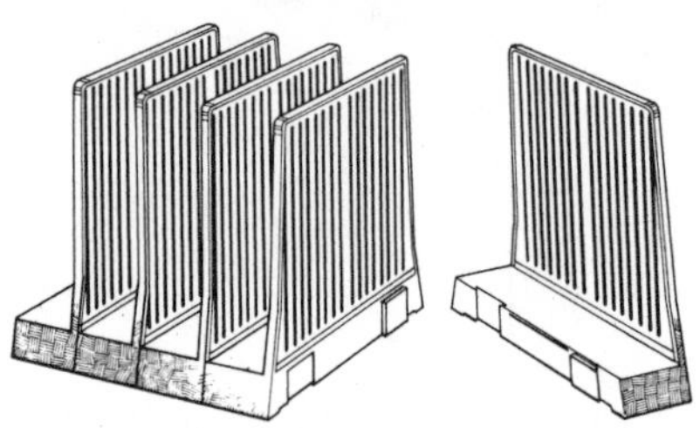

Figure 3-11. Eldon Add-A-File

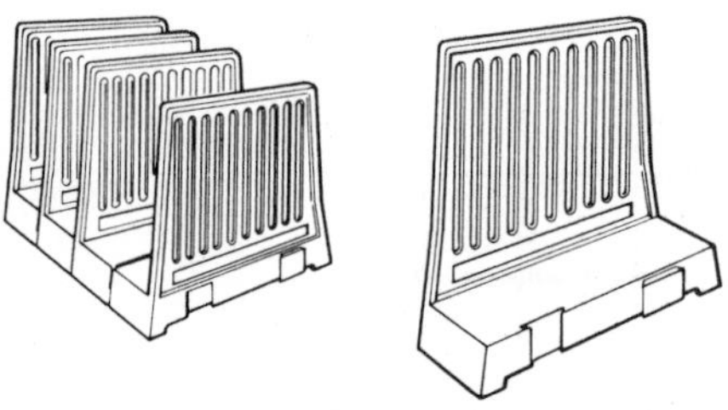

Figure 3-12. Rubbermaid Quicksnap Vertical Filing System

Step files give great visibility to your working files. Figure 3-13 shows the **Sterling Step-Rack**. The **Eldon Step-Up Step Rack** in Figure 3-14 lets you sort different sized papers.

And here's a variation on the step file–instead of slanting up, **Eldon Diagonal Files** in Figure 3-15 have pockets staggered sideways at 45-degree angles.

The **Boorum Wireworks Steprack** in Figure 3-16 is made of steel and comes in four colors.

Fellowes Neat Ideas Active Files in Figure 3-17 and **Fellowes Premier Line Visible Folder Files** in Figure 3-18 show low-cost step files made of corrugated fiberboard with five tiered compartments.

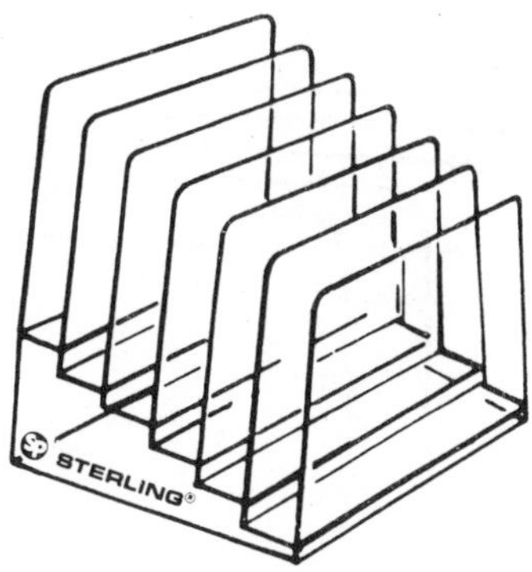

Figure 3-13. Sterling Step-Rack

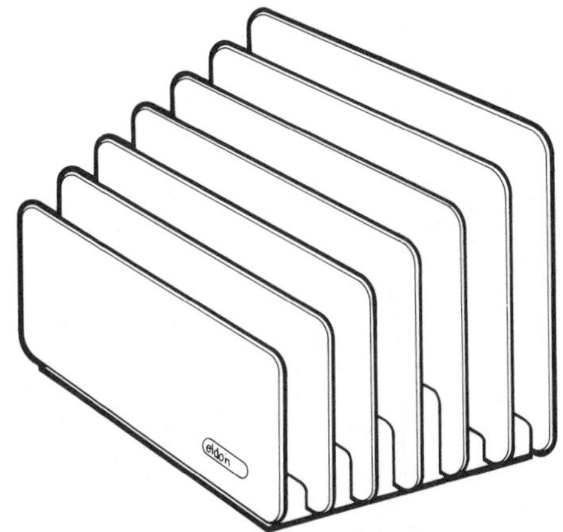

Figure 3-14. Eldon Step-Up Step Rack

The Folder by Eldon in Figure 3-19 makes maximum use of limited space, accommodates letter or legal size and folds flat when not in use.

The Holder by Eldon in Figure 3-20 holds letter or legal size hanging folders.

Fellowes Neat Ideas Folder Files shown in Figure 3-21 holds letter-sized hanging folders, which are included.

Fellowes Neat Ideas Folder Holder in Figure 3-22 is an economical way to keep active manila files close at hand. It's made of corrugated fiberboard and comes in letter or legal size.

Figure 3-15. Eldon Diagonal Files

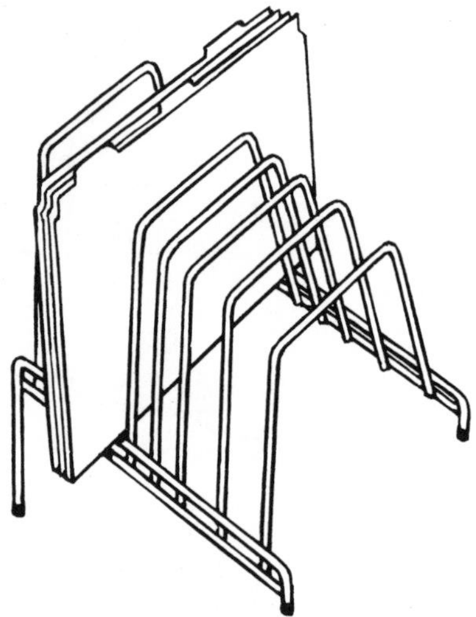

Figure 3-16. Boorum Wireworks Steprack by Esselte Pendaflex

Figure 3-17. Fellowes Neat Ideas Active Files

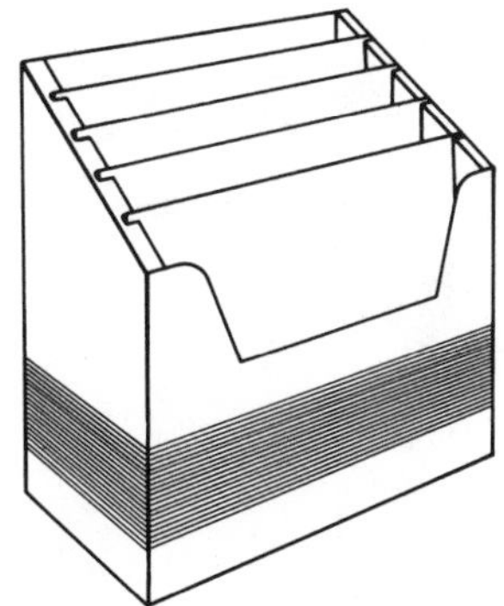

Figure 3-18. Fellowes Premier Line Visible Folder Files

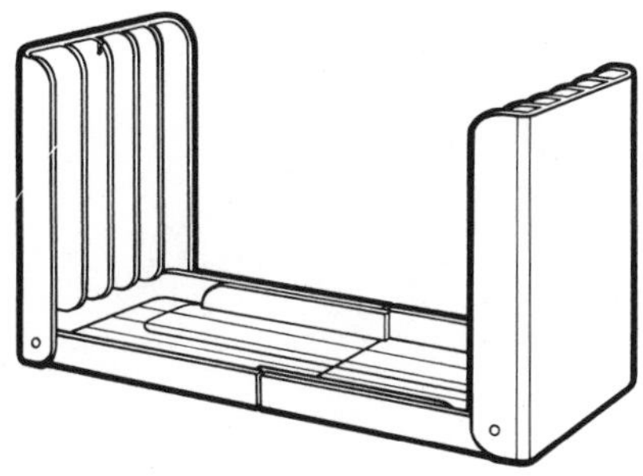

Figure 3-19. The Folder by Eldon

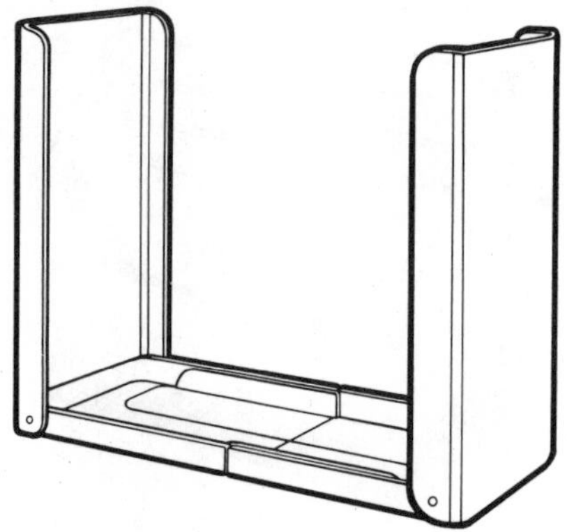

Figure 3-20. The Holder by Eldon

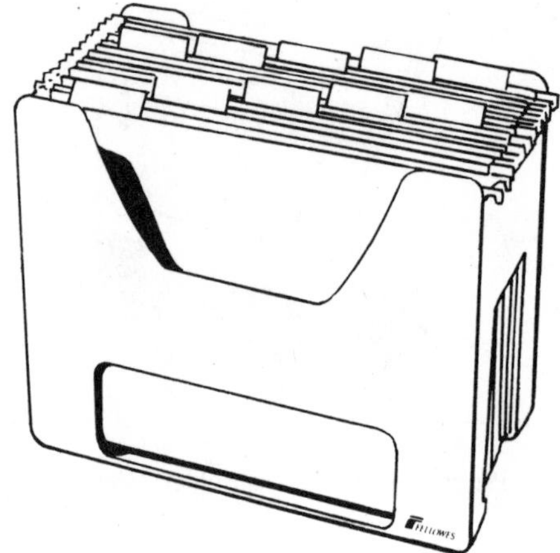

Figure 3-21. Fellowes Neat Ideas Folder Files

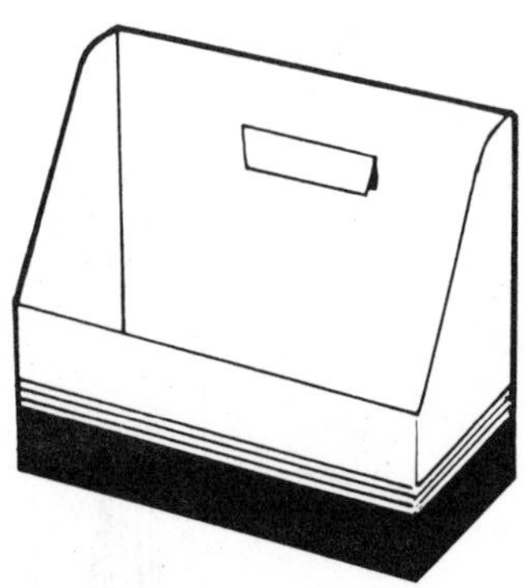

Figure 3-22. Fellowes Neat Ideas Folder Holder

If you need a larger capacity for accessible, hanging folders consider the **Eldon Hot Rack**, in Figure 3-23, which will hold up to 45 hanging folders.

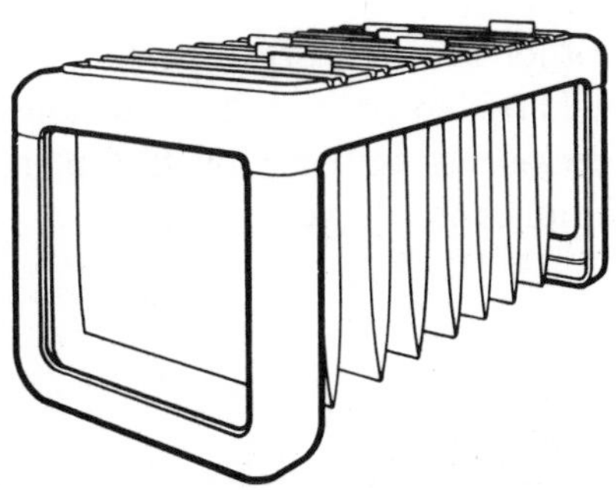

Figure 3-23. Eldon Hot Rack

Boorum Prizm Desktop File Organizer in Figure 3-24 has a sleek, contemporary design.

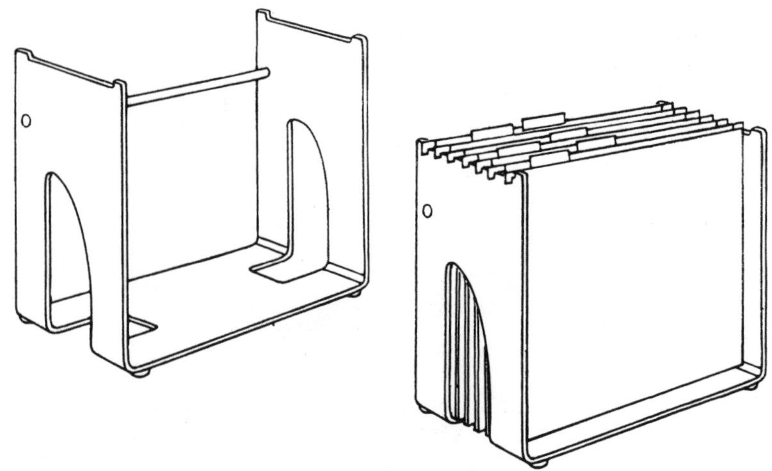

Figure 3-24. Boorum Prizm Desktop File Organizer by Esselte Pendaflex

Other Organizers

Here are some other items to organize your desk and paperwork that you might not know about or might not know their names.

Drawer organizers such as these by **Eldon** in Figure 3-25, can help tidy up the supplies inside your desk.

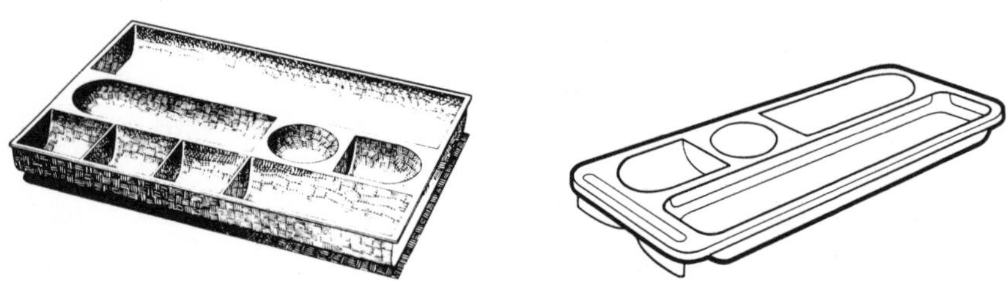

Figure 3-25. Catch'all (left) and Mini Catch'all by Eldon

Stationery holders are great for letterhead, forms and envelopes and come in many different styles and formats. Some sit out in the open and others, like the **Eldon Stationery Tray** in Figure 3-26, fit inside standard desk drawers.

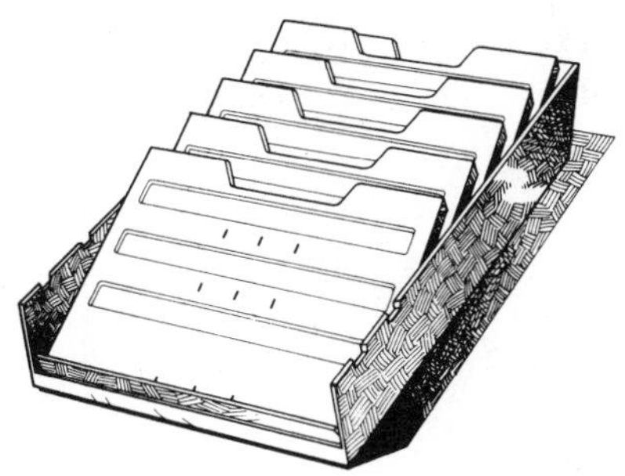

Figure 3-26. Eldon Stationery Tray

The **Evans Collator** in Figure 3-27 is actually designed to manually collate documents but I recommend it for large, bulky, *active* client or project files. It's great for cpa or legal files and comes in 12, 18 or 24 expanding sections. We use it in our office above our printer to store frequently used paper, letterhead and envelopes.

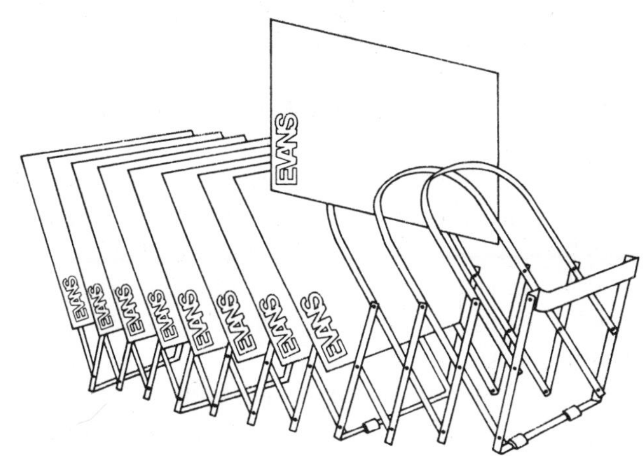

Figure 3-27. Evans Collator

Many organizers, such as the **Eldon Versatilt** in Figure 3-28, are "versatile," allowing you to better organize and hold a variety of materials. This file and sorter system has dividers that can be positioned to accommodate different amounts of materials. Dividers can pivot giving easier access to such items as diskettes, large index cards or forms. Locked vertically, dividers will separate file folders and other paperwork.

Figure 3-28. Eldon Versatilt

If you're short on work surface, try using **wall mount files.** Sometimes these files are referred to as **pockets** and they can be used on walls as well as on sides of desks and filing cabinets. They don't take up much space and they can hit the spot when you need a container for paperwork at the location they will be used. For some examples, see the **Eldon Hot Files and Pockets** in Figure 3-29.

If you have lots of literature or inserts you're pulling together to put into kits or notebooks, consider **literature organizers and sorters.** Your selection will depend on a number of factors: the number of separate inserts you use, the quantity of each insert you need to have on hand, the space you have available, the frequency of use and your budget.

Starting on the low end of need and budget, you might get by with a "mini literature sorter" such as **Fellowes Neat Ideas Desk Top Sorter** in Figure 3-30. Each compartment is one-inch deep. Units can be stacked on a bookcase or shelf. Another low cost solution is **Safco Literature Shelf Trays.**

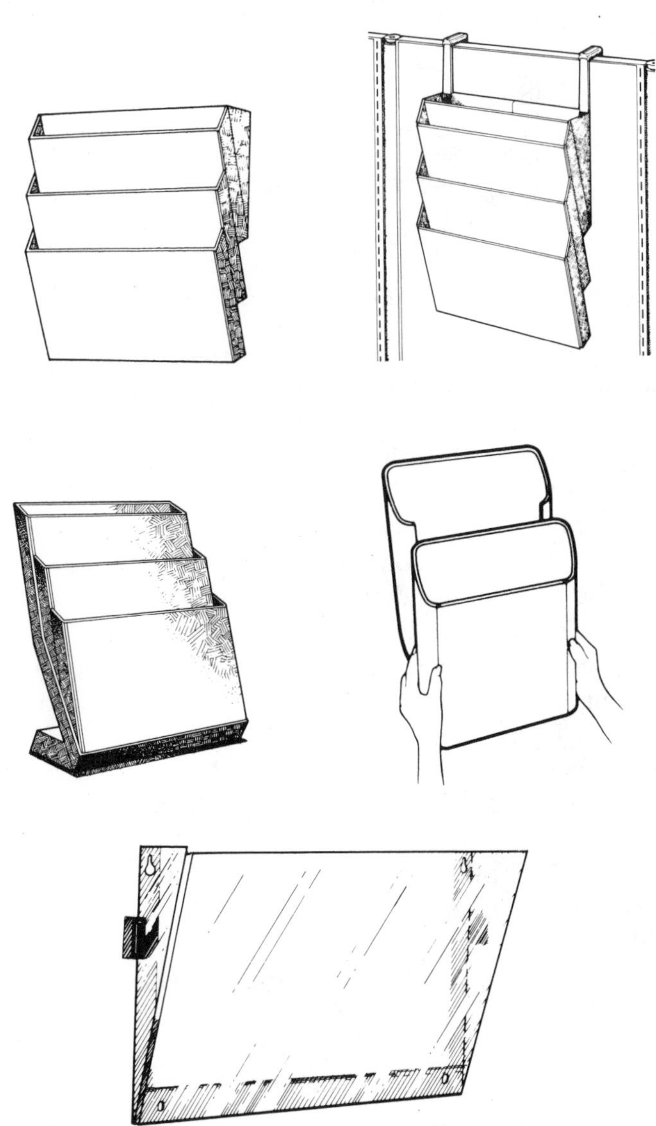

Figure 3-29. Eldon Hot Files and Pockets: Hot File Starter Set and Hot File Hanger Starter Set (top); Hot File Stand and Hot File II Add-On Pocket (middle); Magnetic Hot File (bottom)

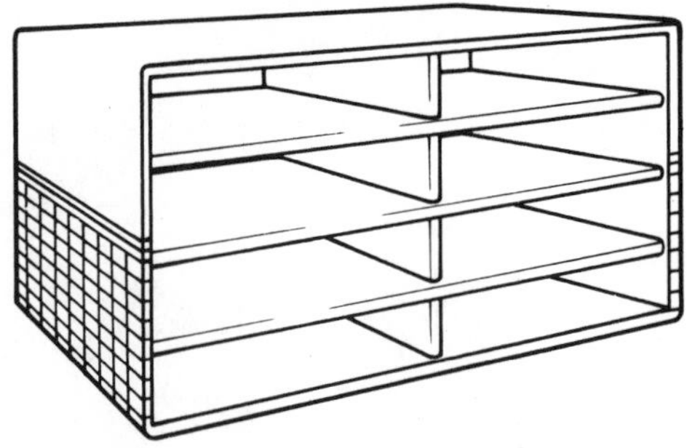

Figure 3-30. Fellowes Neat Ideas Desk Top Sorter

But if you need a more sophisticated solution because you have 24 to 96 different types of inserts to assemble frequently then you're ready for the **Safco Literature Organizer** described in Chapter 9.

Don't forget your basic letter trays, which are useful for in-out boxes or to hold papers to be filed or read. Look for stacking letter trays that leave space between trays and that use supports to connect trays. See the Eldon examples in Figure 3-31.

Eldon also makes a handy tray that sits on top of your computer terminal in Figure 3-32.

To keep other materials, supplies and references neatly organized around your computer and on your desktop consider the Oxford DecoRack in Figure 3-33.

Boorum Wireworks Catalog Rack in Figure 3-34 conveniently stores catalogs, instruction manuals, binders and other bulky reference materials.

If you do any work at a typewriter or computer keyboard, you need a **copyholder**. Figure 3-35 shows you the variety of styles that are available.

Last but not least are three wonderful products by 3M that will help you better handle paperwork. Post-it printed notes as shown in Figure 3-36 eliminate the need to write and rewrite requests for action. (You can also design and print your own custom Post-it messages–ask your printer.)

And finally, two 3M tape products I couldn't live without: Post-it Brand Correction and Cover-up Tape and Scotch Brand Removable Magic Tape. Post-it Tape is a removable opaque white tape for clean and quick copy blockout when you xerox. Scotch Removable Tape is a transparent tape that attaches papers temporarily and removes easily without damaging the material it is attached to. You can write on it with ink, pencil or marker. See Figure 3-37.

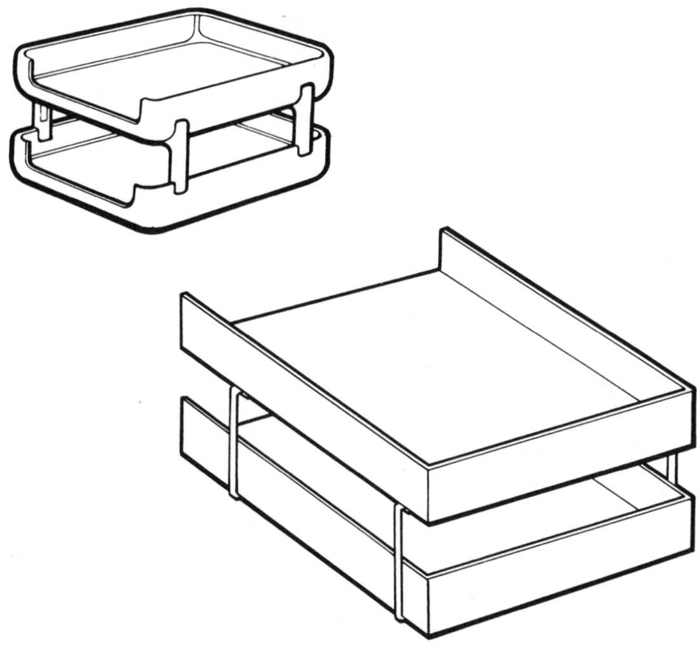

Figure 3-31. Eldon Image 1500 (top) and Eldon Reflection 2000 Letter Trays.

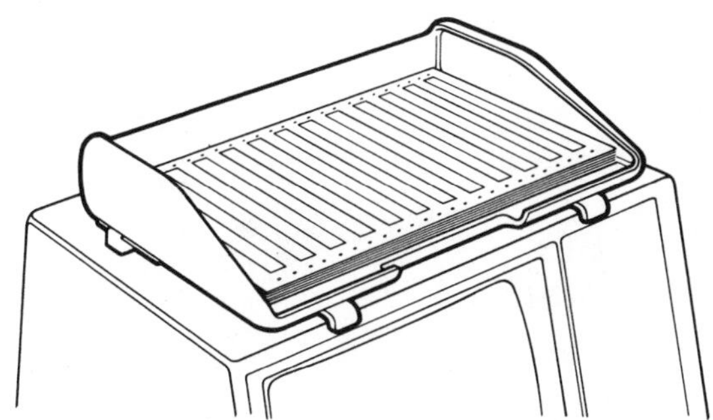

Figure 3-32. Eldon Stackable CRT Tray

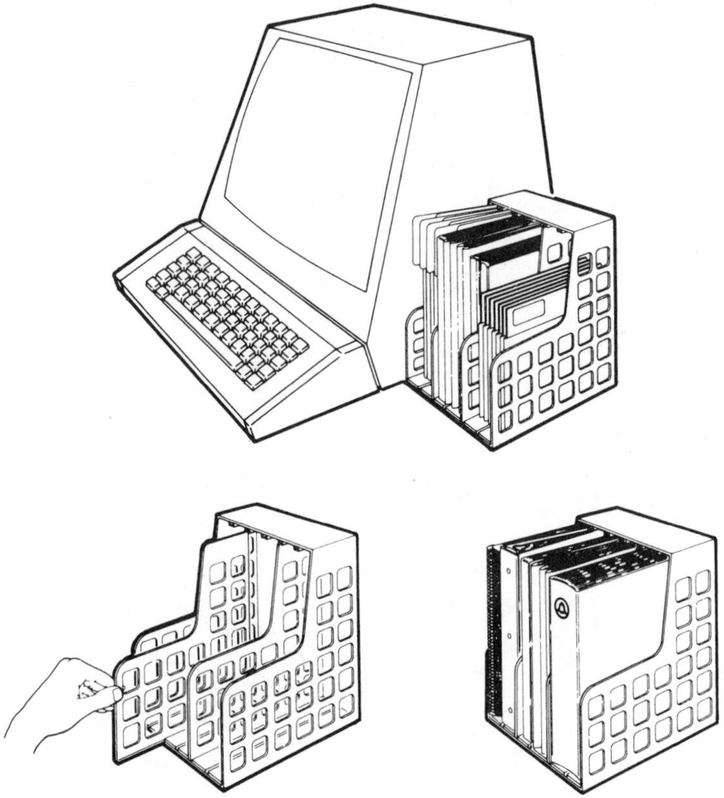

Figure 3-33. Oxford DecoRack by Esselte Pendaflex

Figure 3-34. Boorum Wireworks Catalog Rack by Esselte Pendaflex

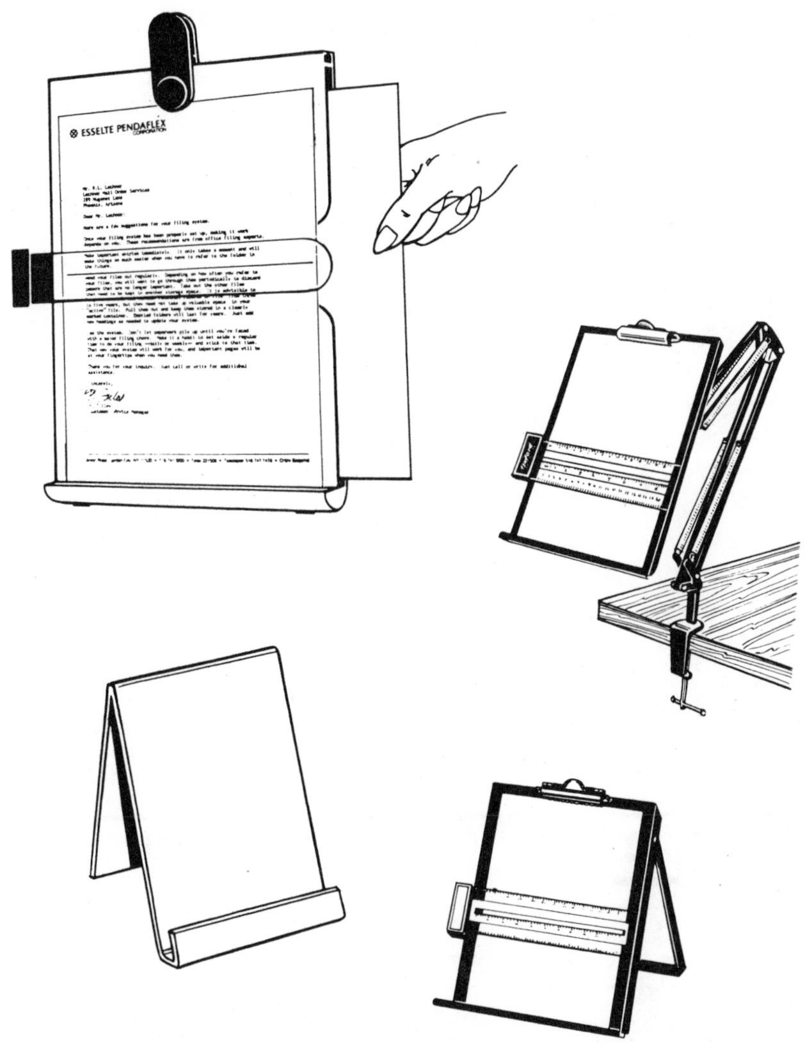

Figure 3-35. Oxford Copyholders by Esselte Pendaflex: Oxford CopyKeeper (top left) has a side storage compartment for "to-be-typed" materials; Oxford Flexible Arm Copyholder; Oxford CopyCaddy (bottom left); Oxford Desk Top Copyholder has a rolling ruler guide

Post-it telephone message pad 7660

To ______________________

Date ____________ Time ____________

WHILE YOU WERE OUT

M ______________________

of ______________________

Phone No. ______________________

TELEPHONED		PLEASE CALL	
WAS IN TO SEE YOU		WILL CALL BACK	
WANTS TO SEE YOU		URGENT	
RETURNED YOUR CALL			

Message ______________________

Operator ____________

Please Copy

Need ____ Copies

Copies To:

Original:

☐ Return to: ____________

☐ File under: ____________

☐ ____________

Post-it copy request pad 7670

Post-it routing request pad 7664

ROUTING - REQUEST

Please

☐ READ — To ____________

☐ HANDLE

☐ APPROVE

and

☐ FORWARD

☐ RETURN

☐ KEEP OR DISCARD

☐ REVIEW WITH ME

Date ____________ From ____________

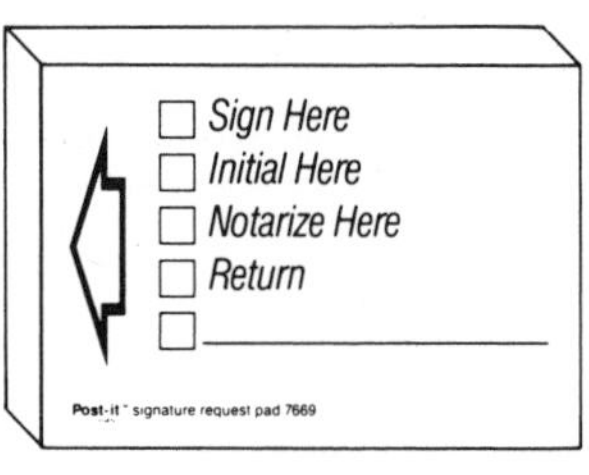

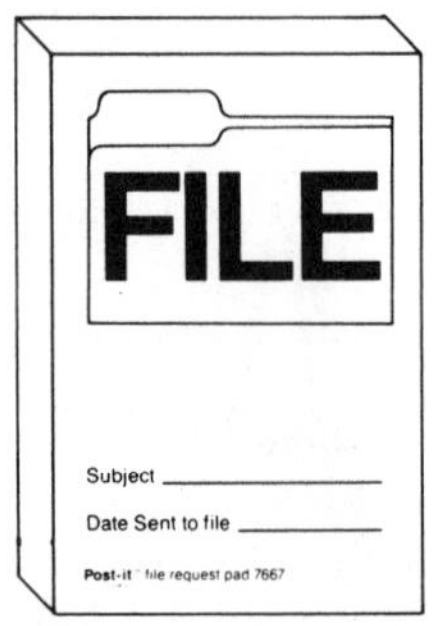

Figure 3-36. 3M Post-it Brand printed Telephone Message, Copy Request, Routing Request, Signature Request, File Request, F.Y.I. and Rush Request Pads

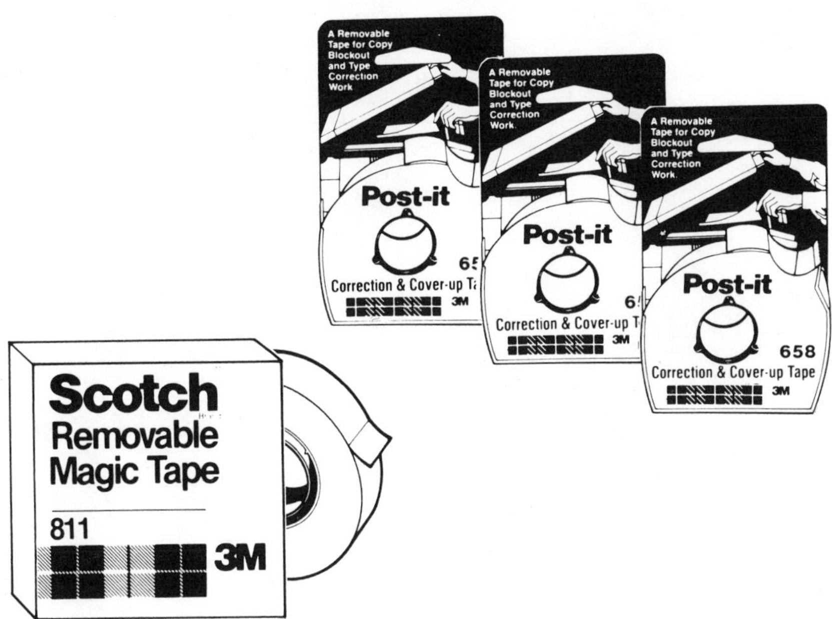

Figure 3-37. Post-it Brand Correction and Cover-up Tape and Scotch Brand Removable Magic Tape

A PRICELESS RESOURCE: CAPITALIZING ON UP-TO-DATE FILES

Quick Scan: They're out of sight, out of mind. Or so you'd like to think until one fateful day when you can't find that all important document. Or until your files are so full that it's physically dangerous trying to pry open files to slip in just one more paper. Find out how to organize your files so that they become an ally not an enemy. Discover what's what in filing supplies.

HOW DO YOUR FILES STACK UP?

For most people, paper files are like skeletons in the closet–bad secrets that no one likes to talk about. Who wants to admit that files are bulging with out-of-date papers, that they are difficult to handle and retrieve and that very often files are misplaced or even lost?

Then there are the *piles*–the papers that never make it into the files. They sit on desktops, in bookcases, on tables, on file cabinets, and yes, even on the floor. Let's see how you stack up in Figure 4-1.

Figure 4-1. YOUR FILES: A QUICK QUIZ

Check "yes" or "no" after each question.

	YES	NO
1. Is filing a real chore?		
2. Would it take a long while to catch up on your filing?		
3. Do you often have trouble finding and retrieving papers -often enough to cause irritation?		
4. Do you keep many papers and/or publications "just in case" someday you may need them?		
5. Is your filing system characterized more by randomness than careful planning?		
6. Are your files inconveniently located?		
7. Do you frequently have trouble deciding what to name files or where to file papers?		
8. Is it difficult to tell what's in each file drawer without opening it up?		
9. Are you afraid to attempt retrieving a document from your files (or piles) while someone is waiting in your office or you're on the phone? (Would you prefer to look without the time pressure of "beat the clock"?)		
10. Are you copy machine happy-do you make unnecessary duplicates of papers?		
11. Are all your filing cabinets/drawers stuffed to the gills?		

If you have at least three "yes" responses, keep reading!

Here are some of the excuses I hear from people who explain why their files are usually not as functional as they should be:

- I don't have a secretary.
- I don't have time/I'm too busy putting out fires.
- Setting up a system is menial, clerical work.
- It's not my job.
- I don't know what to call things.
- I'm creative and my work style is "organized chaos."

FILING PHOBIAS

Besides these excuses, there are three fears people have when it comes to files and piles. I call these fears the "3-Ds." First, people are afraid of Decisions. If you don't know what to call papers, you'll end up calling them nothing. Papers collect in stacks and piles, as well as in drawers and in-boxes.

Second, people are afraid of Discards. Heaven forbid you should throw anything out–you might need it someday.

Third, the fear of Disappearance haunts many. "Filing a paper in my system is like filing it in a black hole–never to be seen or heard from again," one new client told me.

Now that we've psychoanalyzed some filing phobias, here are some valid reasons for *making the time* to set up or revamp your deskside files. Check any that apply to you:

- You look and act more professional and competent when your information is organized.
- Organized information helps you plan your activities.
- It's easier to get work done.
- You feel better when you know where everything is. You have more control over your work.
- You save time looking for things.
- Accessible, fingertip information is a key resource for your productivity, professional image and peace of mind.
- Add some reasons of your own, making them relate specifically to your goals. What will a good filing system help you achieve or accomplish?
  -
  -

CREATING A SYSTEM IN FIVE EASY STEPS

There are five main steps to setting up or revamping your filing system:

1. Categorize files by *active* or *inactive*. For an existing filing system, remove inactive files from your active files.
2. Write out your filing system categories and sub-categories *on paper*. Get input from any others who'll be using the system.
3. Physically set up the system. Have supplies on hand, prepare file labels, purge and consolidate file folders and arrange file folders in your system.
4. Prepare a summary in the form of a file index, map or visual "key to the files," keep it handy and give it to any others who have access to your system. If others are involved, introduce

the system at a special meeting. Be open to comments and suggestions now and at a future follow-up evaluation meeting.

5. Maintain your system. Set up a filing routine for yourself and/or someone else, if you're lucky enough to have some assistance.

We'll go into more detail about these five steps after becoming more familiar with the thought process behind every good filing system.

GETTING STARTED

The hardest part of getting started is having enough incentive. You have to believe this is a top priority or you'll keep putting it off. Filing systems often get put on the proverbial back burner until you've run out of filing space or a crisis occurs.

Understand, too, that the actual filing or clerical work of the process is a small part. We'll be looking at the *mental*, conceptual side of creating or refining a filing system. What follows is a blueprint to guide you in designing your system.

WHAT, WHEN AND WHERE

There are three essential questions to answer about each paper or file:

1. **What** is it? Under what category(ies) does it belong?
2. **When** is it used? How many times a day, a week, a month, a year do you handle it?
3. **Where** should it go? Near your desk? In storage? In a filing cabinet? Which drawer? A notebook? The trash?

The What Question

Going back to question #1, what are the major areas or divisions of your work and/or your work-related information? Start thinking in terms of the largest, *broadest* categories.

One estate planning attorney who is a sole practitioner with a personal computer has designated four main areas of information: clients, business operation, estate planning information and personal computer resources/references. A management consultant has these three categories: business administration (which includes client files), content (for seminars and articles) and marketing/business development. A computer systems engineer has files for communications, software applications and hardware.

Here is a listing of general categories. Check any that might apply to your work. Add your own at the end. Remember to select the *broadest subject areas* (not necessarily specific file names) that apply to you.

Accounts, Customers, Clients or Patients
Background/History
Business Administration
Communications (in company or organization)
Contacts
Legislation
Management
Marketing
Products
Projects
Reference
Research
Resources
Samples
Staff
Support
Volunteers

The When Question

Files can also be categorized on the basis of *frequency*, that is *how often* they are used. There are two basic types: **active** and **inactive**, sometimes also called **open** and **closed.**

Active or open files all belong in your office because you will refer to each of them at least several times a year. You will either add to these files or retrieve something from them. Examples could include your resources, records from this year and active clients or customers.

Working files are active files that are used most often–daily or several times a week. They should be the most accessible to you at your desk or work station. They can go on a credenza, a side table next to your desk or inside the most accessible file drawer. The most active working files can be part of your daily paperwork system, described in Chapter 3.

Inactive, closed or storage files are used infrequently, if at all, and should usually be kept out of your office. If you opt to keep these files in your office, put them in the least accessible locations–in the rear of a file drawer, on a top shelf or in an area separate from your main work area. Whenever possible, remove files to someone else's office or to a designated storage area on- or off-site.

The Where Question

Where files go is a combination of *what* types of files they are, *who* uses them, *when* they are used and *how much room* you have. And you won't know how much room you have until after you have organized your existing system–determining all your category names, how often files will be used and purging your system of unnecessary information. (More on purging later on.)

One of the most important aspects of your deskside filing system is location, location, location. Here are some guidelines to consider when deciding upon location of files:

- Frequency of use usually determines proximity to your desk or main work area. Active files are closest.
- Related items usually go together unless they need to be pulled for storage or for working file status
- Choose appropriate media to store your information–perhaps you want to use notebooks or boxes rather than file folders. Maybe you have large, bulky or odd-sized items that require special filing solutions.
- Security may be a factor; take any necessary precautions to secure confidential information.

Now let's look more closely at the five steps.

THE PROCESS

STEP ONE: ACTIVE AND INACTIVE

Begin by separating piles, or files if you have them, into active or inactive categories. Go through an existing file system and weed out all the inactive files. Discard or store these inactive files.

If you don't have many files, but you have piles of long-term paper build-up and you know some important papers lie buried, go through these piles *quickly*. But don't start spending hours and hours going through long-term paper. You'll never create your filing system. These four steps will help you streamline the process:

1. Get yourself a countdown timer. (An egg timer is fine or you may prefer an LCD countdown timer available at Radio Shack.)
2. Quickly sort out the situation using the timer. This is not the time for a thorough analysis of each and every paper. As my friend and colleague **Maxine Ordesky** says, separate the treasures from the trash. For our purposes here, "treasures" are any papers that will go into active files. Set aside for now "semi-precious" papers that may go into storage. As far as what "trash" to toss at this time, apply my two **Discard Dilemmas** rules:
   1) When in doubt, *save* legal and tax information.
   2) When in doubt, *toss* resource information.
   (For more information on purging, see Chapter 9.)
3. Clear the decks. Put any culled materials temporarily in records storage boxes with lids (such as Fellowes Bankers Boxes). Try to keep the filing area as clear as possible–that way you'll be able to think and work more clearly.
4. As you do this sorting process, be thinking about category and file names and jot each one down on an index card, a Post-it or a sheet of paper. In this way, you'll be more prepared for Step Two.

STEP TWO: THE NAME GAME

Once you have the two most basic groupings of active and inactive, you are well on your way. Continue thinking about category and file names. Try one of three "name games."

It may be helpful to make a picture or chart of these names. Organizer **Nadia Holland** of Systematics recommends drawing an **organization chart**, also known as a "tree directory" in computer circles. Suppose you have three major categories called People, Products, Promotion. Your chart might look like the one in Figure 4-2.

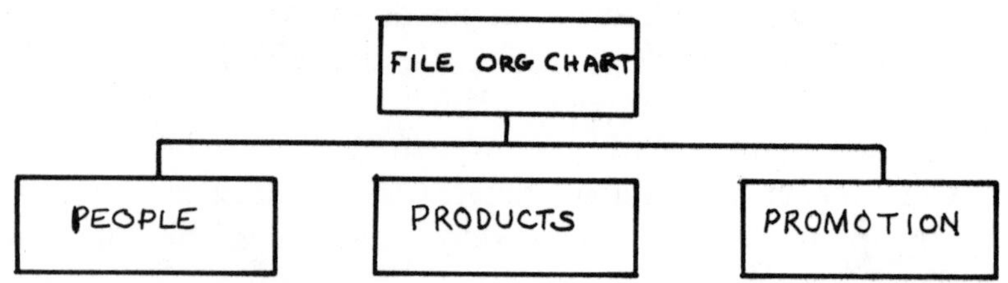

Figure 4-2. File Organization Chart

Writing in pencil, you would then draw lines and fill in the boxes with the next largest, broadest category names. Figure 4-3 shows how it might look now.

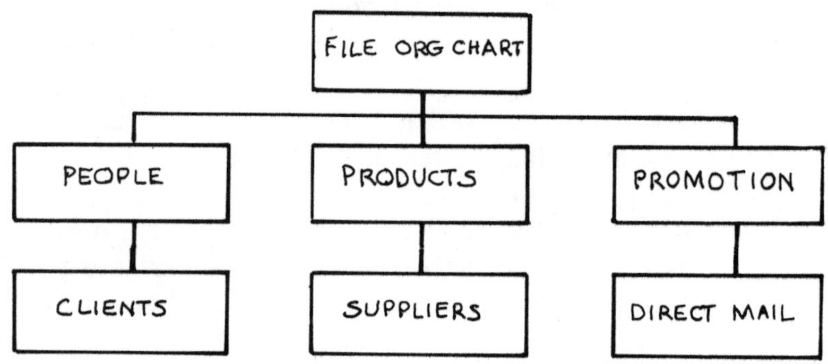

Figure 4-3. Expanded Organization Chart

If you're just setting up your system for the first time (or feel like it's the first time) you may want to use **index cards.** Buy colored cards and use one color for each of the major categories. Put each file name on the appropriately colored card and put it with the other cards. Spread out the cards and arrange them alphabetically or by subject. You'll use the cards later to make up your filing system labels.

If you have a computer, a **word processing program** will be helpful. Besides being able to easily move words around, many word processing programs such as WordPerfect let you sort (arrange) words alphabetically.

Look at the existing file folders or your stack(s) of papers to be filed. See if file names suggest themselves to you. Look for patterns, groupings, combinations that go together. Be creative but don't create categories that you won't remember later. Don't try to think of *every* file name right now; this is not your final system–it's only the beginning.

Designing a System on Paper

After playing with one or more of the above name games, you may be ready to design your system on paper.

Write down file names in a listing that shows how they all fit together. Don't worry about alphabetical order at this point (unless you're listing actual names of people or companies).

Start with one of your major category areas, say, Resource Information. Now look at the File Chart (Figure 4-4) which will help you organize your file categories and names and show how they are related.

Figure 4-4. FILE CHART

MAJOR CATEGORY (OR DRAWER NAME):

HEADING	SUBHEADING	SUBHEADING

Use the File Chart as a guide (xerox it if you want). Using pencil, (or your computer, if you're lucky enough to have one), write down a major work category from your filing system. Now complete what you think will be the main headings. Leave plenty of space between headings as shown in Figure 4-5. Select names for headings that make sense to *you* (and anyone else using the system). Stick with unadorned nouns for headings, if possible.

Figure 4-5. MAIN HEADINGS

MAJOR CATEGORY (OR DRAWER NAME): Resource Info.

HEADING	**SUBHEADING**	**SUBHEADING**
Contacts		
Manuals		
Products		
Warranties		

Look at Figure 4-6 to see the subheadings that have been added.

Figure 4-6. ADDED SUBHEADINGS

MAJOR CATEGORY (OR DRAWER NAME): Resource Info.

HEADING	**SUBHEADING**	**SUBHEADING**
Contacts	Stores	
	Consultants	Answers on Computers
	Service	
Manuals		
Products	Hardware	
	Software	
Warranties		

As you chart out headings and subheads you'll start to see which names belong together and which ones need additional subheads. You're creating your own file design. Don't get too carried away with elaborate headings and subheads. Usually one heading and two subheads are usually plenty. Keep your design simple!

Now complete the file chart for one *major category only.* Then, when you're ready, do a chart for each of your other major categories in your filing system. Remember, nothing is etched in stone; your file chart is only a guide.

STEP THREE: PUTTING IT ALL TOGETHER

Now it's time to physically set up your system–a time-consuming task that's nice to share with someone else, if you have the luxury.

Pull out your File Chart or index cards, which you can use as a map. Go through each heading and subhead. Put a star by any that you think will be up to one-inch thick and two stars by any that will be up to two inches thick.

Make sure you have the right supplies on hand (see also the chapter resource guide). The following are particularly important and are minimum suggested quantities:

One box of hanging file folders, (generally 25 to a box), they come with or without tabs

Hanging "box bottom" file folders, one-inch capacity, one box of 25, no tabs included

Hanging box bottom file folders, two-inch capacity, one box of 25, no tabs

Plastic tabs for any hanging folders that don't come with tabs. Tabs come in two-inch or 3½-inch lengths–I prefer the 3½-inch size.

If you're going to color code your files, get colored plastic tabs or buy colored plastic windows (to use with clear plastic tabs).

Third-cut Interior folders, (100 per box); interior folders are cut lower than ordinary manilla folders so that the folders sit inside the hanging folders without sticking up; they come in a variety of colors

Self-adhesive file folder labels; if you're color-coding your files, buy the colored labels

Color coding by drawer or by major category can be helpful, especially when you go to refile a folder. We use blue for our business and administrative files, for example, and yellow for our resource information files. You're less likely to misfile a folder in the wrong drawer with color coding. You can also see at a glance the type(s) of folders in a particular drawer. Keep your color coding scheme as simple as possible, however.

Hanging file folders, especially the one- and two-inch box bottoms, work great as your major headings. Inside each box bottom folder, place several interior folders, which can serve as your subheads. Any subheads that are thick can be given their own box bottom folders, too. Avoid using only one interior folder per hanging folder; too many hanging folders will take up too much space and you won't take advantage of the heading/sub-heading classification system, which adds to greater retrievability.

Working on one major category at a time from your File Chart, indicate which of the headings and subheads will take regular, one-inch or two-inch hanging folders. (Most of your subheads will take interior folders.)

With your File Chart as a guide, type or print the hanging folder labels using all capital letters. (For more ideas about labeling, see Figure 4-7 called "Creative Labels for Hanging Folders.")

Figure 4-7. CREATIVE LABELS FOR HANGING FOLDERS

Colleague **Beverly Clower** of Office Overhaul uses a **Kroy lettering machine** to create large, legible labels. She uses 18- and 24-point size wheels in the Helvetica bold all caps font style. The 24-point size is for headings and the 18-point size is for major subheads. Kroy produces black lettering on clear (or white, if you prefer), self-adhesive strips cut to size. Each strip is then affixed to the white label insert.

If you have access to a **personal computer** with some desktop publishing capabilities, you could prepare your label names with the font and style of your choice. Print them directly on an 8½-by-11-inch sheet of "crack 'n peel" (self-adhesive paper used for labels).

Or if your printer won't accommodate crack 'n peel, print onto your normal paper, which will become the master. Then use the master to xerox onto the crack 'n peel (make sure your copier will accept crack 'n peel-most high speed copiers should).

If your copier will accommodate it, you might also try xeroxing onto "65 lb. card stock," a heavier grade of paper that you could use instead of the furnished white label inserts.

With any of these options (other than Kroy) you'll have to spend time cutting the labels on a paper cutter.

Insert the labels into the hanging folder plastic tabs. Go through your File Chart and see which headings and subheads require hanging folders. Put in order the hanging folders you had marked on your File Chart. Insert the plastic tab on the inside front cover at the far left for headings. For subheads, you may wish to place the plastic tab a little over toward the right, as shown in Figure 4-8. Also note that you should stagger any tabs that would block other tabs. If you have selected a box bottom folder, insert the cardboard reinforcement strip in the two slots located on the bottom. Set up your new hanging folders in a file drawer. Place existing file folders inside the new hanging folders.

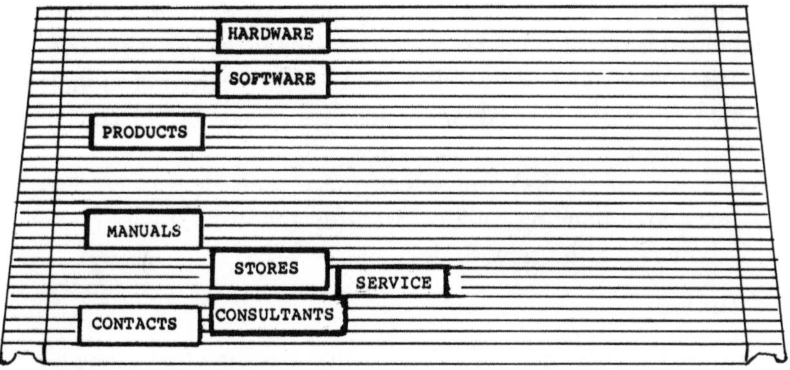

Figure 4-8. Position hanging folder tab headings on the left and subheadings to the right. Notice that the tab subheadings, "Consultants," "Stores" and "Service," are staggered for greater visibility.

Now type labels for new interior folders. Before you affix them on the interior folders, place the three types of folders in front of you: left-cut, center-cut and then right-cut (assuming you are using third-cut folders). Pull folders in order of left-cut, center-cut, and right-cut. Don't always start at the left every time you come to a new hanging folder; keep going where you left off. That way you won't end up with a lot of extra right- or center-cut folders when you're done. In addition, you will maintain good visibility in your system by staggering folders in this way. Now affix the labels.

For interior folders that you know will be handled frequently and will risk dog-earring, cover the label area with either self-adhesive plastic that you'll have to cut to size or use pre-cut label protectors listed in the resource guide.

Arranging Folders

You can arrange your file folders in a number of ways: alphabetically, numerically or by frequency of use. You might even arrange your folders in a combination of ways. For example, you might use a basically alphabetical setup but group frequently used folders in a special, accessible location, for example, in the front of your file drawer.

Certain kinds of information work better alphabetically. For example, client or customer name files work best in an alphabetical system.

On the other hand, subject files do not always have to be in strict alphabetical order. It may be more convenient to place files you use more often in a more accessible location, irrespective of alphabetical sequence. Frequently-used subheads, too, may be placed out of alphabetical order within their hanging folders.

Whichever method(s) you select, place your interior folders into their respective hanging folders. Transfer any unfiled papers you can at this point into the new folders.

Fine Tuning

You may have noticed that your existing files haven't yet undergone a complete and thorough purge. There's a good reason for this. It's better to set up a *functional* system first and fine tune later. Do your fine tuning now.

Go carefully through each of your existing, *active* folders in your system. Do you really need this information? How accessible does it have to be? Could a folder be consolidated with another folder? Use a timer and allot a specified period of time, from 15 minutes to an hour and a half on a given day. Or try giving yourself a goal, say, five folders in fifteen minutes.

You may find you need to add new labels (or delete others). Add them to your File Chart in a different color. Don't take time out to type or print the labels right now. Jot down subheads in pencil on new folders.

When you have completed the purge for one complete subject area, type or print any remaining labels and attach them to the new folders.

STEP FOUR: SUMMARY AND INTRODUCTION

Now that you've physically set up your system, make sure you can tell the types of files you have in each drawer without having to open each one. You need a summary of your file drawer contents. Such a summary could be as simple as labeling each drawer with main headings.

Beverly Clower makes a "key to the files," which is a map or diagram of file cabinets and drawers. See Figure 4-9.

A simple listing on paper, such as your File Chart or a "file index," could suffice. Or keep a listing on your computer that can be easily updated. Be sure to print out at least one "hard copy" on paper.

Train anyone who'll be using your filing system. Have a special meeting or training session to introduce the system. Distribute a file index, file chart, key to the files or other listing. If appropriate, show how to borrow files by leaving an **out guide** in the place of the missing file. See Figure 4-10.

STEP FIVE: MAINTENANCE

The trick to a productive filing system is a regular maintenance program by you or someone you designate. Your program should be fairly routine and involve only a minimal amount of time–famous last words! But let's see how it can be done.

Start by making some decisions in advance about your file maintenance program. Answer the following questions:

1. Who's going to do your filing?
2. Will you file some or all papers "as you go"? Which ones?
3. If you plan to file papers in batches, how often and when specifically will filing occur?
4. How many times a year will you purge your files and transfer inactive files into storage? During which months or quarters?

Too many professionals and offices have *no* filing maintenance guidelines. Don't wait until an emergency, crammed file cabinets or a move forces you to take stock. It may be too late or you may be

KEY TO THE FILES

Cabinet 1: Next to Shirley's Desk	Cabinet 2: Next to Ann's Desk
OFFICE ADMINISTRATION GENERAL INFO/SOURCES	BOARD OF TRUSTEES MINUTE BOOKS COMMITTEES
INSURANCE PERSONNEL	CONTRIBUTIONS FINAN. ASSISTANCE
AGREEMENTS/CONTRACTS	ESTATE FILES
REPORTS/STUDIES	BUILDING PROJECTS

Figure 4-9. A "key to the files," such as the one above, is distributed to everyone in an office using or accessing an office filing system.

in the middle of a top priority project that prevents you from devoting what will now require a large chunk of time.

Adopt a **purge prevention policy** such as the one developed by **Derrick Crandall**, president of the American Recreation Coalition in Washington, D.C. Crandall implemented an ongoing, self-policing, purge prevention policy to limit office file cabinets to two, lateral, five-drawer units. He explains, "It's so easy to become a walking encyclopedia of nonessential stuff. It's more time effective to go elsewhere for information, even if it takes 24 hours to get it than having to purge files in two to three years. It's a terrible waste of time to prune that stuff–better to deal with it the first time around."

Set up your own maintenance system. Until your system takes root, write it down on your daily to-do list or in your calendar.

Decide how many minutes a day or a week you (or someone you designate) will spend on it. Which day(s) will you choose and which time(s)? Be specific. Make it a habit. Take a look at the Quick Chart (Figure 4-11) for other ideas.

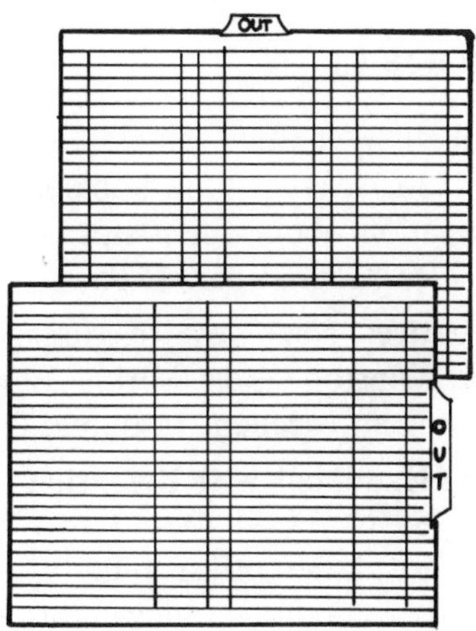

Figure 4-10. Two different styles of out guides, which function as library cards for your filing system

Figure 4-11. QUICK CHART: FILE MAINTENANCE TIPS

Here are some tips to make filing easier:

- Immediately after you read a paper or an article you want to save and file, jot down the subject or file name in the top right corner. This will save you time, especially if the paper is not filed right away so that you or an assistant don't have to re-read the paper before it's filed.
- If the information in the article will probably be obsolete after a period of time, indicate a discard date in the top left corner. This will help you easily toss old papers without having to reread them.
- As an experiment, keep track of papers or files that you actually go back and refer to. Jot down an "R date"–the date you referred back to a paper or file for information. At the top of the paper or file write "R" followed by the date. If you start to see several R dates, maybe you need to move this information so that it's more accessible. On the other hand, seeing no R dates, you may decide to discard more papers and files. If nothing else, R dates may show you how often or little you actually refer to files.

The longer you wait to either set up or implement your maintenance system the easier it is for paper to accumulate once again. Get tough on paper!

RESOURCE GUIDE

BOOKS AND BOOKLETS

How to File published by Esselte Pendaflex Corp., Clinton Rd., Garden City, NY 11530. A great little booklet with lots of photos, examples and information about filing tips, supplies and systems. 800/368-2077 or 516/741-3200. Paper. $4.95

The Organized Executive: New Ways to Manage Time, Paper and People by Stephanie Winston (New York: Warner Books, 1985). The chapter on filing is an excellent resource. Paperback $7.95.

Records Management Handbook with Retention Schedules. Fellowes Manufacturing Co. 1789 Norwood Ave., Itasca, IL 60143, 312/893-1600. While geared for large office filing systems, this booklet provides useful records retention/purging information applicable to smaller systems. Free.

FILING SUPPLIES

FOLDERS

Hanging folders, like the Smead folder in Figure 4-12, are made of durable, green paper stock or in colored stock. Pendaflex Hanging Folders also come in plastic.

Scoring in the middle of the front and back flaps of some hanging file folders such as Pendaflex allow you to bend back the flaps so that the folder can be propped open in the file drawer until the contents are reinserted. See Figure 4-13.

The basic hanging folder is v-shaped but scoring and folding along the bottom edge will increase your storage capacity. To really increase the capacity so that you can more easily use the hanging

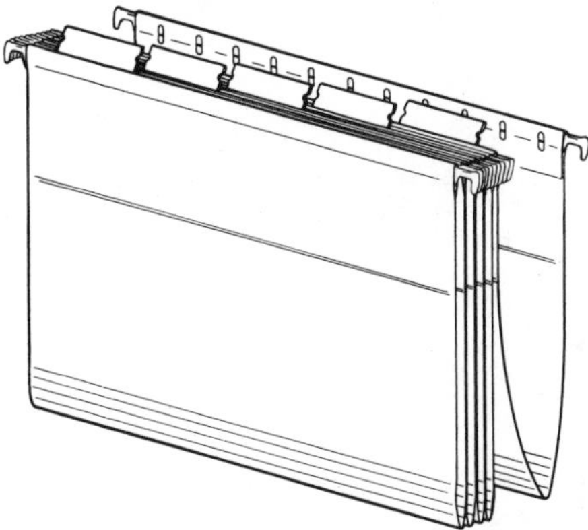

Figure 4-12. Smead Flex-I-Vision hanging folders are scored at the bottom for a full two-inch expansion.

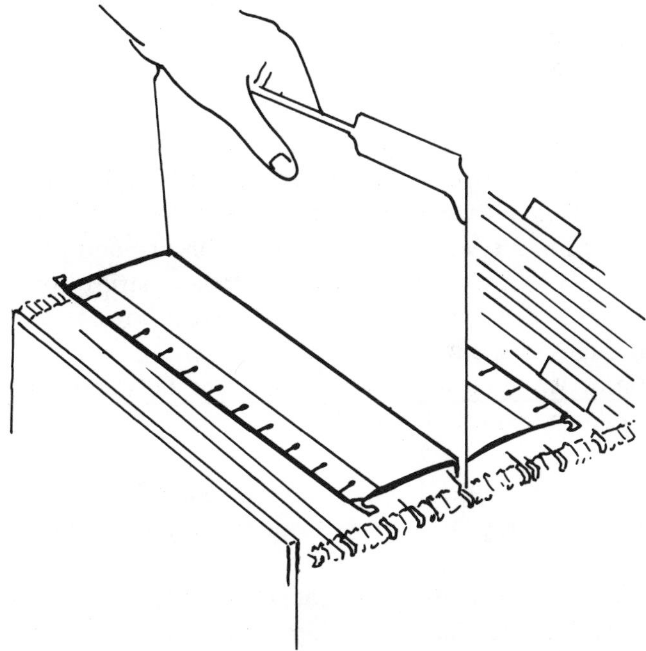

Figure 4-13. Scoring in the middle of Pendaflex hanging file folders lets you bend back the flaps to "mark your place" in a filing drawer when you temporarily remove a file.

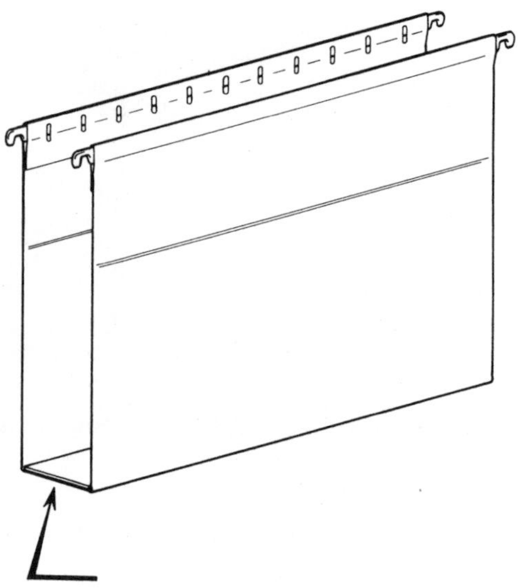

Figure 4-14. Smead Flex-I-Vision box bottom folder

folder as a container for several file folders (or for catalogs) use a **box bottom folder**, which, depending on the manufacturer, come in one- to four-inch capacity, letter or legal size, and two-inch for computer printout size. Pendaflex box bottoms come in the standard green or in other colors. Special cardboard strips reinforce the "bottom" edge of box bottoms. On the Smead box bottom the strip is pre-installed. See Figure 4-14.

Pendaflex Hanging Box File is a blue box bottom with sides that prevent papers and other materials from slipping out. See Figure 4-15.

Pendaflex also makes hanging folders that will meet a variety of different filing storage needs for: invoices, x-rays, computer printouts, checks and magnetic media.

The **Pendaflex Hanging File Jacket** in Figure 4-16 lets you file small items with standard sized papers so that they won't slip out. Notice the easy-access, cut-away front.

Pendaflex Interior Folders come in manila and five two-tone colors. They are slightly shorter than standard file folders, so they won't obscure the hanging folder tab.

Figure 4-15. Pendaflex Hanging Box File

Figure 4-16. Pendaflex Hanging File Jacket

For manila folders that are handled frequently, consider getting those with **reinforced** tabs such the one in Figure 4-17.

If you hole punch papers, rather than keeping them loose in folders, you probably use fasteners. Figure 4-18 shows Smead folders

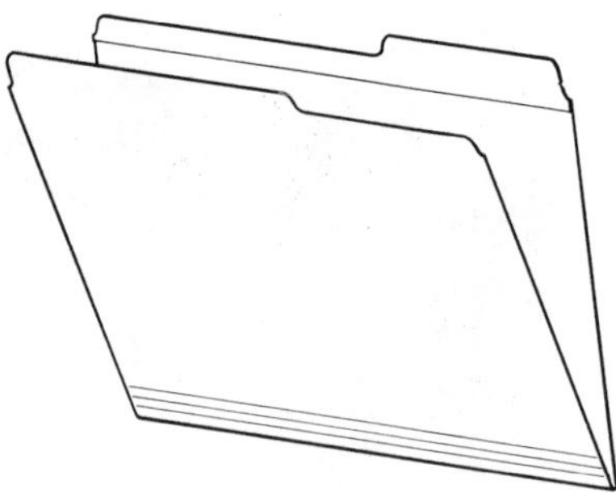

Figure 4-17. This Smead manila folder with the reinforced "two-pli" tab has extra durability. Notice also the scoring along the bottom which permits 3/4-inch expansion.

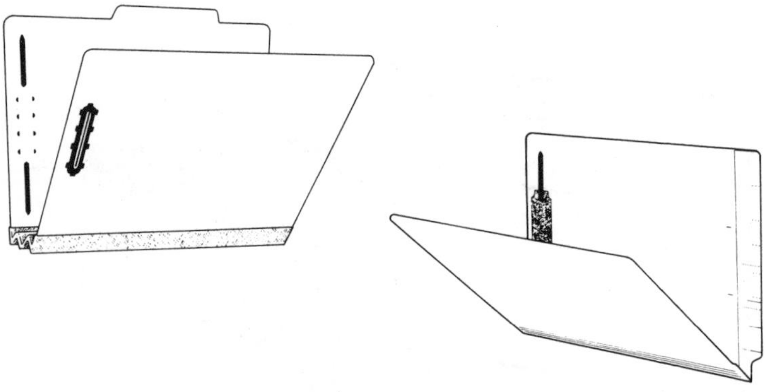

Figure 4-18. Smead folders with two different styles of fastener: the "K" fastener (on left) is clinched into slots by eight tabs and the "B" fastener has a strong fiber base that bonds to inside surface of folder

with the fasteners already attached. Why would you use these folders? They're essential for important papers that have legal or tax implications where you just can't take a chance on losing any paper. Generally, you'll put papers in reverse chronological order–i.e., the most recent papers are on top–and in that order they will stay securely. Hole punched papers take up less space, which is particularly important in businesses where bulky files are the order of the day.

The **Pendaflex Hanging Partition Folder** (shown in Figure 4-19) is really two folders in one—a hanging folder and an interior folder. But what an interior folder! You can group related papers in different sections of the folder by attaching two-hole-punched papers to fasteners on the six sides of the partitions and/or by placing unpunched papers in the three sections created by the partitions.

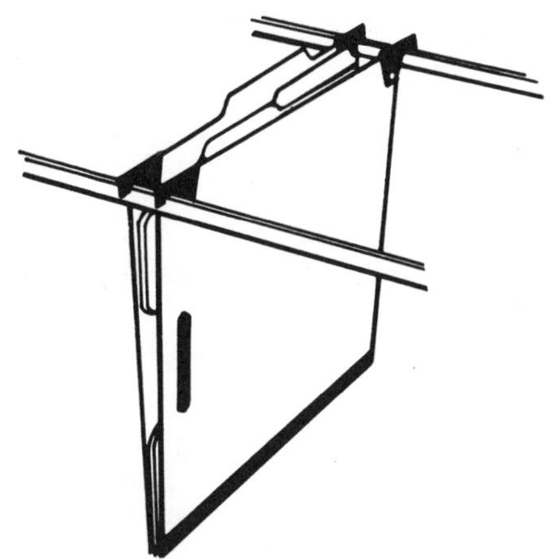

Figure 4-19. Pendaflex Hanging Partition Folder

Wherever you'd use several interior folders for one client or project, the **partition folder** (hanging or non-hanging) is great. The partition folder, also called a **classification folder**, is made of heavy duty pressboard. Different styles are available from different manufacturers. You can get from one to three partitions, some of which are pocket dividers. See Figure 4-20.

If you frequently pull files out of the filing cabinet and take them to different locations, you may want to use folders that have three sides to protect the contents. The **file jacket** comes in two styles—flat or expansion. File jackets can be used within your filing system or as part of the daily paperwork system discussed in Chapter 3. Oxford file jackets come in manila and in ten colors. See Figure 4-21.

Much sturdier than the file jacket, the **file pocket** in Figure 4-22 has accordion style sides called "gussets" that allow for more expansion and use. The file pocket can fit inside a file cabinet, on

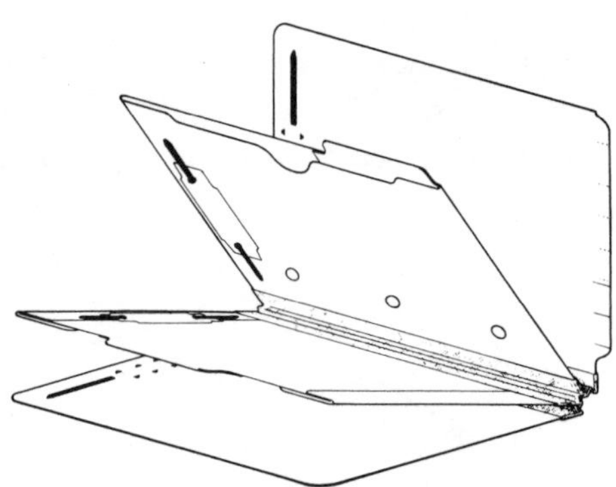

Figure 4-20. This Smead Classification Folder comes with pocket style dividers.

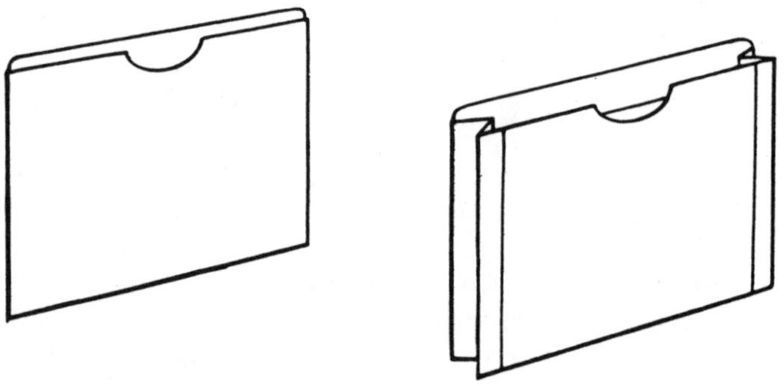

Figure 4-21. Oxford Manila File Jacket (on left) and Oxford Expandable Manila File Jacket

a shelf or in a metal collator (see Chapter 3). The file pocket will hold several related file folders together or other bulky materials, including catalogs and books.

The **expanding wallet** is similar to the file pocket except it has a flap with a tie or an elastic cord. It is used for carrying, transporting or storing old records. Wallets come with or without internal dividers or "pockets." I use wallets with pockets to store my annual tax and business records. See Figure 4-23.

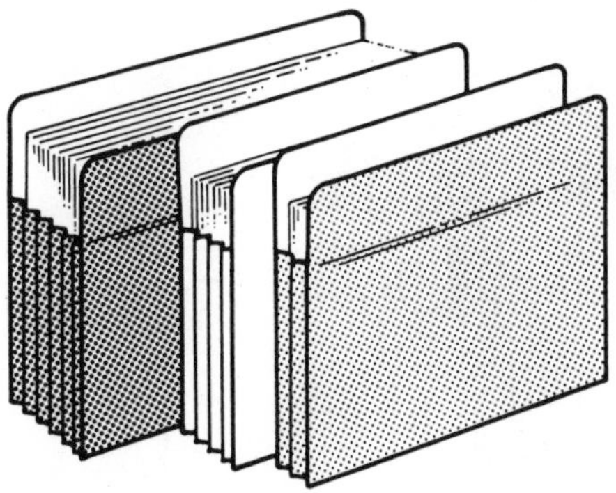

Figure 4-22. WilsonJones ColorLife File Pockets

The **expanding file** is similar to the wallet in terms of construction (except you can get it without the flap). The expanding file is a box-like, multi-pocket file with pre-printed headings such as A-Z, 1-31 and Jan-Dec. Figure 4-24 shows an example. If you're looking for an extremely durable material for an expanding file, check out **WilsonJones ColorLife Expanding Files** in a good office supply catalog or **CaseGuard** in the **Law Publications** catalog (800/421-3173; in California, 800/858-7474; in Los Angeles, 213/558-3933). Speaking of materials, take a look at Figure 4-25 to see the different types and grades of materials for file folders.

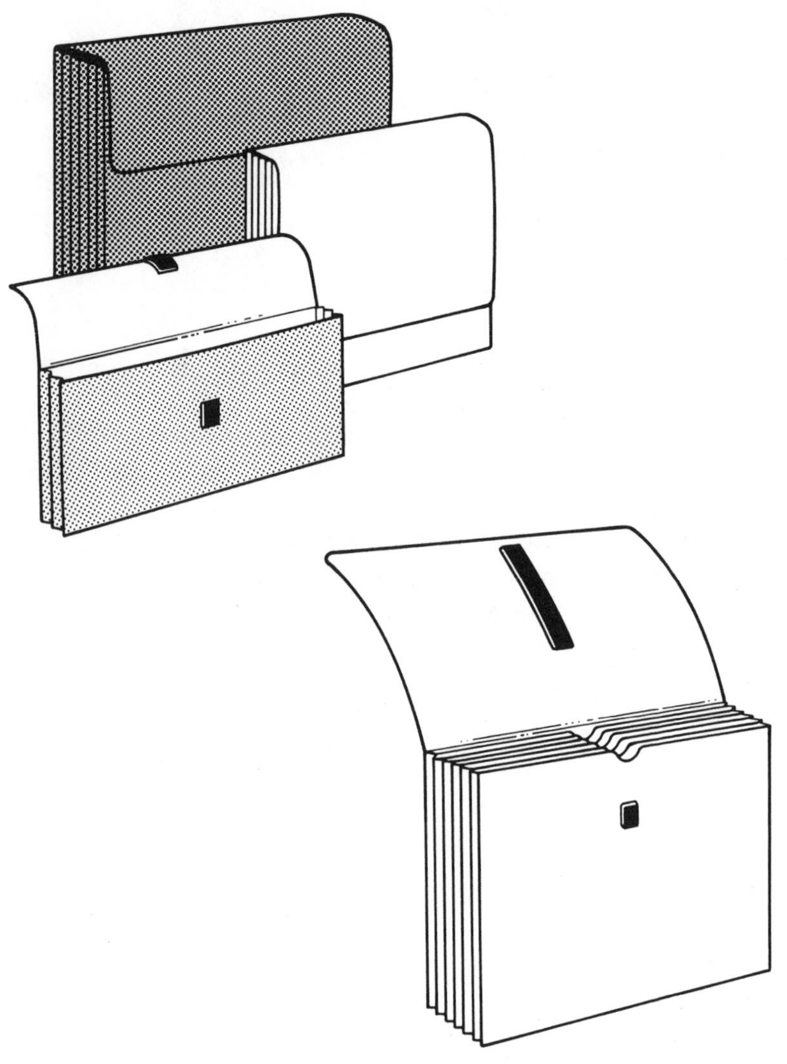

Figure 4-23. WilsonJones ColorLife Expanding Wallets with single pocket and six pocket styles

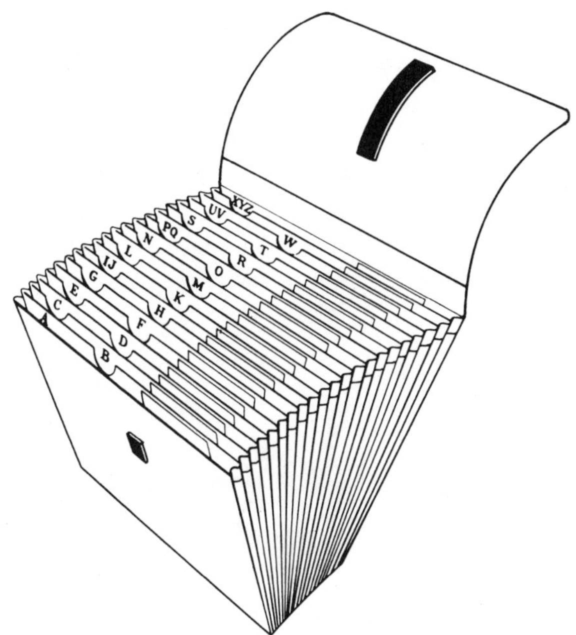

Figure 4-24. WilsonJones ColorLife Expanding File

Figure 4-25. FILE FOLDER MATERIALS (Reprinted with permission of Esselte Pendaflex Corp.)

3 COMMON TYPES OF PAPER FOR FOLDERS:

Manila is semi-bleached stock that resists tearing, folding and bursting. It's available in 9½- and 11-point thicknesses (more about point sizes momentarily).

Kraft is durable, smooth, unbleached stock that offers greater strength and rigidity. The tan color resists soiling. It comes in 11 and 17 points.

Pressboard is hard, dense, long-lasting that offers superior strength and comes in 25 points.

MORE ABOUT POINTS AND FOLDER PAPER STOCK

Bearing in mind that a point is all of .001 inch....

9½ points Medium weight.
11 points Heavy weight. Available in manila and kraft.
17 points Extra heavy weight. Available in kraft.
25 points Superior weight and thickness. Available in pressboard.

OTHER SUPPLIES

You'll need **hanging file frames** (see Figure 4-26) to support your hanging folders, unless your filing equipment already has them. Most come notched at half-inch intervals that you can break off to fit your drawer. But since most never break off easily, I recommend having your supplier cut them to size for you. Be sure to get the right size frame; Pendaflex drawer frames come in not only letter and legal but also check, invoice and jumbo x-ray sizes.

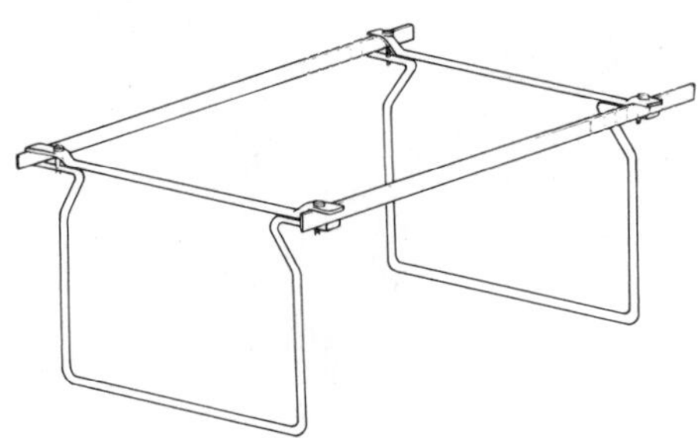

Figure 4-26. Smead Steel Frame for hanging file folders

Pendaflex Links and **Stop Clamps** in Figure 4-27 are useful accessories that will help you better manage and separate your hanging file folders. Made of stainless steel, links fasten hanging folders together so you can prevent between-folder misfiles. Stop clamps fasten to frame rails to separate groups of folders or to keep folders from sliding along the frame.

Hanging folder **tabs** generally come in one-fifth or one-third cut. I recommend "third-cut" because of the larger label surface. **Pendaflex Insertable Tabs** come in clear (white) and seven colors–blue, green, orange, pink, red, violet and yellow. Or if you prefer, get the clear **Pendaflex Snap-On Tabs**. They're easier to attach but if you're using color coding, you'll need to also buy and insert **Pendaflex Colored Plastic Windows**. Use these windows, too, in any existing clear tabs that you'd like to color-code. **Pendaflex Printed Label Inserts** let you save labeling time. Inserts are printed A-Z for name, subject and alphanumeric filing; States for geographic files; and Months (Jan.-Dec.) and Daily (numbered 1-31) for follow-up, sequential or chronological filing.

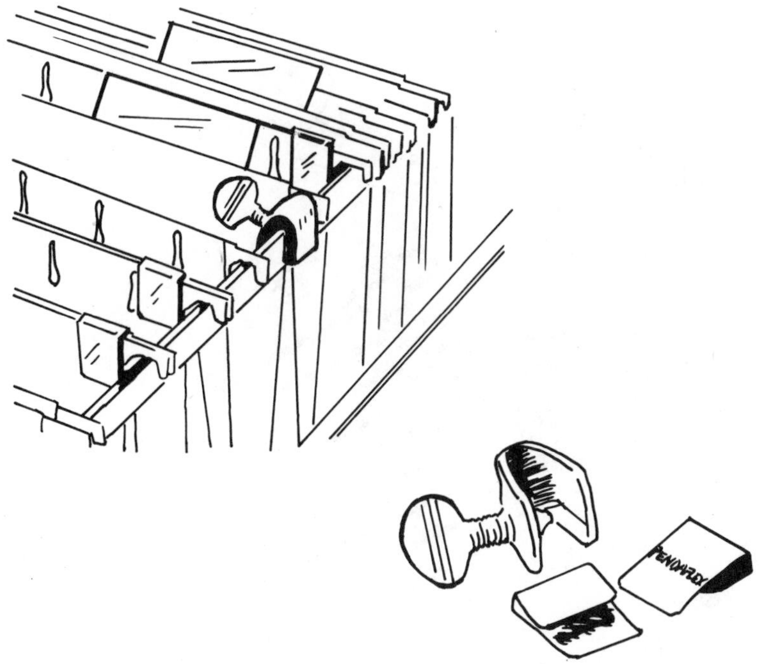

Figure 4-27. Pendaflex Links and Stop Clamp

Label protectors will help you keep file folder labels and tabs clean and resistent to wear and tear. **Smead Seal & View Label Protectors** ($4.50 for a box of 100) are made of a clear, Mylar laminate and should be available in your office supply catalog.

You can also get label protectors by mail order from the **Business Finance Forms** catalog (800/621-2184 or in Chicago, 312/663-9777) and the **SYCOM** catalog (800/356-8141 or in Wisconsin, 800/356-9152). If you only need a few and don't mind cutting them yourself, look under "Sheet Protectors" in an office supply catalog and then look for clear, self-adhesive, plastic sheets that you can cut to size.

And here's a new twist on labels. 3M has just come out with **Post-it Brand Removable File Folder Labels** (Figure 4-28) for both file folders and hanging file folders. Use them for temporary labels or for ones you change frequently. Try them, also, whenever you're setting up or revamping a filing system.

Figure 4-28. Post-it Brand Removable File Folder Labels

5 POWERFUL COMPUTING: ORGANIZING YOUR IBM PERSONAL COMPUTER FILES

Quick Scan: Both you and your computer will never be the same when you learn the basics of organizing and maintaining your computer files. Gain full value from your automation tool by discovering how computer files should be organized on hard disks and floppies and which computer products can help you the most. This chapter is for anyone who uses an IBM personal computer or compatible, has DOS version 2.1 or higher or OS/2 and has, or plans to have, a hard disk.

One day, when the glow of using a computer wears off, you may discover you're having trouble getting around your computer. Files are hard to find. Naming and organizing your files is confusing. Somehow you thought the computer would make everything easier, certainly easier than dealing with all the paperwork on your desk and in your cabinets.

The bad news is that just like paper files, computer files need to be accessible, up-to-date, properly categorized and regularly maintained. Your computer can slow down dramatically whenever computer file organization and maintenance is poor (or non-existent).

But the good news is both you and your computer will function better when your personal computer files are in good working order. And it's not hard to learn how to organize your files.

If your computer has DOS 2.1 or higher, then you already have access to a built-in organization system called *tree-structured directories*. These directories make up a classification system that comes with your computer. They're called "tree-structured" because a diagram of them resembles a tree–an upside-down tree to be exact.

STARTING AT THE ROOT OF THE MATTER

Just as you start with the root of a tree, so, too, tree-structured directories start with the **root directory**. This is the first and main directory; all other directories "branch off" from the root.

Technically, there is only one directory, the root directory. All the other directories are really **subdirectories**. All of your subdirectories grow and expand as you add files to them.

A directory or subdirectory (the terms are often used interchangeably) is a specific area on your disk that stores files, usually related files. Compare it to a drawer or a section of a drawer in your filing cabinet that holds a particular grouping of files. All subdirectories are related to one another, too, because in the tree-structured directory system, they all descend ultimately from the root directory. Some subdirectories are on the same level, some have their own subdirectories and those subdirectories can have their own subdirectories, ad infinitum.

If the terms "root directory" and "subdirectory" are still confusing, compare them to their counterparts in a paper filing system. Think of the root directory as your entire filing cabinet with no dividers for major sections or categories. All contents will be thrown together unless you include groupings such as dividers or drawers called subdirectories in the computer world.

The tree-structured directory system is similar to the one you set up for your paper files in Chapter 4. In a well-organized paper filing system you group related files together under headings and subheadings. You do much the same thing with your computer files, whether they're on floppies or your hard disk, when you group them in subdirectories.

You can draw a picture of your tree-structured directories, just as you drew a chart for your paper files in Chapter 4. Think of this drawing as a "family tree" for your computer that shows how everything is related. The Directory Tree Chart in Figure 5-1, adapted from my computer's tree-structured directories, will help you see the relationships between five of my major subdirectories.

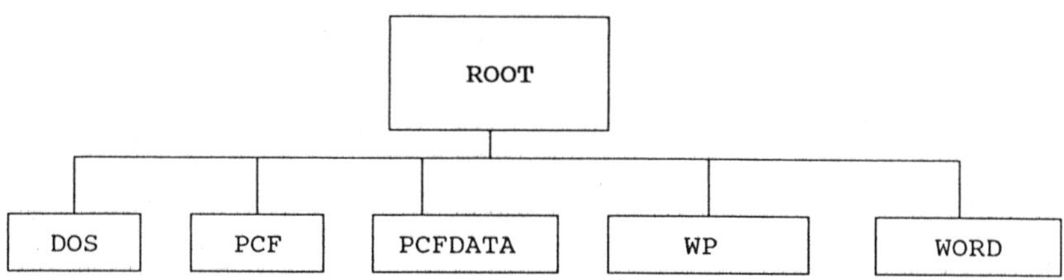

Figure 5-1. Directory Tree Chart adapted from my computer

AN ORGANIZED ROOT DIRECTORY

The root directory is the place that files will automatically go until you set up your subdirectories. The purpose of the root directory, however, is *not* to store files. An organized root directory works like a table of contents for your entire hard disk.

Most importantly, **don't put all of your files in the root directory.** Just as you shouldn't put all your eggs in one basket, you're asking for trouble by putting all of your files in the root directory. For one thing, the root directory is limited as to the number of files it can hold. All your files simply wouldn't fit. And for another, even if your files didn't exceed the limit, you'd spend a lot of time trying to locate files. There is a better way to organize your system. Tree-structured directories let you group related files together so that your root directory doesn't become the local dumping ground. Your root directory should contain the names of your first level subdirectories plus miscellaneous files that your programs require and three DOS files–command.com, config.sys and autoexec.bat. Put the rest of your DOS files in their own subdirectory branching off from the root directory called \DOS.

Most of all, remember that the root directory is not a place to put miscellaneous files. Check your root directory from time to time to make sure you haven't accidentally saved a file there that belongs in a subdirectory.

To see the files in your hard disk root directory from anywhere on your computer, go to any DOS prompt (e.g., **a>** or **c>**) and type **dir c:** and tap **<ENTER>**. By the way, \ by itself means "root directory." The command **dir c:** means display the listing for your root directory. If you want to see one screen at a time type **dir c:\ /p** ("p" stands for "pause"). To see the rest of the listing, tap any key to unfreeze the screen and continue scrolling. The listing will show files and/or subdirectories. **<DIR>** indicates a subdirectory.

Instead of scrolling down the screen, you can see the contents of the entire directory several columns *wide* by typing **dir c:\ /w** or if you want to include a pause: **dir c:\ /w/p**. To see only subdirectories, type **dir c:*** and tap **<Enter>**.

ORGANIZING YOUR SUBDIRECTORIES

I suggest several guidelines when you name and organize your subdirectories. The most important one is this: **Keep your program files and data files separate.** Program files are the software programs you purchase and data files are what you create. Put each program file in its own separate subdirectory (e.g., one for your word processing program and another for your spreadsheet program). Group your data files on other separate subdirectories (e.g., one for each client or for the type of work). If you are a professional writer, for example, keep your word processing program in its own subdirectory and keep your articles on at least one other subdirectory. A professional writer as well as a consultant and speaker, I have subdirectories called "BOOK," "WRITE," "CONSULT" and "SPEAK," all under my WordPerfect data subdirectory called "WP." See Figure 5-2.

If you have too many subdirectories, however, you may want to put data subdirectories *under* their corresponding program subdirectories. Taking the previous example, look at Figure 5-3 to see how it would now look.

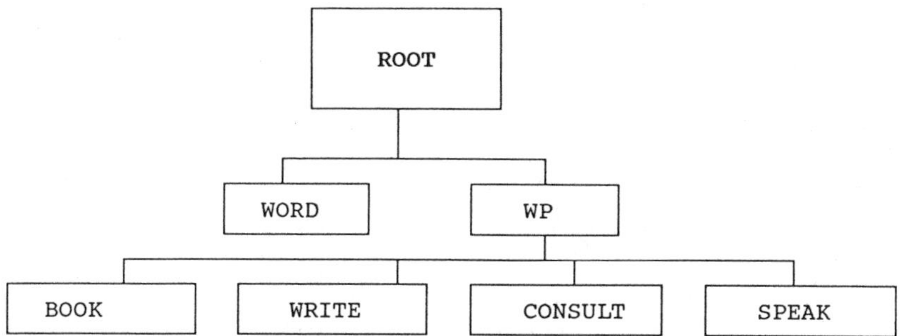

Figure 5-2. On my computer I keep my WordPerfect program in its own separate subdirectory, "WORD." I keep data files in their own subdirectory called "WP," which then in turn has grouped data files into their own task specific subdirectories. WORD and WP are on the same level; the four subdirectories shown here are all on the same level, one level down.

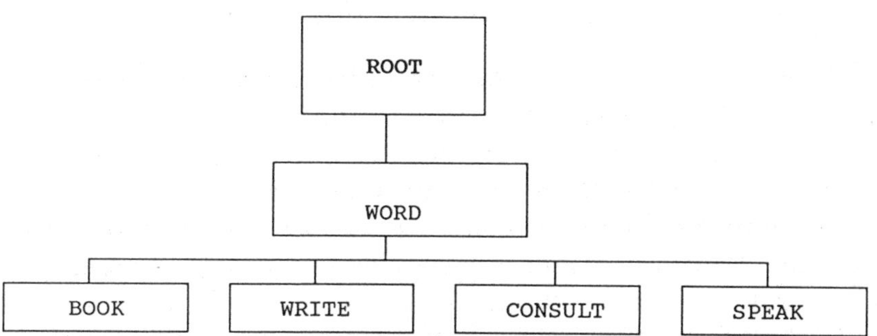

Figure 5-3. In this arrangement, the application program resides in the subdirectory, "WORD." The data file subdirectories are under the WORD subdirectory.

If you share your computer with other people who are using the same programs, it also makes sense to arrange program subdirectories followed by data subdirectories. For an example of what your subdirectory organization might look like see Figure 5-4.

Another solution for multiple users would be to keep your programs in directories on your hard disk and have each individual put their own data files on separate floppies. Make sure each file will fit on just one floppy and your computer performance is fast enough.

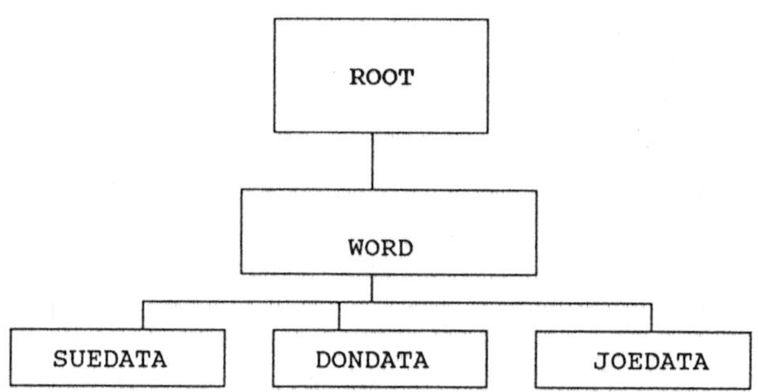

Figure 5-4. Subdirectory organization with shared computer word processing program

If possible, don't go more than three levels down from your root directory. Keep your subdirectory structure as simple as possible–simple enough to let you find and use files easily. As a general rule, **don't have any more than one screen full of data files per subdirectory.** When you have more than one screen full of names, it may be time to think of creating a new subdirectory–either a subordinate or a parallel one. Or, it may be time to delete files or move them into archival storage. If you really must have numerous files, just remember that you and your computer can slow down considerably trying to locate them.

IT'S ALL IN A NAME–A PATH NAME, THAT IS

One reason to keep your tree structure as simple as possible is to help simplify naming and locating individual files. Let's see why.

Just like a person, each individual file has both a name and an address. A computer file name is similar to a person's name in that both are made up of letters of the alphabet. A computer file name, however, can include numbers as well as letters but is limited in length. You can only use eight characters in a file name, plus a period followed by three additional characters for an "extension."

A name alone is not enough. Both a person and a file need more than a name to make them truly accessible. An *address* is necessary to locate a person as well as distinguish one person from another. John Jones on Maple Street isn't the same person as John Jones on Elm Street. An address is a *path* to someone's door, starting with the state, going to the city, then to the street and number and finally to the individual.

A computer file needs an "address," too. A **path name** is the address for a computer file. Your computer locates a file by following a path from the "drive" you're in (usually "A" or "B" for floppy drives and "C" or "D" for hard disk drives), on next to the root directory, then through any subdirectory name(s) and finally to the actual file name.

Just as the U.S. Postal Service likes to use certain abbreviations, so does your computer. When typing out a path name, start with the letter name of the drive you're in followed by a colon. Use a backslash symbol \ every time you want to indicate the different parts of your path name. The first backslash indicates the root directory. Each additional backslash tells the computer to go down to a new subdirectory level. The last name is the file name itself.

Here's an example. Go back to the Directory Tree Chart in Figure 5-1. C:\WP\BOOK\CHAPT1.D1 is the full path name for my Chapter 1 file. **C** is the drive name for my hard disk, the first \ stands for the root directory, **WP** is the first level subdirectory, **BOOK** is the second level subdirectory and **CHAPT1** is the actual file name with the **.D1** extension. The ".D1" extension, which means "Disk 1," lets me easily identify and back up all the D1 chapter files onto a backup floppy I call "Disk 1." I use a "D2" extension for all remaining book files that I back up onto "Disk 2."

And just as there can be a John Jones who lives on Maple as well as one who lives on Elm, so, too, you can have the same file name (or the same file) in two different subdirectories. If I wanted, I could have a copy of CHAPT1 in my WRITE subdirectory, too. The path name lets you locate the correct file. Your computer will not, however, let you create the same file name if it already exists in the same subdirectory you're in.

You also can't have two first level subdirectories with the same name, for example, \BOOK and \BOOK. But with two different first level subdirectories, you could have two second level subdirectories with the same name. For example, the following would be acceptable: \REPORTS\MAY and \EXPENSES\MAY.

To keep your path names simple, keep down the number of subdirectory levels. Since many times you'll need to type out the complete path name to "call up" (retrieve) a file, you'll want to do as little typing as possible.

Fortunately, you don't always have to type out the full path name when you want to call it up. Just as sometimes when you're filling out a form, for example, a doctor's intake form, you might not need to list your state of residence. But you better know where you are at all times.

The same holds true for computers. **Know where you are**–especially which subdirectory you're in. Let's suppose you're in a particular subdirectory and you're using a file from that directory. If you want to switch to another file in the same directory, you need only specify the file name. But if you want to call up a file from a different directory, you have to follow the correct "path."

Let me show you what I mean. Once again, here's the full path name for the CHAPT1 file: C:\WP\BOOK\CHAPT1.D1. If you're in the CHAPT1 file but you want to call up CHAPT4, no problem. Simply save CHAPT1 and call up CHAPT4. (In some word processing programs, such as WordPerfect, you may not have to save a file first before calling up another; in WordPerfect, for example, you can either open a window or switch to a different screen to call up a different file.)

If, however, you want to call up a file called MEMOS88, which is located in the CONSULT subdirectory, under the WP subdirectory on the C drive, you'll have to let the computer know you want to go to the CONSULT subdirectory.

To be sure, it's much easier calling up different files in different subdirectories when you're in the same program. Both CHAPT4 and MEMOS88 have at least one subdirectory in common–WP. It's kind of like living in the same city, but on different streets. Just as it's easy getting around city streets using local transportation, it's just as easy changing to a different subdirectory in the same program.

At other times, however, you may want to work on a file that's in another program. To do that, you may have to exit one program entirely, start another program and then make sure you're in the right subdirectory containing the file. A utility program, such as SoftwareCarousel, lets you temporarily exit a program you're working in, quickly switch to another program and be able to resume your place in the original program.

MAY I SEE A MENU, PLEASE?

There's another easy way to switch into a different program subdirectory. After you boot up (start your computer) you should see a **menu** or listing of all your main computer application programs. If you don't have such a menu on your computer, consider buying a menu utility program such as Fixed Disk Organizer (FIDO) or DOS 4.0 (see the next section). Figure 5-5 shows a sample menu screen from FIDO which can list up to 45 programs and applications.

Master Menu

Date: December 3, 1989
Time: 21:33:00

1. WordPerfect 5.0
2. WordPerfect 4.2
3. PC-File/R
4. Hard Disk Backup
5. XTREE
6. DOS commands

Figure 5-5. A FIDO (Fixed Disk Organizer) menu screen such as this one lists programs that can be loaded just by tapping the appropriate number on the menu.

You don't have to reboot the computer to see your menu. It should automatically appear on your screen whenever you exit a program.

MULTITASKING: BEYOND MENUS

A menu utility basically groups all of your applications together and lets you "point and shoot" to load a selected program. Multitasking goes beyond a menu in two important ways.

First, multitasking allows you to load more than one program at once. So when you choose a program you don't have to wait for it to load–the computer is basically switching from one pre-loaded program to another. This is called "context switching" or "concurrency."

Second, in multitasking you can run a program in the "background" while you're working on another program in the "foreground." This means, for example, that you can continue to work on a report in your word processor at the same time your database management program is sorting names and addresses in alphabetical order.

If you only work in one program or you rarely need to switch between programs, you don't need multitasking. But if you'd like to be able to switch frequently or to do work in the background, multitasking is the way to go.

As of this writing, you have three options: 1) buy a multitasking software program, 2) buy **OS/2**, the new IBM operating system, or 3) buy a Macintosh that has Multi-Finder.

DOS IS NOT A DIRTY WORD

DOS, (which stands for Disk Operating System), is an essential program for your computer. DOS is a collection of commands that let you operate your computer–specifically, your hard and floppy disks.

Think of DOS as a language with special words and codes that allows you to organize and coordinate all the operations related to your disks, your programs and your files. Compare DOS to a foreign language that helps you get around in a foreign country (in this case, your computer, which just may on occasion feel like a foreign country!). Knowing even a few key words and phrases can give you greater mobility, confidence and control. Control over what? In the computer environment you'll need control over information–managing, storing and retrieving it. DOS provides built-in file and information management tools. These tools help you control the information in your computer files. DOS lets you copy, erase, rename, back up, search, sort (in alphabetical or numerical order) and protect your files from accidental erasure.

What's more, DOS lets you list files in each directory, make a new directory, remove a directory and change to a different directory.

FILE MANAGEMENT THAT KEEPS DOS TO A MINIMUM

Knowing how to take full advantage of DOS is a lot like auto mechanics; it might be nice to know your carburetor from your master cylinder and how to change your oil but you don't need the specifics of auto mechanics to drive your car.

It doesn't hurt to understand generally how DOS works but there are some wonderful file management utility programs that will do most DOS functions for you simply and easily–in plain English. And starting with version 4.0, DOS itself has become easier to use.

Whether you have a 4.0 version or a file management utility, knowing a few of the basic DOS commands can be very helpful and time efficient. There are a number of good DOS books and classes available. I recommend starting with **Running MS-DOS** by Van Wolverton. Consider also getting *Personal Computing*'s "DOS Card" that contains a handy summary of basic and advanced DOS commands. (To get a copy of the card, send $3 to DOS Card, *Personal Computing*, Ten Holland Dr., Hasbrouck Heights, NJ 07604.)

FILE MANAGEMENT THAT USES DOS TO THE MAXIMUM

I must admit, there's a certain thrill learning to understand and use DOS. It's like cracking a secret code. In fact, DOS commands look an awful lot like code, rather than English.

But once you crack the code, you'll discover tempting shortcuts to incorporate into your computer routine. Take the **batch file**.

A batch file is like putting an automatic transmission into a stick-shift car; it does routine, repetitive tasks for you automatically. For example, it can automatically bring up a menu of your main programs on your screen shortly after you have started your computer. A batch file can help you simplify your work by reducing the number of keystrokes to perform a computer operation. A batch file contains a series of DOS commands or instructions to carry out an operational computer job such as starting your computer.

Every time you boot up (start) your computer, DOS follows a certain procedure. You can alter this procedure by creating a batch file called **AUTOEXEC.BAT** that has all the commands you want carried out. (Translated, AUTOEXEC.BAT means "AUTO" short for automatic; "EXEC" is short for execute or carry out; "BAT," short for "batch," has to appear as an extension on every batch file.).

Your AUTOEXEC.BAT file can include commands such as setting the date and time as well as taking you to your main menu of programs. If you are only using one program all the time, you could have AUTOEXEC.BAT take you right to that program. When you boot your computer, DOS automatically checks to see whether there is an AUTOEXEC.BAT file; if there isn't one, DOS carries out its own simple start-up procedure. The AUTOEXEC.BAT file lets you customize this procedure.

You may also want to include another useful command as part of your AUTOEXEC.BAT called **PROMPT PG**. No, this isn't a typo. This may well be one of the oddest *looking* commands but it certainly is one you should have. This funny looking command tells you where you are in your tree-structured directory system when you're in DOS. It's like those directory maps in shopping malls showing all the stores and a little red dot that says, "You are here."

Normally, all you'd see on your computer screen is the letter of your default drive before a greater than sign. It would look like this: **C>** and is pronounced "C prompt." All you'd know is that you are in your C drive, as compared with say, your A or B drive.

With the PROMPT PG command added to your AUTOEXEC.BAT, however, instead of just seeing C> you'd be supplied with additional information about your current directory. Let's say you are in your root directory. Your location or "system prompt" would now read:

C:\>

As you may remember, the backslash symbol– \ –stands for the root directory. You now know that's where you are on the C drive. If you were in a subdirectory for your WordPerfect word processor (\wp) on the C drive, your system prompt in DOS might read:

C:\wp>

You can add PROMPT PG to your AUTOEXEC.BAT file through a word processing program such as WordPerfect or through Edlin, the built-in DOS text editor.

A USER-FRIENDLY DOS: IBM DOS 4.0

If you're really opposed to learning and typing odd-looking symbols and codes, IBM has made it easier for you through IBM DOS 4.0–a whole new generation of DOS.

Instead of having to remember DOS commands, you can easily select them from pull-down menus. You can even use a mouse to select the command or file management function you want.

IBM DOS 4.0 is graphic from pull-down menus to a graphic representation of your tree structured directories.

RESOURCE GUIDE

FILE MANAGEMENT UTILITY PROGRAMS

Also called "file managers" and "DOS shells," these programs let you move, delete, copy and rename files easily without having to master the DOS commands. You really want to have at least one of these invaluable programs when you're cleaning out your hard disk. (By the way, the terms "file manager" and "file management program" are also used for simple database programs, which are described in Chapter 8.)

Diskette Manager II is a disk library management system that creates a catalog of the files on each floppy (up to 200 floppies) and allows you to store text comments about the files. You can print disk labels from the catalog. $99.95

Lassen Software, Inc.
468 Manzanita Ave., Suite 5
Chico, CA 95926
916/891-6957

DOS2ools has a full range of features and includes 43 programs. *PC Magazine* reviewer Vincent Puglia called DOS2ools "the most complete set of intelligent utilities I've ever encountered."
E-X-E Software Systems
8855 Atlanta, #298
Huntington Beach, CA 92646
714/662-2535

KeepTrack Plus has an excellent selective backup feature that lets you split files between disks. It also has a good range of file management features. Besides an operating manual, the program also comes with a special manual called *Guide to Disk Organization,* which is very helpful for anyone who owns a hard disk. $79.
The Finot Group
2390 El Camino Real, #3
Palo Alto, CA 94306
800/628-2828

Norton Commander is described as a DOS shell that helps you manage your hard disk and has many special features not found in similar programs. You can create menus as well as view and edit files. It's easy to learn and use and is suitable for a wide range of computer users–from novice to experienced.
$75
Peter Norton Computing, Inc.
2210 Wilshire Blvd., #186
Santa Monica, CA 90403
213/453-2361

Q-DOSII Version 2.0 has speed plus versatile file management features. $69.95
Gazelle Systems
42 North University Ave., Ste. 10
Provo, UT 84601
800/233-0383; 801/377-1288

XTreePro is a file manager I have been using for several years and is considered to be a mainstay of file managers. Its visual representation of DOS' tree structure can't be beat and has been hailed by many as its most important feature. The only negative I've encountered is you can't back up a large file, such as a database, onto more than one floppy. The program is very easy to use–this one is friendly. $49.95.
Executive Systems
15300 Ventura Blvd., Ste. 305
Sherman Oaks, CA 91403
800/634-5545; 800/551-5353 (in Calif.); 818/990-3457

MENU UTILITY PROGRAMS

Direct Access, along with PreCursor was selected as *PC Magazine*'s Editor's Choice. $89.95
Delta Technology International
PO Box 1104
Eau Claire, WI 54702
715/832-0958

Fixed Disk Organizer, also known as FIDO, as in the dog's name, is an easy-to-use IBM menu utility. I use it on my computer.
IBM
800/447-4700; 800/447-0890 (Alaska and California)

PreCursor, Version 3.0 helps you design menus easily to organize your programs and batch files. You can list up to 121 entries. The program also has a password feature for security. It was selected as *PC Magazine*'s Editor's Choice. $69.95
The Aldridge Co., Inc.
2500 CityWest Blvd., Suite 575
Houston, TX 77042
713/953-1940

MULTITASKING SOFTWARE PROGRAMS

Multitasking programs offer you some exciting possibilities. Beware, though, that installing such programs can be complex.
Here are ones that have received favorable reviews:

Concurrent DOS can support up to 10 users. $295 to $395
Digital Research Inc.
Box DRI
Monterey, CA 93942
408/649-3896

Deskview 2.01 offers a mouse-and-windows environment. $129.95
Quarterdeck Office Systems Inc.
150 Pico Blvd.
Santa Monica, CA 90405
213/392-9701

PC-MOS can support up to 25 users. $195, single-user version
The Software Link Inc.
3577 Parkway Lane
Atlanta, GA 30092
404/448-5465

SoftwareCarousel, a program that provides concurrency for 10 different programs, in combination with **DoubleDOS**, a program that lets you do work in the background, provide an economical, multitasking, concurrent environment. $31.98, SoftwareCarousel; $27.98, DoubleDos
SoftLogic Solutions
One Perimeter Road
Manchester, NH 03103
800/272-9900 or 603/627-9900

Windows 386 has a Macintosh-like environment that runs multiple MS-DOS applications. $195
Microsoft Corp.
Box 9097017
Redmond, WA 98073-9717
206/882-8080

FURTHER READING

The following magazines are excellent sources of computer information, providing news and views on the latest programs, updates and versions:

MicroAge Quarterly is a quarterly magazine for business users of microcomputers. It focuses on problem-solving articles on office automation and computer applications oriented toward small and medium size businesses. For information contact:
MicroAge Computer Stores, Inc.
Box 1920
Tempe, AZ 85281
602/968-3168

PC Computing, America's Computing Magazine is a monthly magazine on personal computing aimed more at active PC users than experts. It provides shortcuts and secrets designed to increase productivity.
Ziff-Davis Publishing Co.
80 Blanchard Rd.
Burlington, MA 01803
617/221-0300

PC Magazine, The Independent Guide to IBM-standard Personal Computing, comes out every two weeks and features in-depth product reviews and industry trends. The "Editor's Choice" designation helps you quickly spot winning products and programs. A one-year subscription (22 issues) costs $39.97–for subscription information contact:
PC Magazine
PO Box 54093
Boulder, CO 80322
303/447-9330

PC World is a monthly that is well-designed and easy-to-read. There are plenty of reviews and features. $29.90 for one year.
PCW Communications, Inc.
501 Second St.
San Francisco, CA 94107
415/243-0500

Personal Computing, The Personal Systems Magazine, is a monthly magazine for professionals and managers who use personal computers as a tool in day-to-day business tasks. *Personal Computing* details hands-on computing tips and techniques, personal computing management strategies, product trends and manufacturer profiles and product analyses. $18 for one year.

VNU Business Publications, Inc.
Ten Holland Drive
Hasbrouck Heights, NJ 07604
800/423-1780, in Florida, 800/858-0095

Sacra Blue is the monthly newsletter/magazine for the Sacramento PC Users Group, Inc., one of the largest computer clubs in the U.S. To get a subscription, you pay $25 to join the group.
Sacramento PC Users Group, Inc.
Attn: Membership Director
PO Box 685
Citrus Heights, CA 95611-0685

Hard Disk Management in the PC and MS-DOS Environment by Thomas Sheldon (New York: McGraw-Hill, 1987). This book expands upon the organizational areas covered in this chapter. You'll learn more about DOS commands, tree-structured directories, menus, batch files, data protection strategies and organizing a hard disk to suit your needs. Paperback, $24.95

Inside OS-2 by Gordon Letwin (Bellevue: Microsoft Press, 1988). If you have IBM's PS-2 computer, you'll need to learn about the next generation of operating system software. OS-2 picks up where DOS leaves off. Because the author helped design OS-2 software, he'll help you understand it–from the inside out. Paperback, $19.95

Running MS-DOS: The Microsoft Guide to Getting the Most Out of the Standard Operating System for the IBM PC and 50 Other Personal Computers by Van Wolverton (Bellevue: Microsoft Press, 1988). This book is considered the definitive source on MS-DOS. It's highly readable, with excellent illustrations. The well-organized chapters, table of contents and descriptive index make this book a handy reference source, as well. Paperback, $19.95

Note: With all of the software listed in this chapter as well as the following chapters, you should always check the latest version to see the additional features offered by the latest product.

6 MAKING THE MOST OF YOUR MACINTOSH FILES

Quick Scan: If you use a Macintosh Plus (Mac Plus), a Macintosh SE (SE), or a Macintosh II (Mac II), this chapter will help you better manage all the documents and applications you're accumulating. Discover how to take full advantage of the file management features that are built right into the Mac. See how to make the best use of your hard disk and high-capacity, 3½-inch disks.

HFS AND HOW TO USE IT

Several years ago, Apple introduced a tool to help you better organize all of your application and document files. It's called the **Hierarchical File System** (HFS).

HFS is a filing system for your computer that lets you organize applications and documents inside file folders. Just as a good paper filing system groups related papers and files logically together, so, too, HFS encourages you to group related applications, documents and folders together.

Whether you're using high capacity floppy disks or a hard disk, HFS is a lifesaver. This filing system helps you better manage the large numbers of files and folders that come with the increased storage you now have available.

What's nice about HFS is that you have a system that lets you group files logically by categories (folders) and subcategories (folders "nested" inside folders) that make sense to you. This beats scrolling through a long list of several hundred files at a time–which is what Mac users had to do before HFS.

DO YOU HAVE HFS?

See if you have HFS on your Mac. How can you tell? If you're using at least System version 3.2 (which came out in 1986), you have it.

Speaking of which, are you using the right **System** and the right **Finder**? As of this writing, you should be using at least System version 6.0.2 and Finder version 6.1. If you're not, buy yourself the **Apple Macintosh System Software Update** (called the **System Update** for short), version 6.0. Or check with your dealer for the latest System Update that you need for your machine.

Both the System file and the Finder file are necessary to operate your Macintosh. These two files (together known as "System files") should reside in your System Folder. The System file contains HFS–and tells your Mac and all the applications you use how to organize and store files. The Finder uses information from the System file, including the HFS information, to help you work easily with disks, applications, folders and files.

It's important to update your system files and make sure you aren't using multiple system files. **Lloyd Pentecost**, computer consultant and owner of **Answers on Computers** in Santa Monica, California, stresses the importance of this updating process. "One of the first things I do with a client is check all version numbers of all the systems and utilities. I make sure there aren't duplicates. People often don't realize they're adding all these systems to their computer when they update their computer."

Dan Shoff, an Apple dealer senior systems consultant, explains why this is dangerous. He says, "The main problem we find is that customers load multiple System files onto their hard disk, which invariably causes their hard disks to crash–at which point customers get angry. It's very important to have only one set of System files–one system and one finder that are compatible with one another."

Shoff also points out that all machines don't necessarily need the latest versions. "It just depends on your machine and your applications."

If you've ever updated and upgraded your System and Finder before, you'll find upgrading with System Update 6.0 is much easier and simpler. The System Update also lets you keep intact any fonts, desk accessories and utilities that you've previously customized. System Update 6.0 costs $49 and is available from your Apple dealer. (If you don't want or need the documentation, you may be able to get the System Update by itself for free from dealers, user groups or on–line services.)

HOW THE "HIERARCHY" IN HFS WORKS

HFS is a *hierarchical* system because it lets you group files and folders in a multi-level hierarchy. You see the first or top level of the hierarchy when you open a disk and you view all the applications, folders or documents in the **disk window**. Each of these folders, applications or documents you first see is at the first level (sometimes also known as the **root directory**). Look at Figure 6-1 for an example of a disk window at the first level.

If you were to open up one of the folders, you would see the second level of the hierarchy. Open up a window for a second level folder and you'll see the third level. Figure 6-2 illustrates these "nested" folders at the three levels.

There is an easier way of moving through the different levels of your hierarchy within an application rather than double-clicking on folder names in a series of windows. First, pull down the File menu and select Open, which will open a **standard file dialog box** (as shown in Figure 6-3) and provide you a listing of the folder's contents. The dialog box only shows you what's in one level at a time–namely, files or folders. But by placing the mouse pointer on the disk or folder icon at the top and holding down the mouse

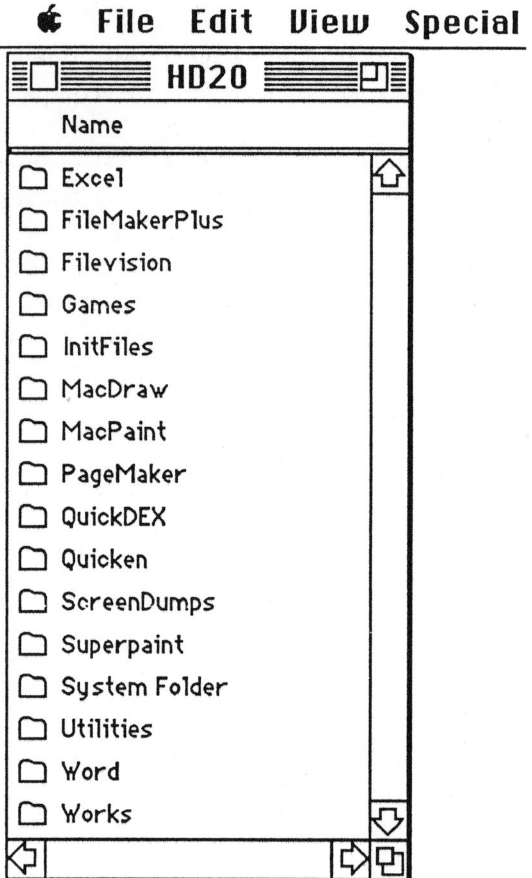

Figure 6-1. Disk window at the first level

button, you can see the different levels of the hierarchy—that is, the different levels of the nested folders. (See Figure 6-4.)

What you get is a pull-down list (which looks similar to a pull-down menu). But instead of listing commands, the list shows you the path through the hierarchy, all the way back to the first level. (By the way, the first and highest level is always the last one on the pull-down list and is the name of the disk you're using.)

This little pull-down list shows you all the different levels in order. To get to a different level, you simply drag the mouse to the

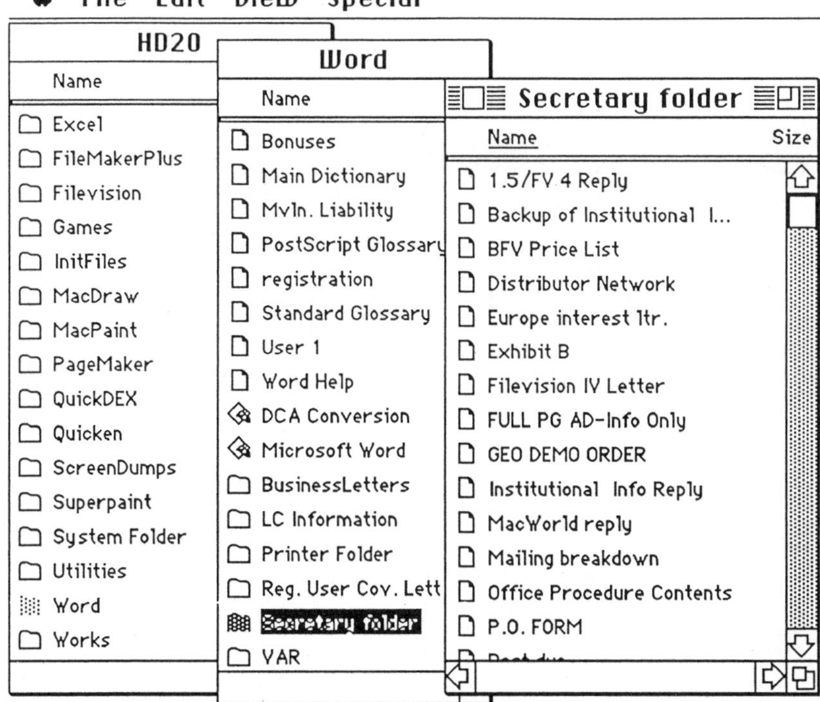

Figure 6-2. "Nested" folders showing the first three levels of the hierarchy

level you want (or from the keyboard, press the Command key and the Up or Down Arrow).

NAMING NAMES

The name you give a document or folder may depend in part upon your use of dialog boxes and whether you're scrolling to see long lists of files and folders.

Bear in mind that file and folder names in dialog boxes are in alphabetical order but special characters (such as periods, commas and asterisks) and then numbers precede letters. The order goes like this: first, special characters; second, numbers; and third, letters.

This is good to know if you want to have the files you use most often at the top of the dialog box. You simply tack on a special

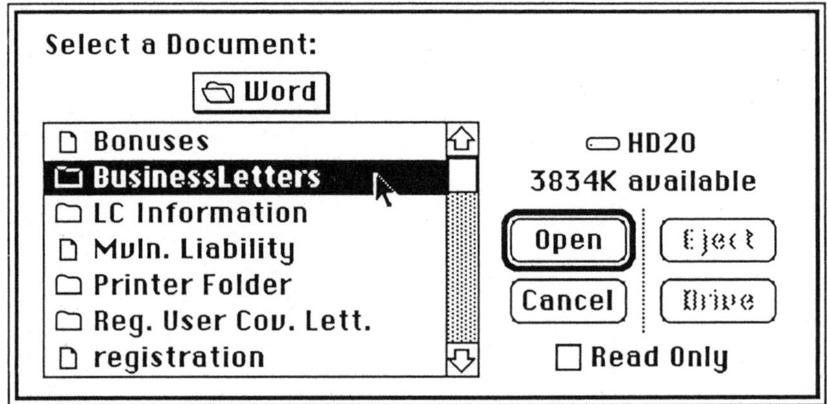

Figure 6-3. Standard file dialog box

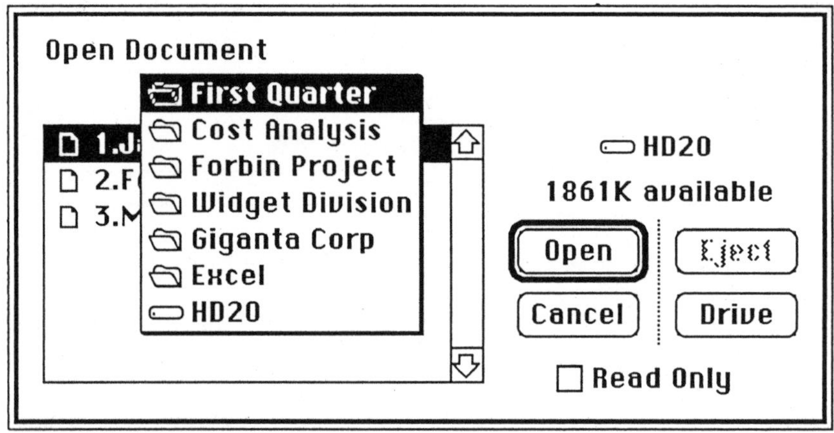

Figure 6-4. Different hierarchy levels using the mouse pointer on the folder icon

character or number to the name. For example, you could easily change the folder name "Report" to ".Report" or "1Report" to move up the folder in the dialog box. See Figure 6-5.

HFS lets you repeat file names–provided you put each of those files in different folders. Let's suppose you have three files called "Mileage Report." With HFS you could keep a Mileage Report in three different folders–for example, one for Mary, another for John and still a third for Chris.

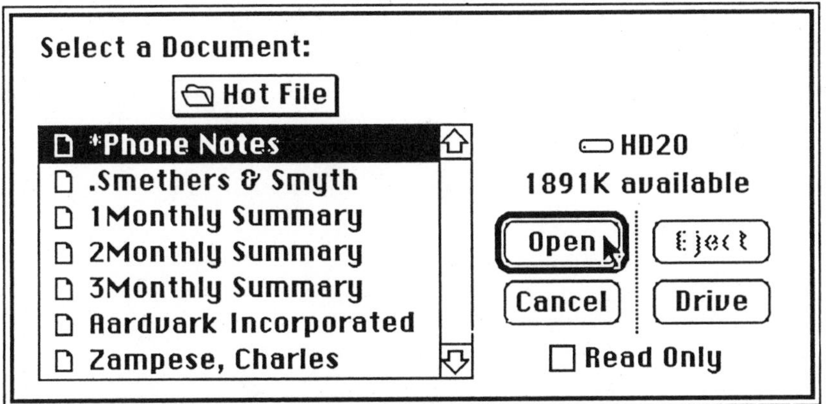

Figure 6-5. Use of special characters and numbers in names

HFS makes sure you don't replace any file you've previously created with the same name. You'll be asked whether you want to replace the existing file. If you click OK, you'll destroy the original file and replace it with the new one. Incidentally, it's not a good idea to give documents the same names as applications. Disks should also have their own, individual names.

There are only a few restrictions to the names you choose. Remember not to use more than 27 characters (including spaces) for a disk name and no more than 31 characters for a document or folder name. Don't use colons in your names.

PUTTING APPLICATIONS IN GOOD ORDER

There are three main locations in which you can place your applications: a disk window, the desktop and a folder.

APPLICATIONS IN YOUR DISK WINDOW

Whether you're working on a hard disk or on a floppy disk, Figure 6-6 illustrates how you can place applications (depicted as application icons) in the window of the disk you're using. The disk window shows the top organizational level of HFS.

Applications stored outside a folder in your disk window should generally be only for applications you use daily that don't have their

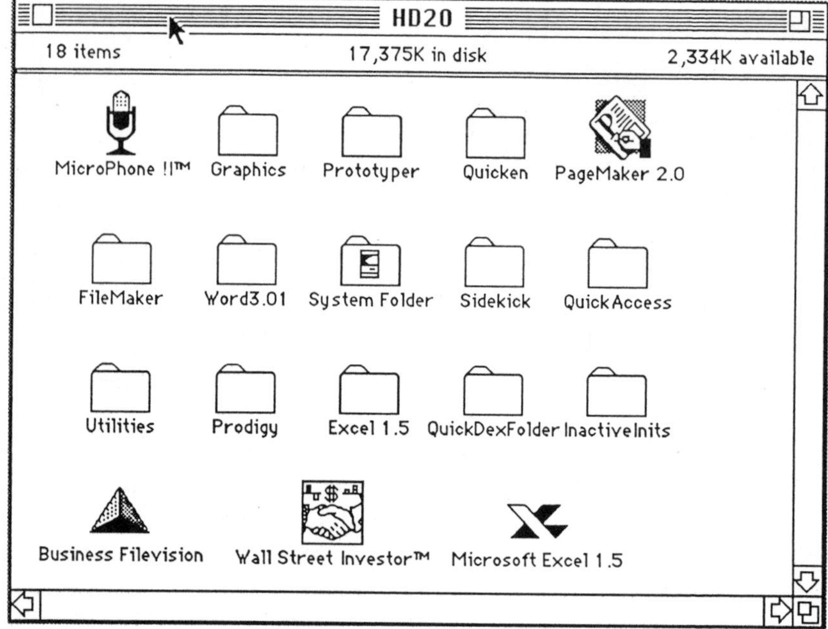

Figure 6-6. Applications in a disk window

own auxiliary files or utilities. Storing applications in this way makes saving files easier. You also won't have to navigate out of a folder when you open files inside an application.

I know one Mac user who keeps all his applications in the disk window. He places the ones he uses regularly in the visible part of the window and the ones he doesn't are kept out of sight, at the bottom of the window, available through scrolling. What he's doing is grouping them by frequency of use, using the standard, "By Icon" view.

If, however, you have an application that uses auxiliary files (such as a word processor that has extra dictionary files), you're not going to want to clutter up the disk window with all these files. You have a couple of options. You could place these auxiliary files in the System Folder since the application will look there for them, after not finding them at the application's location. Or you could put both the application and these files in their own folder–a method we'll be discussing shortly.

If you don't have a hard disk, you can put your applications on 3½-inch disks. If your computer has two 3½-inch disk drives, you could keep related applications on one disk, which would serve as your startup disk. Your applications would appear in the window of this disk. Documents could be kept separately on another disk.

If you only have one disk drive, you can create special disks organized by task that combine related applications and the documents created with them. Since each of these disks will also be serving as a startup disk, be sure to include the System Folder on each one. (The System Folder contains the System and Finder files.) Don't forget to leave at least 50K of available space on any startup disk.

APPLICATIONS ON YOUR DESKTOP

If you use just a few applications on a regular basis, say four or less, consider moving those applications from your disk window onto the desktop itself. The desktop is the first thing you see after loading the Finder. You'll usually see a light gray surface that has a menu bar at the top, a disk icon in the top right corner and a trash can icon in the lower right corner. (I've changed the gray desktop to white for the illustrations.)

You'll save some keystrokes by not having to open your disk window each time you want to call up an application. It's also easier to find a few applications on your desktop rather than having to look through lots of application and folder icons in your disk window. See Figure 6-7. Be careful, however, you don't accidentally throw them in the trash can, which is nearby.

Your desktop can also be used to temporarily store a group of selected applications, as well as folders or documents, that you may be using on a particular day. What's nice is you can pull the icons you want from different disks and "drag" them all to the desktop. There's no need to keep windows open. It's easy to put the icons back; first select them, then select "Put Away" from the File menu and the Finder does the rest. It's like having all of your current paperwork and projects on your desk, right in front of you for easy

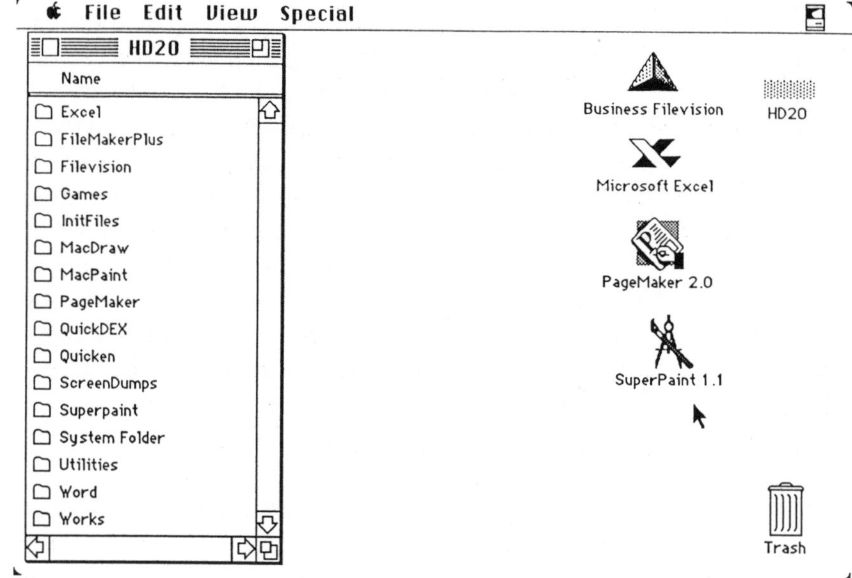

Figure 6-7. Applications on the desktop

access, and then having an assistant put everything away for you when you're finished.

APPLICATIONS IN FOLDERS

We've talked about storing frequently used applications (with their icons) outside folders on the desktop and in disk windows. Let's see some situations where you might want to store applications in folders (and then keep those folders in disk windows–the first level of HFS).

You should store most of your applications (including work applications and utilities) in folders. Documents, though, should generally not be kept in the same folder as applications. You could, however, have a folder for each application (and its supporting applications or utilities) and then nested folders for the application's documents. But you may be better off putting all applications in one folder and then setting up separate folders for each application's documents. These methods can work if your applications aren't sharing data.

Users whose work involves sharing of data often group related applications and documents in a project or task folder that describes a type of work that's being done. You might have a Presentations folder, for example.

If you have many project folders, however, that each need to use a particular application, you're probably not going to have space to keep more than one copy of that application on your disk. In that case, you could group similar applications together. A word processing application folder could contain a word processor, a spelling checker and an outlining program, for example.

Take a look at Figure 6-8 to see how applications can be stored in folders in the disk window, the top organizational level. Store utilities in their own folder, which you can keep inside the Application folder, or if you use utilities frequently, store the Utilities folder also in the disk window.

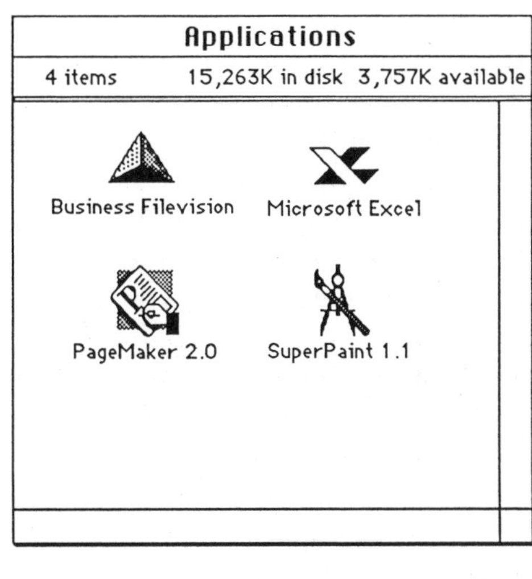

Figure 6-8. Applications in folders in the disk window

As you can see, you have quite a bit of flexibility with HFS. For additional flexibility, consider using **Multi-Finder**, which comes with the latest System Update. Multi-Finder can replace your Finder and give you the ability to load as many applications as memory will allow and to switch easily between them at the click of the mouse.

One word of warning: if you purchased any Mac software before January 1986, confirm compatibility of your software applications with HFS. Contact any manufacturers of software that could apply.

And here's an important tip: don't keep any applications you rarely use, especially space-hungry work applications, on your hard disk.

DEALING WITH DOCUMENTS AND FOLDERS IN HFS

When it comes to organizing documents, just like applications, HFS gives you tremendous flexibility. With flexibility, however, comes the opportunity for too many choices and if you're not careful, chaos can quickly take over.

Organizing your documents with HFS is a lot like organizing your papers in a filing system. There's no one right way to set up a system. What's most important is thinking in terms of meaningful category names to you. Where would *you* logically file and find documents and folders? Under what names?

You also want to make sure you don't accumulate too many documents in any one folder. When that happens, files become difficult to find. That's when you may need to subdivide large folders into smaller ones. But if you have too many small folders, your system can become too complex. It's all a matter of balance and good design whether you're using a paper filing system or the Macintosh Hierarchical Filing System.

To keep your HFS as simple and as accessible as possible, follow two guidelines. First, limit the number of documents you keep in each folder, especially any folder that you use frequently. Some experts suggest keeping no more than one dialog box full of files so that you don't have to scroll to another screen. Of course, you can always use the View menu to help you view the contents in a text view that compacts and groups more information in one window than you can see in a dialog box. Charles Rubin and Bencion Calica in their book *Macintosh Hard Disk Management* recommend you should create a new folder when you have more than 20 files on a disk or in a folder.

The fewer files you have in a folder, the faster it is to find files–especially the files you use most often. And that's the secret: keep files you use most often, most accessible. If a folder is crowded with files you rarely use, both you and your computer will slow down. Yes, you can use the Find File utility, but it won't be as fast for you as having a smaller, well-organized folder (and HFS) system. Get in the habit of moving old or rarely used files to archival or storage folders and disks.

Second, limit your number of nested folders. Although technically you can go more than 50 levels deep with HFS, beware of creating too complex a system that takes too much time to use. In general, you won't want to go more than three levels deep.

CREATING FOLDERS

Start by setting up your first level folders in your disk window. Use names that reflect the major kinds of work you do and how you like to group that work. General folders called "Correspondence," "Reports" and "Graphics" may be just fine. Perhaps, however, these may be too general and you'll need to go immediately to a second level of folder within each one to break it down further.

You might, instead, want to be more specific with your first level folder names. For example, give them the names of specific projects, clients or customers. Then break each one down into second level folders–representing the different activities connected with each.

These second level folder names can be identical, provided they're used in different first level folders. Suppose, I have two speaking engagements, one for IBM and another for GE. My IBM first level folder could have three second level folders called "Correspondence," "Notes" and "Seminar Materials" and so could my GE first level folder.

DESKTOP MANAGEMENT

As a Mac user you probably have two desktops: the traditional one where you do your paperwork and your Macintosh screen or working environment, which is also called a "desktop." We'll be looking at ways to manage your Macintosh desktop more effectively, so that you can do computer organizational tasks more easily and productively.

The Mac desktop is the main staging area for your computer work (just as your desktop may be the main area for your paperwork). The Finder is the system application used to create the desktop and manage what happens on the desktop, such as organizing documents, creating folders, viewing windows and starting applications.

FIVE FINDER MENUS

You can do these and many other desktop management tasks using the commands or mini-applications located in five Finder pull down menus along the top edge of your desktop: **Apple**, **File**, **Edit**, **View** and **Special.**

APPLE MENU

Mini-applications called **desk accessories** (DAs) are included in the Apple menu. Let's look at three that help with file management.

The **Control Panel** will let you design your own desktop, set the date and time and use a "RAM cache" to speed up your work. The Control Panel lets you choose these and other options to customize your computer to your specifications.

Find File helps you locate any application, folder, document or resource on a disk. It's particularly helpful in an HFS environment where you may have many files nested many levels deep in folders and when you just can't remember where you put a file. Find File not only locates a file for you but it furnishes a brief summary about it. You'll learn when you created the file, when you last modified it, the size of the file, the space the file takes up on your disk and where it's located. If you want, Find File will put the file right on your desktop.

You can use Find File from the desktop or when you're in a file or an application.

Scrapbook is a desk accessory that lets you store bits and pieces of text and graphics that you use frequently or in many files. You might store such things as pictures, letterheads or boilerplate (standard portions of text that are plugged into different documents).

Not only can you store text and graphics, you can cut, copy and paste them using the commands in the Edit menu (which we'll be discussing soon).

Incidentally, you can have up to 15 desk accessories in the Apple menu. You can install a DA (desk accessory) directly into an application using the Font/DA Mover program usually found in your System folder. An excellent utility called "Suitcase" allows you to go well beyond the 15-DA limit (see the chapter resource guide.)

FILE MENU

This menu has ten useful file management commands, which are used with icons and windows (as opposed to documents, folders and applications).

New Folder creates a new folder to hold applications, documents or other folders.

Open is used with icons to open documents into windows and to start applications.

Print lets you print documents by first selecting their icons.

Close lets you close the active window, leaving a highlighted icon and the next active window, if there is one.

Get Info gives you a brief summary of a selected icon. You can add information of your own as well as edit certain items in the summary (lock/unlock, the application memory size and the text summary itself).

Duplicate makes copies of items you select.

Put Away returns items on the desktop back to their original folders or disks.

Page Setup is used with the Print Catalog command to print *directories.* A directory is a listing of the contents in a disk or folder. The listing could be alphabetical, pictorial (with icons) or chronological. Page Setup lets you select page specifications for directories only. It doesn't work with documents you want to print from the Finder. Each application has its own Page Setup command that governs its documents. When in other applications, the Page Setup command calls up an application-specific dialog box that contains other specifications besides those found in the Page Setup command used for directories.

Print Catalog prints the active directory window in any "view" you've selected for the window. (We'll discuss the View Menu shortly.)

Eject is used to eject the diskette that is currently selected, or if no disk drive is selected, the last one in the series of one or more drives.

EDIT MENU

Besides helping you edit text in standard documents, the Edit Menu also is useful for editing three types of desktop management information: 1) the names of disks, applications, folders and documents; 2) the text in "Get Info" windows; and 3) the text and pictures in desk accessories such as Scrapbook and Note Pad.

Many of the Edit commands are used with the **Clipboard**, a special holding place for material you "cut and paste." The Clipboard (generally stored in the computer's memory) is used with the Scrapbook file (located on the current startup disk) by means of a desk accessory program such as Scrapbook (an Apple DA) or Smart Scrap. The Scrapbook file contains frequently used pictures and text.

Undo undoes one of the editing commands you just used from the Edit menu. It can undo something you just did in a desk application, such as typing something incorrectly.

Cut deletes material (text or graphics) and puts it in Clipboard. Any other previous material in Clipboard will be replaced.

Copy makes a copy of the selected material, which then goes to Clipboard. Once again, any previous material is replaced.

Paste inserts the material from Clipboard.

Clear deletes material without putting it in Clipboard.

Select All lets you select all the icons either in the active window or on the desktop.

Show Clipboard reveals a window showing you what's currently in Clipboard.

Incidentally, you may notice that most of the file and edit commands listed in the pull-down menu have a special symbol followed by a letter. That symbol stands for the Apple or command key. When you press the command key and at the same time tap the appropriate letter, you can more quickly perform an edit function rather than pulling down the File or Edit menu each time. Since you probably use the file or edit commands very often, it makes sense to use these shortcuts.

VIEW MENU

This menu lets you see directories (listings) of disks and folders and even the trash in different "views." Through these different views, you can see more directory information at a glance and in more organized ways. The View menu makes it easier to find, copy, move and even rename files in your active directory window.

Each **By Small Icon** listing has a small icon on the left followed by its icon name. If you have many documents or applications, the By Small Icon view, shown in Figure 6-9, lets you see them quickly.

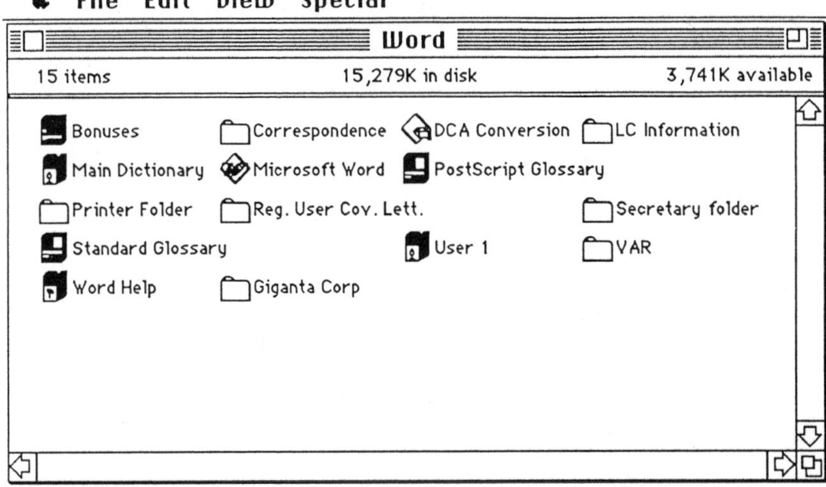

Figure 6-9. By Small Icon View

The **By Icon** view in Figure 6-10 resembles the desktop with its icon only display. This is a useful view if you only have a small number of applications, folders or documents.

By Name gives you an alphabetical listing. If you're good at remembering names–application, folder or file names, that is–then you should like this view. See Figure 6-11.

By Date arranges your window contents chronologically by the date you most recently created or modified an application, folder or file. See Figure 6-12.

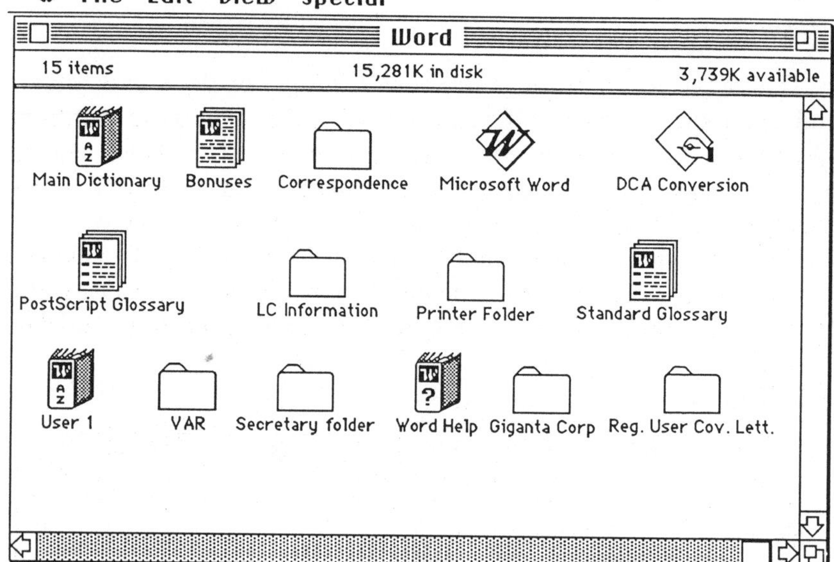

Figure 6-10. By Icon View

By Size lists applications and documents in order of their size so you can see which ones are taking up the most space. Folders are also listed but their size is not included. Folders are, however, listed alphabetically and they follow the listing of applications and documents. See Figure 6-13.

By Kind groups applications, folders and documents separately. Each document also shows which application created it. See Figure 6-14.

SPECIAL MENU

Finally, the Special menu offers important desktop management tools.

Clean Up arranges icons neatly in an active directory window or on the desktop. Clean Up is used when the By Small Icon or By Icon view is in effect. Clean Up is called up by selecting the "Clean Up" command in the "Special" pull-down menu. If you hold down the Option key while selecting the Clean Up command, the icons

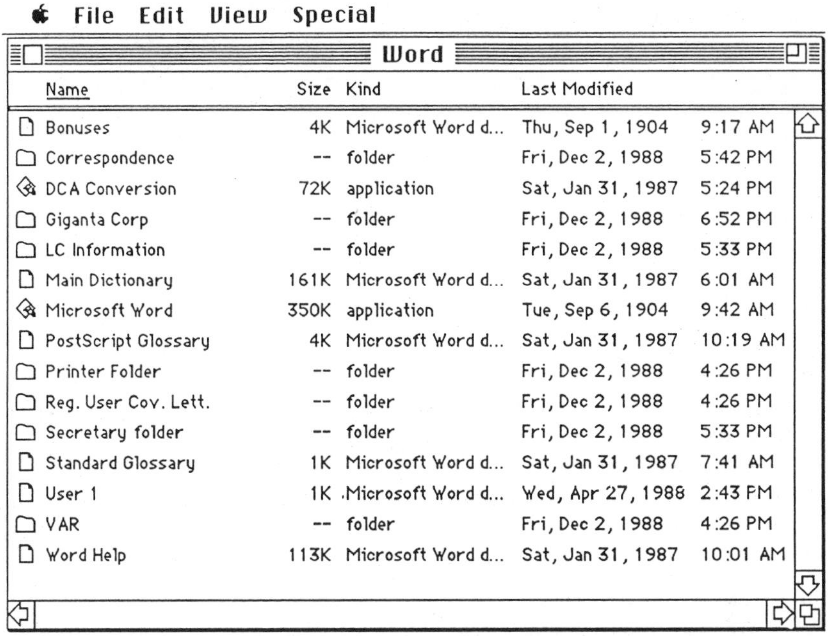

 File Edit View Special

Word

Name	Size	Kind	Last Modified	
Bonuses	4K	Microsoft Word d...	Thu, Sep 1, 1904	9:17 AM
Correspondence	--	folder	Fri, Dec 2, 1988	5:42 PM
DCA Conversion	72K	application	Sat, Jan 31, 1987	5:24 PM
Giganta Corp	--	folder	Fri, Dec 2, 1988	6:52 PM
LC Information	--	folder	Fri, Dec 2, 1988	5:33 PM
Main Dictionary	161K	Microsoft Word d...	Sat, Jan 31, 1987	6:01 AM
Microsoft Word	350K	application	Tue, Sep 6, 1904	9:42 AM
PostScript Glossary	4K	Microsoft Word d...	Sat, Jan 31, 1987	10:19 AM
Printer Folder	--	folder	Fri, Dec 2, 1988	4:26 PM
Reg. User Cov. Lett.	--	folder	Fri, Dec 2, 1988	4:26 PM
Secretary folder	--	folder	Fri, Dec 2, 1988	5:33 PM
Standard Glossary	1K	Microsoft Word d...	Sat, Jan 31, 1987	7:41 AM
User 1	1K	Microsoft Word d...	Wed, Apr 27, 1988	2:43 PM
VAR	--	folder	Fri, Dec 2, 1988	4:26 PM
Word Help	113K	Microsoft Word d...	Sat, Jan 31, 1987	10:01 AM

Figure 6-11. By Name View.

in the selected window will be arranged more neatly and compactly within the window.

If you can't wait to "empty the trash" or you simply need more space on your disk immediately, then use **Empty Trash**. Of course, the trash is automatically emptied every time you shut down.

Use **Erase Disk** to delete the contents of a disk other than your startup disk. Erase Disk will also "initialize" a disk–prepare or format the disk so that it's ready to receive information.

Set Startup sets the conditions for the next restart of the computer. It allows you to specify being under the control of the Finder or under Multifinder. Under Finder, Set Startup takes you automatically to one pre-designated application after starting the computer (without stopping at the Finder first). Under Multifinder, Set Startup allows you to specify that several applications are loaded automatically upon startup.

Use Minifinder... lets you group together applications and documents you use most often or those you'd use together for a specific task.

 File Edit View Special

Word

Name	Size	Kind	Last Modified	
Giganta Corp	--	folder	Fri, Dec 2, 1988	6:52 PM
Correspondence	--	folder	Fri, Dec 2, 1988	5:42 PM
LC Information	--	folder	Fri, Dec 2, 1988	5:33 PM
Secretary folder	--	folder	Fri, Dec 2, 1988	5:33 PM
Printer Folder	--	folder	Fri, Dec 2, 1988	4:26 PM
Reg. User Cov. Lett.	--	folder	Fri, Dec 2, 1988	4:26 PM
VAR	--	folder	Fri, Dec 2, 1988	4:26 PM
User 1	1K	Microsoft Word d...	Wed, Apr 27, 1988	2:43 PM
DCA Conversion	72K	application	Sat, Jan 31, 1987	5:24 PM
PostScript Glossary	4K	Microsoft Word d...	Sat, Jan 31, 1987	10:19 AM
Word Help	113K	Microsoft Word d...	Sat, Jan 31, 1987	10:01 AM
Standard Glossary	1K	Microsoft Word d...	Sat, Jan 31, 1987	7:41 AM
Main Dictionary	161K	Microsoft Word d...	Sat, Jan 31, 1987	6:01 AM
Microsoft Word	350K	application	Tue, Sep 6, 1904	9:42 AM
Bonuses	4K	Microsoft Word d...	Thu, Sep 1, 1904	9:17 AM

Figure 6-12. By Date view

Use **Restart** (on the Mac II) when you want to change to a different startup disk. Restart saves your latest information, ejects the disk you no longer want to use, empties the trash and restarts your computer.

You can also switch to a different startup disk by using either of the following:

- Hold down the Option key while you're opening an application that's on another startup disk. This is a useful way of switching if you're using a hard disk.
- Hold down the Option and Command keys while you're double-clicking the Finder icon on the disk you're switching to.

Shut Down prepares your computer for an orderly shut off. It turns off a Mac II, but not a Mac, a Mac Plus or a Mac SE.

 File Edit View Special

Word

Name	Size	Kind	Last Modified	
Microsoft Word	350K	application	Tue, Sep 6, 1904	9:42 AM
Main Dictionary	161K	Microsoft Word d...	Sat, Jan 31, 1987	6:01 AM
Word Help	113K	Microsoft Word d...	Sat, Jan 31, 1987	10:01 AM
DCA Conversion	72K	application	Sat, Jan 31, 1987	5:24 PM
Bonuses	4K	Microsoft Word d...	Thu, Sep 1, 1904	9:17 AM
PostScript Glossary	4K	Microsoft Word d...	Sat, Jan 31, 1987	10:19 AM
Standard Glossary	1K	Microsoft Word d...	Sat, Jan 31, 1987	7:41 AM
User 1	1K	Microsoft Word d...	Wed, Apr 27, 1988	2:43 PM
Correspondence	--	folder	Fri, Dec 2, 1988	5:42 PM
Giganta Corp	--	folder	Fri, Dec 2, 1988	6:52 PM
LC Information	--	folder	Fri, Dec 2, 1988	5:33 PM
Printer Folder	--	folder	Fri, Dec 2, 1988	4:26 PM
Reg. User Cov. Lett.	--	folder	Fri, Dec 2, 1988	4:26 PM
Secretary folder	--	folder	Fri, Dec 2, 1988	5:33 PM
VAR	--	folder	Fri, Dec 2, 1988	4:26 PM

Figure 6-13. By Size view

Word

Name	Size	Kind	Last Modified	
Bonuses	4K	Microsoft Word d...	Thu, Sep 1, 1904	9:17 AM
Main Dictionary	161K	Microsoft Word d...	Sat, Jan 31, 1987	6:01 AM
PostScript Glossary	4K	Microsoft Word d...	Sat, Jan 31, 1987	10:19 AM
Standard Glossary	1K	Microsoft Word d...	Sat, Jan 31, 1987	7:41 AM
User 1	1K	Microsoft Word d...	Wed, Apr 27, 1988	2:43 PM
Word Help	113K	Microsoft Word d...	Sat, Jan 31, 1987	10:01 AM
DCA Conversion	72K	application	Sat, Jan 31, 1987	5:24 PM
Microsoft Word	350K	application	Tue, Sep 6, 1904	9:42 AM
Correspondence	--	folder	Fri, Dec 2, 1988	5:42 PM
Giganta Corp	--	folder	Fri, Dec 2, 1988	6:52 PM
LC Information	--	folder	Fri, Dec 2, 1988	5:33 PM
Printer Folder	--	folder	Fri, Dec 2, 1988	4:26 PM
Reg. User Cov. Lett.	--	folder	Fri, Dec 2, 1988	4:26 PM
Secretary folder	--	folder	Fri, Dec 2, 1988	5:33 PM
VAR	--	folder	Fri, Dec 2, 1988	4:26 PM

Figure 6-14. By Kind view

RESOURCE GUIDE

DESKTOP AND FILE MANAGEMENT DESK ACCESSORIES AND UTILITIES

Cat-Mac is a disk cataloging utility application that's so easy to use, it has no instruction manual. Cat-Mat shows files graphically as they fit into HFS structure. The "Save As Text" feature lets you save catalogs and use them with other applications. From $10 to $24.95, depending on the levels you select.
Phoenix Specialties, Inc.
2981 Corvin Dr.
Santa Clara, CA 95051
408/733-9625

Disk Ranger is a fast catalog utility application that makes catalogs of the files on your hard and floppy disks. The application includes many features, including sorting capabilities, duplication elimination and disk label printing.
$49.95
Graham Software Co.
8609 Ingalls Circle
Arvada, CO 80003
303/422-0757

DiskQuick is a lightning-fast catalog utility that has a database interface so you can quickly look up files in a catalog that has been downloaded to your database program. It comes with a clearly written manual. $49.95
Ideaform, Inc.
PO Box 1540
Fairfield, IA 52556
515/472-7256

DiskTools Plus, is a powerful desk accessory that includes seven useful accessories. "DiskTools II," the major disk accessory in the program, greatly improves upon Finder; in fact, you may rarely need to use Finder again. DiskTools II uses simple, function icons to let you easily create folders; find, rename, copy, move or delete documents and applications; install files and applications without having to go through the folder structure; and find information about

files. Other DAs include "Calendar," "PhonePad," "Print Text" and "Windows." $49.95
Electronic Arts
2755 Campus Dr.
San Mateo, CA 94403
415/571-7171

Disktop is a useful DA that lets you do Finder functions without having to leave an application or document. $49.95
CE Software
801 73rd St.
Des Moines, IA 50312
515/224-1995

myDiskLabeler is a disk labeling utility that easily lets you create meaningful and versatile disk labels. $44.95
Williams & Macias, Inc.
3707 S. Godrey
Spokane, WA 99204
800/752-4400 or 509/458-6312

QuicKeys and DialogKeys is a macro utility program that lets you bypass the mouse and more quickly perform commands and desktop management tasks. $99.95
CE Software
801 73rd St.
Des Moines, IA 50312
515/224-1995

SmartScrap & The Clipper are two excellent DAs that offer significant improvements to the standard Macintosh Scrapbook and Clipboard DAs. Replacing Scrapbook altogether, SmartScrap features a "Table of Contents" that displays many Scrapbook pages. SmartScrap lets you have many Scrapbook files on a disk and lets you select any portions of files. The Clipper doesn't replace Clipboard but you have access to many features, including the ability to modify pictures.
Solutions International
29 Main St. (PO Box 989)
Montpelier, VT 05602
802/229-0368

Suitcase allows you to go beyond the 15 DA limit set by Apple. With this program, you can install as many DAs (not to mention fonts and Fkeys) as you want. $59.95
Software Supply
599 N. Mathilda Ave.
Sunnyvale, CA 94086
408/749-9311

Switcher Construction Kit lets you switch between up to eight programs at the click of a mouse. If you use several programs every day, Switcher gives you the fastest method of calling them up. Through the special feature "Always Convert The Clipboard," you can easily cut and paste between applications. $19.95
Apple Computer, Inc.
20525 Mariani Avenue
Cupertino, CA 95014
408/996-1010

DATA ACCESS/DATA RECOVERY

Eureka! is a file-finding utility that's great for locating files whose names you may have forgotten or that may be buried deep within your HFS. It installs into a spare DA slot and can be selected from your Apple menu at any time. $24.95
Personal Computer Peripherals Corp.
6204 Benjamin Rd.
Tampa, FL 33634
800/622-2888 or 813/884-3092

HFS Locator Plus is a combination file finder and file management DA. HFS Locator Plus lets you look for files in many different ways. Locator gives you useful file information including HFS location, the size and the type of file. Locator can also perform file management functions such as creating folders as well as moving, copying, deleting and renaming files.
PBI Software, Inc.
1163 Triton Dr.
Foster City, CA 94404
415/349-8765

Sonar is a fast, text retrieval program that can search folders full of word-processed documents. It also does indexing.
Virginia Systems Software Services, Inc.
5509 W. Bay Court
Midlothian, VA 23113
804/739-3200

BOOKS, CATALOGS, REFERENCES

Hard Disk Management for the Macintosh by Nancy Andrews (New York: Bantam Books, 1987) is easy to read and understand. The book comes with three utilities, LOCKIT, WHEREIS and BACKUP. $34.95, paper

MacGuide is a terrific quarterly guide/magazine that features reviews and listings of more than 3,000 Macintosh products. The guide is very well organized with helpful numerical ratings, thorough reviews, excellent feature articles. This is a user friendly publication that goes out of its way to help the reader. $4.95 for one issue; $14.85 for a one year subscription (four issues)
MacGuide Magazine
818 17th Street, Suite 210
Denver, CO 80202
303/825-8166

Macintosh Hard Disk Management by Charles Rubin and Bencion Calica (Indianapolis: Hayden Books, 1988) is superb. Rubin and Bencion write clearly and the book has many helpful techniques, illustrations, examples and resources. $19.95, paper

Macintosh Plus, **Macintosh SE** and **Macintosh II manuals** are filled with excellent illustrations, examples and shortcuts. Sure the Mac is friendly enough so you don't *have* to read the manual, but you'll really benefit from doing so. At the very least, take a peek at the Contents pages and read selected chapters.
Apple Computer, Inc.
20525 Mariani Avenue
Cupertino, CA 95014
408/996-1010

The Macintosh Buyer's Guide is an excellent resource for learning about software and hardware for the Mac. $20, newsstand price for one year; $14, subscription price for new subscribers.
Redgate Communications Corp.
Attn: Circulation Dept.
660 Beachland Blvd.
Vero Beach, FL 32963-1794
800/262-3012

MacUser is an excellent Macintosh monthly magazine that provides the latest in Macintosh software, peripherals and usage. This is a very practical, hands-on publication. $3.95 per newsstand copy; $19.97 for a one-year subscription (12 issues)
MacUser
PO Box 52461
Boulder, CO 80321-2461
415/378-5600

Macworld is a wonderful monthly magazine with top quality design and well-written columns and feature articles. $30 for a one-year subscription (12 issues)
PCW Communications, Inc.
501 Second St.
San Francisco, CA 94107
800/525-0643: in Colorado, 303/447-9330

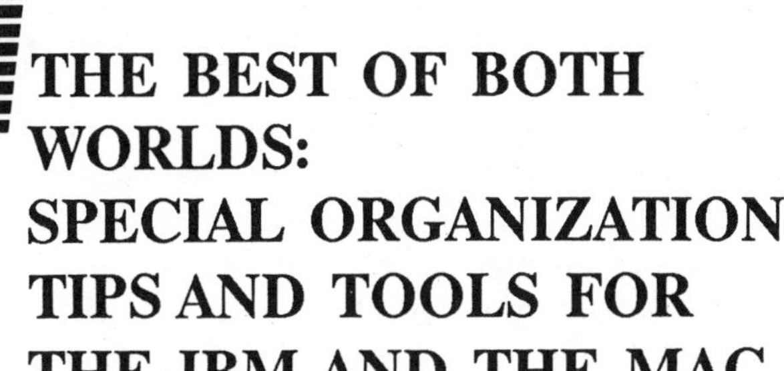

7 THE BEST OF BOTH WORLDS: SPECIAL ORGANIZATION TIPS AND TOOLS FOR THE IBM AND THE MAC

Quick Scan: Read this chapter if you want to protect yourself against computer disaster because yes, it can *happen to you. You'll learn the best protection for your personal computer comes from computer file maintenance, clean hard disks, organized floppies and a sound backup routine. Besides some simple techniques, you'll also discover some indispensable software programs that make it all much easier. Read this chapter whether you own a Macintosh, IBM or IBM compatible personal computer. Products are grouped by computer type in the chapter resource guide. (The term "IBM" is used throughout this chapter to denote both IBM and IBM compatible personal computers.)*

When it comes to good organization, computers are like file cabinets, only worse. If your file cabinets are jam packed, your hard and floppy disks are probably, too. But as long as you've got space on your disks, what's the problem? Let's see why you shouldn't wait until all your space is gone.

THE REWARDS OF COMPUTER FILE MAINTENANCE

Regular computer file maintenance is essential. Not only will it be easier to find files, but you can improve the productivity and speed of your computer–particularly your hard disk.

Just as with manual systems, try to keep most accessible only the files you're regularly using. Only these files should be kept in your current subdirectories or your Mac folders. It's so easy to start stockpiling files that you never use. At that point, you'll soon discover you have trouble finding files that are needed.

BIGGER IS BETTER, RIGHT?

If you've ever been tempted to substitute a bigger hard disk for computer housekeeping chores, think again. You may have also been tempted at one time or another to buy another file cabinet for all your papers and files. Or perhaps you've bought a bigger house to accommodate all the "stuff" you've accumulated (you may remember the famous George Carlin routine).

If you're behind in your housekeeping, a bigger hard disk is just going to make matters worse. Just as with file cabinets, you can only tell how much space you need *after* you have purged your files. Once you've cleaned out your hard disk, see if you have 75 percent or higher filled with current programs and files. If so, a larger or additional hard disk may be very appropriate.

By the way, when was the last time you cleaned out your hard disk? Have you *ever* cleaned it out? Since for most of us, out of sight means out of mind, it's particularly easy for computer files to accumulate.

There are three reasons to take the time and trouble to clean out your hard disk:

1. to speed up your computer
2. to speed *you* up (locating files becomes difficult when your IBM directories or Mac folders are full of files that you aren't using)
3. to make more room on your hard disk.

KEEP IT CLEAN

The best computer file maintenance is done as you go–deleting duplicates and out-of-date files, storing inactive files on backup media and having a backup routine that you use regularly. But if you're like most people, you probably will need to sit down once every six months to a year and do a thorough spring cleaning. Where do you begin and how do you proceed?

- Before you do any "house cleaning," print a hard copy of your root directory so you can see at a glance all the names of your IBM subdirectories or your Mac first level folders.
- Go through each main IBM subdirectory or Mac folder and see if you recognize any files you can delete. (Now's the time to remove those extra backups that your word processor may automatically make.)
- Look more closely. Are there any files you're no longer using but you'd like to keep in archival storage? If so, back these up on floppies. Or perhaps you have a backup device or program that can "tag" these specific files and back them up collectively. For files that are very important, make *two* archival copies that are kept in different locations.
- Consolidate any files you can–i.e., group separate, related files together in one new file or a Mac folder. For example, instead of having every letter in a separate file, group all '89 letters together or all letters to a client together. In the IBM environment, depending on your version of DOS, a file could take up to 8,000 bytes of memory even though it looks in your directory listing as if the file only has say, 100 bytes. (Each file under DOS is allocated a certain minimum number of bytes, whether or not those bytes are actually used and whether or not those bytes appear to be included in the number of bytes next to the file name on your directory.)
- Make hard copies of catalogs or directory listings and keep them near your labeled backup media. If you back up your hard disk with a program that contains a catalog feature, print out the catalog when you complete your backup. If you're using 5¼-

inch floppies, print out the directory listings and tape them to the jackets holding the floppies.

A CLEAN HARD DISK

There are two steps to cleaning out your hard disk. First, you'll need to eliminate, transfer and consolidate files, which we've just discussed.

Second, you should **optimize** your hard disk using a software program such as Disk Optimizer in order to regain your original speed. The more you use your hard disk, the slower it becomes. The reason for this is that every time you want to save information, your computer stores the information wherever it will fit. Actually your computer stores pieces of the information in **clusters,** wherever it can find room on your hard disk. The information in a file may start out as one cluster but through use, the file becomes many clusters that are scattered all over the hard disk. This results in slower access time, which you'll notice especially when you call up a file.

A software program, such as Disk Optimizer, can reorganize the clusters on your hard disk, grouping them all together. **Mike Lamanno**, owner of Graphix Data Products in Santa Monica, California, and a computer service expert, suggests optimizing at least once a week. He says optimizing not only keeps your access time from slowing down, but it also saves wear and tear on your computer. If your disk is optimized, your computer doesn't have to scramble around looking for all the clusters of a file and therefore, your computer doesn't have to work as hard.

FLOPPY ORGANIZATION

Most of our discussion about computer file organization has focused on your hard disk. But chances are good, you'll still be using floppies from time to time. Here are some tips to prevent you from floundering in floppies.

As a general rule, separate program files from your data files. Group data files together by subject, task or client or by a common IBM subdirectory or Mac folder name.

Keep floppies in plastic storage cases specially designed for floppy disks. Get the kind with plastic dividers and stick-on labels to group different types of files. For extra security, buy cases with locks and keys. See Figure 7-1.

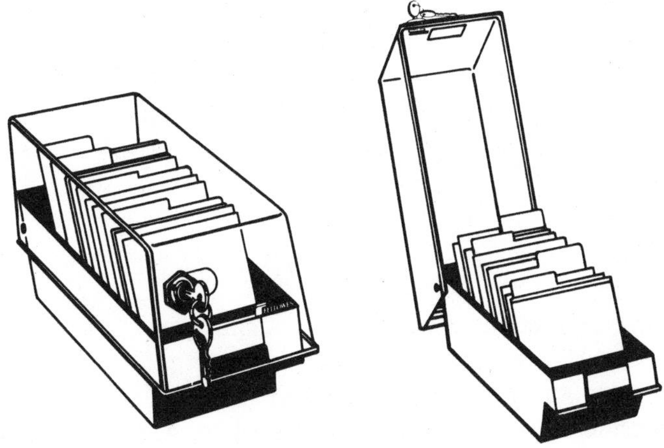

Figure 7-1. Fellowes Econo/Stor 40 Diskette Filing Tray

Keep a set of up-to-date, printed **directories** for all your floppies. As used here, a directory is a table of contents for your floppy. For the 5¼-inch floppy format, tape each floppy directory to its jacket. It's a good idea to keep a set of printed directories in a nearby notebook or folder, whether you're using 3½- or 5¼-inch floppies. Hard-copy directories can save you the time of inserting floppies and scanning their directories when you want to see what's on them.

If you have hundreds of files, you may want to consider color coding. Use colored diskette labels or buy diskettes that come in colors. Sentinel makes diskettes in 10 different colors.

When you label a diskette always date it. In fact, anytime you work on a disk, write the date on the label. Use a thin, permanent felt-tip marker, such as a Sharpie pen, instead of a pencil or ball-point pen, that could damage the diskette.

And finally, when you buy diskettes, buy the best. But price and name-brand recognition are not necessarily the key factors. A *New York Times* column by Peter H. Lewis suggested that disks manufactured by Syncom Technologies in Mitchell, South Dakota, are very high quality. Syncom sells its disks under the Platinum label, as well as other names.

Whatever you do, avoid generic, dirt-cheap disks, that carry no manufacturer's name. These disks are said to have high failure rates–as high as 20 percent. High quality disks have no more than a one percent failure rate.

One test conducted by Memory Control Technology Corp. (Memcon) and reported in *Personal Computing* magazine found that the following manufacturers passed with flying colors: BASF, JVC, Memorex, Kodak, Nashua, Sony and 3M.

BACK IT UP!

You can't talk about computer file maintenance without talking about backups. For our discussion here, a backup is a duplicate copy of computer data (programs and files) that is stored on another medium besides the primary one you're using. There are two parts to making backups: establishing a **backup routine** and selecting a **backup device.** The backup device or medium you select isn't half as important as whether you actually use it.

WHY BOTHER?

Why do you have to bother backing up your work when you have a hard disk–isn't it solid as a rock? Computer expert Paul Somerson responds by saying, "Hard disks used to be expensive and unreliable. That's all changed. Today they're inexpensive and unreliable."

You never backed up your filing cabinet; why should you back up your computer files? First, the chances of wiping out your computer data are much greater than losing your hard data. Second, it's too easy today *not* to backup. (And why tempt fate anyway?)

Backups are *insurance* for valuable, current data that would either require more than an hour to re-enter or would be next to impossible to recreate exactly as inputted the first time. Whenever I'm producing original, creative material, I not only save it on my hard disk, but I save it onto a special backup floppy as well. That floppy goes home with me each night.

By the way, since I'm saving this material frequently and onto two different media–a procedure that requires many steps–I use a **macro** to automate the process. A macro is a quick, shorthand method of doing many operational steps with just a few keystrokes. With

WordPerfect, my word processing program, I was able to create a "save" macro that lets me press just two keys (the Alt key and the letter "S") to quickly perform an operation that would normally require pressing at least 35 different keys!

Besides making additional copies of important information, backups can serve as **storage** for less important information that is not being used and is taking up too much space on your hard disk. Once you've backed up this archival information, then you can delete it from your hard disk or a working floppy. Make two archival backup copies if the information is very important and keep the copies in separate locations–for example, at home and at the office.

Good backups will let you conduct business as usual even if your hard disk crashes or your entire computer is in for repair.

HOW OFTEN, HOW MUCH?

Your backup routine depends on how often files change, the number of files you modify a day, the kind of information or application and how easy your backup device is to use. It may also depend upon whether you keep any hard copy that would enable you to recreate computer files. Based on these criteria, check any of the following that you think would apply to your situation:

- Each day back up any data, IBM subdirectories or Mac folders or applications you have modified that day.
- Have two rotating sets of complete backups where the most current set is off site (at home, for example, if your office is not in your home). As soon as you make your most up-to-date backup, take it off site and bring back now the older backup set.
- Do a complete backup every day.
- Do a complete backup every week.
- Do a complete backup every month.
- Have three complete sets of programs and data: one you're working with, and two current backups–one on-site and an additional backup kept off site.

Data processing departments generally keep daily files Monday through Thursday, make a weekly backup on Friday and do a monthly backup every fourth week. Copies of weekly and monthly backups are kept off site as well as on site. My recommendation is **always have at least one complete, current backup off site.**

ADDITIONAL TIPS FOR A BETTER BACKUP ROUTINE

Following these simple backup tips can save you many headaches down the long haul. Check off all the ones you already do; circle those you will incorporate into your routine after reading this section:

- Always back up new software.
- Always back up newly *installed* software, particularly if you made any special installation procedures. (Also keep a record of the answers you gave to installation questions in case you need to reinstall the program.)
- Make two backups of files that change every day. Make the backups as you go, saving each file twice, on your hard disk and on a floppy). Or make your backups at the end of the day from a daily, written list of modified files.
- Carefully *date* and label all backup media; use color coding if necessary.
- When you install a backup device, test it out with a some junk files before betting your life on it.
- Use dated hard copy as important backup.
- Have two current sets of all important work–one should be off site.

TYPES OF BACKUP

Your backup routine should include **selective** as well as **complete** backups. Selective or partial backups are used to copy individual files, programs or data. An **incremental** backup is a type of selective backup that copies only files that have changed since your last complete backup. (If your backup device can do incremental backups, you will save time–keep this feature in mind when you select a backup device.)

Complete or "full" backups are used to copy the entire contents of your hard disk and would be useful if you had a system failure and you had to restore the data on your hard disk. Backup devices do complete backups in one of two ways: **image** or **file-by-file.** Image backups make a mirror-image copy of your hard disk and are very fast. The disadvantage is that you might not be able to restore an image backup to a different hard disk other than the original. (If, for example, your hard disk crashes and can't be repaired, you may possibly be unable to transfer your image backup to a new hard disk.)

File-by-file backups, while slower, don't have that problem. Not only are they more reliable, they also make it easier to find backed-up files. New technology is aiming for faster, file-by-file backups. File-by-file backups can be used for selective as well as complete backups.

TYPES OF BACKUP AND STORAGE DEVICES

If you're confused about which backup device to choose, you're not alone. Selection criteria as well as the two basic types of devices are described here; specific brands and models receiving favorable computer magazine reviews are listed at the end of this chapter.

Selection Criteria

When it comes to choosing a backup device these are the key criteria you should consider:

- ease of use (if it's not easy to learn and use, you won't bother with it)
- speed (how much of your time will it take?)
- capacity (how much do you need now and in the foreseeable future?)
- portability (are you going to be removing and transporting the device frequently and if so, how far?)
- operator monitored (or does it "run in the background" by itself?)
- compatibility (with other office computers)
- security
- performance
- reliability/verification (what kind of error checking does it have?)
- For IBM users: DOS or non-DOS format (often faster, more condensed and more reliable in a non-DOS format although you won't be able to use non-DOS files until they are "restored" back to a DOS format)
- additional hardware required (the cost factor aside, what kind of space do you have for more hardware?)

- file-by-file or image (you may need both, but at the very least have file-by-file)
- cost (what are your budget restrictions?)

Go back and check off all the criteria you *must* have and compare them to your budget and your information needs to determine the price you're willing to pay.

TYPES OF BACKUP DEVICES

All backup devices are one of two types–**disk** or **tape.**

Disk devices are generally faster in terms of backup speed than tape devices. It's also easier and faster to locate backed up data on a disk. But disks usually cost more and hold less data than tapes.

Tape backup devices use a magnetic tape similar to the kind used in audio recording. Most backup tapes are housed in cartridges.

Seven Disk Backup Devices

Of the seven disk backup devices, using **floppy disks** in combination with **DOS commands** is the least expensive disk backup device. Unfortunately, it's also the slowest.

Using **floppies** in conjunction with a **hard disk backup utility program** is an inexpensive, reliable choice, though once again, not super fast. But if you have a fairly small hard disk (10 or 20 megabyte) or you use and back up only a small number of files, this could be a good choice. It has worked for me. When I had a 10-megabyte hard disk, I backed it up in eight to 10 minutes using Fastback, a software program that continues to get good reviews. Now that I have a 40 megabyte hard disk, I'm still using Fastback (although I've upgraded to Fastback Plus). I make incremental backups daily in combination with full backups every quarter.

A **second hard disk** can function as a backup device as well as a duplicate computer system, provided you keep the second disk completely up to date. If your main hard disk should crash, you've got the second one ready to go. (Most likely you would have to send your hard disk, not the entire computer out for repair.) You can get an *external* hard disk or two *internal, half-height* hard disks. Warning: Never rely solely on a second hard disk on site; you also better have a backup copy of data off site.

A fourth alternative is a **removable hard disk** instead of a conventional hard disk. Such a hard disk is housed in a sealed unit. While faster than many other backup systems, a removable hard disk is slower than the standard hard disk and will not hold as much data. It is faster and has longer media life than the next alternative, but it is considered to be much more fragile. ("Auto-parking" and "head-locking" features, however, help to minimize the fragility of removable hard disks.)

Removable cartridge disk systems use specially designed, more rugged "cartridge disks," which are like large capacity floppies housed in cartridges. These disks can hold from 12 to 20 megabytes each. The Bernoulli Box is an example. Cartridge disk systems provide removable, large capacity storage. These systems use their own controllers (compared to those that use floppy disk controllers) and can therefore, write more data on a disk.

There are two types of removable cartridge disk systems–flexible and hard. Removable flexible cartridges appear to be more durable.

While perhaps the most cost-effective solution for removable mass-storage, these systems are considered slow and somewhat susceptible to media wear.

Hard disk cards are faster than floppy disks or tape backup units. They are cost effective, too. Easy to install, a hard disk card slips into an empty computer slot. It's the equivalent of having a second hard disk. A hard disk card can be moved from computer to computer but it is inconvenient to switch it frequently. To use a hard disk card as your *only* backup storage device is foolhardy since you want media that you can and *will* store off site.

The **optical disk**, also called the **optical cartridge drive** or **WORM** (Write Once, Read Many) is a new backup system that stores *hundreds of megabytes* (some store *gigabytes*) and provides special security that prevents records from being altered. A WORM can store information more densely than any other backup device (as of this writing) but it can't be erased or rewritten. It is also a random-access device but it takes ten times longer to find information randomly. It's expensive but this technology can store more information than any other medium and does so in a way that protects and secures data at the highest level.

New technology is being developed that will take off where WORM has begun. A "floptical" drive (a cross between floppy and optical technology) may replace WORM drives completely. The distinct advantage will be that you can write to floptical media many times.

Tape Backup Devices

Tape backup systems for personal computers include a variety of special **tape drives** and **tape cartridges.** ("Open-reel" tape systems are the standard for mainframe computers.) Tape backup is fairly fast and reliable but it has a number of disadvantages. For one thing, tape drives and cartridges are not standardized (which is only a problem if you work on several different types of hardware). For another, many cartridges need formatting (i.e., preparing) before use, which takes time. Tape backup units also do not store or restore files as quickly as disk backup systems.

But you can't beat the *capacity* of tape systems. Today's standard size of ¼-inch tape data cassettes come in lengths of 300, 450 and 600 feet which can store correspondingly 30, 45 and 60 megabytes of data.

Be aware that even as you read this page, new and updated backup and storage technologies are emerging.

RESOURCE GUIDE

IBM OR IBM COMPATIBLE PRODUCTS

DISK BACKUP AND STORAGE DEVICES

Bernoulli Box is a removable cartridge disk system that continues to get good reviews. It consists of a special 10 or 20-megabyte cartridge disk inserted into its own disk drive. It comes with its own programs and clear documentation. Installation is easy. The original Bernoulli Box does weigh in at 46 pounds, however, and is the size of an IBM PC; Bernoulli Box II is considerably lighter and features a slim, 5¼-inch cartridge. You can buy a one- or two-drive model ranging in price from $1,440 to $2,500.

Iomega Corp.
1821 West 4000 South
Roy, UT 84067
801/778-1000

Mountain Computer Drive Cards are hard disk cards that slip into an empty slot in your computer. They come in 20- and 30-megabyte sizes and are easy to install.
Mountain Computer, Inc.
240 Hacienda Ave.
Campbell, CA 95008
800/458-0300

Passport is a removable hard disk selected as a *PC Magazine* "Editor's Choice." It is built for high performance and portability and includes auto-parking and head-locking to protect against head or disk damage. Internal unit, $659; external unit, $399; Micro Channel business PS/2 unit, $759; 20MB disk, $595; 40MB disk, $795.
Plus Development Corp.
1778 McCarthy Blvd.
Milpitas, CA 95035
408/434-6900

Backup Utility Programs

While most of these programs are designed to be used with floppy disks, some of them (such as Fastback Plus) can be used with other media, including tape cartridges.

Back-It has been rated as a good program with good speed. It formats disks during backup. It tells you approximately the number of diskettes you'll need. Unfortunately, it does not keep a hard disk index. It also doesn't allow you to quickly restore a single file. $79
Gazelle Systems
42. N. University Ave., #10
Provo, UT 84601
800/233-0383, 801/377-1288

DataCare was favorably reviewed in *PC Magazine.* $99
Ellicott Software Inc.
3777 Plum Hill Ct.
Ellicott City, MD 21043
301/465-2690

DS Backup + is a good program that is relatively fast. You cannot format disks as you go, but the program will pause to let you format in the middle of a backup.

Design Software, Inc.
1275 W. Roosevelt Rd.
West Chicago, IL 60185
312/231-4540

Fastback Plus is a powerful, fast and flexible program that I'm using. I've been a Fastback user for years (I started with the standard version and was thrilled to upgrade to the "Plus" version). To give you some idea of Fastback's speed, consider this: you can back up a full 10-megabyte hard disk in just eight to nine minutes compared to DOS which takes nearly 30 minutes. (Other backup utility programs take from 13 to 22 minutes for 10 megabytes.) It does complete or selective backups and incremental backups. Fastback formats disks as it copies and will let you print a catalog of the backed up files. Besides the useful manual, there is a help line with "user friendly" assistance. $189 ($159 for regular Fastback)
Fifth Generation Systems
1322 Bell Avenue, Suite 1A
Tustin, CA 70809
714/259-0541

Intelligent Backup rates high for beginners or busy professionals who don't have a lot of time. It is an automated program that reminds you when to do your next backup. $149
Software Laboratories, Inc.
202 E. Airport Dr., #280
San Bernardino, CA 92408
714/889-0226

Take Two, favorably reviewed in *PC Magazine*, is a menu-driven backup program that offers speed and flexibility. $165.
United Software Security Inc.
8133 Leesburg Pike, #800
Vienna, VA 22180
800/892-0007

TAPE BACKUP DEVICES

Genoa's Galaxy 3260 was selected as *PC Magazine*'s second choice (out of 13 reviewed tape backup systems). This is an easy-to-use system with friendly documentation and on-line help that will do mirror-image or file-by-file backups. $1,400.

Genoa Systems Corp.
73 E. Trimble Road
San Jose, CA 95131
408/945-9720

Maynard's Maynstream 20 is a 20-megabyte portable tape backup system that is about the size and weight of a library card-file drawer (it weighs six pounds to be exact). It backs up a 10-megabyte hard disk in about 21 minutes. The tape cartridge doesn't need pre-formatting (some others can take 40-minutes). Installation is easy and comes with good documentation. $1,595 (and $195 per controller card for each computer). There is now a Maynard Maynstream for the PS/2 (which was a *PC Magazine* "Editor's Choice") with a 60-megabyte tape at $1,695.
Maynard Electronics
460 E. Semoran Blvd.
Casselberry, FL 32707
305/331-6402

Mountain FileSafe Series 7120 was selected as a *PC Magazine* "Editor's Choice" for the PS/2. It is fast and easy to use. It comes with a 120-megabyte tape cartridge. $2,395
Mountain Computer Inc.
360 El Pueblo Rd.
Scotts Valley, CA 95066
800/458-0300 or 408/438-6650

Sysgen QIC-File is a tape backup system that has been *PC Magazine*'s "Editor's Choice." Its main attraction is an automatic selective backup feature that works in the background to back up any files that have changed. It will do mirror-image or file-by-file backups. QIC-File also has a small "footprint"–it's small and compact at 2 inches high, 6 inches wide and 9¾ inches deep. $1,495.
Sysgen Inc.
47853 Warm Springs Blvd.
Fremont, CA 94539
415/490-6770

Tecmar QIC-60H is a 60-megabyte tape backup system whose vertical design makes for a compact fit next to your computer. This a full-featured system that can do file-by-file or image backups.

Additionally, its image backups can be restored to disks other than the original disk–a real plus. $2,144
Tecmar, Inc.
6225 Cochran Rd.
Solon, OH 44139
216/349-1009

SPECIAL ORGANIZATIONAL UTILITY PROGRAMS

A number of specialized utility programs will help you correct specific file and data problems you may encounter on your computer.

Hard Disk Maintenance Utilities

Cubit expands the capacity of your hard disk (will also work for floppies) through data compression. It is based on the space-saving techniques used on mainframe computers. Cubit stores up to twice as much data on the same amount of disk space. $69.95
SoftLogic Solutions Inc.
One Perimeter Road
Manchester, NH 03103
800/272-9900 or in New Hampshire, 603/627-9900

Disk Optimizer will speed up your hard disk by reorganizing scattered data into contiguous clusters. $69.95
SoftLogic Solutions Inc. (See above.)

Disk Technician will repair bad sectors before or even after a hard disk crash. It can prevent hard disk errors and recover lost data. A head-parking routine is included, an important safety feature when you turn off or move your computer. One reviewer wrote, "This could be the best investment you ever make." $99
Prime Solutions Inc.
1940 Garnet Ave.
San Diego, CA 92109
619/274-5000

SpinRite is a utility program designed to tune up your hard disk and test it for flaws. $59
Gibson Research Crop.
22991 La Cadena
Laguna Hills, CA 92653
714/830-2200

Data Recovery

Mace Utilities, Version 4.1 will recover deleted files and restore a formatted hard disk. It comes with all kinds of file management and hard disk maintenance utilities that will unfragment files and sort/squeeze directories. $99
Pace Mace Software
400 Williamson Way
Ashland, OR 97520
800/523-0258
503/488-0224

The Norton Utilities 4.5 has become a standard for its ability to recover deleted files. It performs other hard disk maintenance functions. The "Advanced Edition," which is for the hard disk, includes a disk optimizer and a directory commenter. $150
Peter Norton Computing, Inc.
2210 Wilshire Blvd.
Santa Monica, CA 90403
800/365-1010 or 213/453-2361

Data Access

File Facility also known as **Filefac** is a low-cost IBM program that helps you find data files no matter which directory they're on. $19.95
IBM Personally Developed Software
PO Box 3280
Wallingford, CT 06494
800/IBM-PCSW

Gofer is a full-text retrieval software program that lets you find a word (or group of words) and copy it to another document. This program doesn't take up valuable space on your hard disk because it doesn't create an index. This memory-resident program works great for occasional searches or if you don't have hundreds of files to search. $59.95
Microlytics
300 Main St.
East Rochester, NY 14445
716/377-0130

IN.SIGHT, Version 2.02 retrieves documents by word, phrase or matching letter combination. $95
Pearlsoft Inc.
PO Box 638
Wilsonville, OR 97070
503/682-3636

LIST is a fast, inexpensive file search utility that scans forward, backward and sideways through files. This is a shareware program available directly from Vernon D. Buerg. $15
Vernon D. Buerg
456 Lakeshire Dr.
Daly City, CA 94015
415/994-2944

Magic Mirror quickly reformats and transfers data between incompatible programs. The data is stored in a memory buffer and then transferred to a target program. $99.95
SoftLogic Solutions
One Perimeter Road
Manchester, NH 03103
800/272-9900 or in New Hampshire, 603/627-9900

Memory Lane, Version 1.3, is a full-text retrieval program that creates an index to help you find text quickly and efficiently. It's especially useful if you do searches frequently and have long or many files. $99
Group L Corp.
481 Carlisle Dr.
Herndon, VA 22070
703/471-0030

Swap converts word processing files from one format to another. $79.95
Wiley Professional Software
605 Third Ave.
New York, NY 10158
212/850-6398

Zoo Keeper, besides its clever name, is a clever way to locate files on your hard disk. Zoo Keeper lets you create 40-character descriptors for any of the files on your hard disk whose eight-

character names may be a bit baffling. If you forget what you called a file, Zoo Keeper will look for your description of it. $75
Polaris Software
613 West Valley Parkway #323
Escondido, CA 92025
800/338-5943

ZyINDEX Professional is a file-indexing program that creates an index of almost all the words or specified combinations of words in your files and their location. The program indexes up to 5000 files. $295. (ZyINDEX Plus indexes up to 15,000 files and multi-user systems and costs $695.)
ZyLAB Corp.
233 E. Erie St.
Chicago, IL 60611
312/642-2201

MACINTOSH PRODUCTS

DISK BACKUP DEVICES

Bernoulli Box disk cartridge/drive system offers models ranging from 10 to 40 megabytes of backup storage. The **Bernoulli Box** disk cartridge system is a reliable, highly rated backup system. From $1,299 to $2,299.
Iomega Corp.
1821 West 4000 South
Roy, UT 84067
801/778-1000

Backup Utility Programs

Copy II for the Macintosh is a program that makes archival backups and also copies software without making parameter changes. $39.95
Central Point Software, Inc.
9700 SW Capitol Hwy, Suite 100
Portland, OR 97219
503/244-5782

DiskFit is a hard disk backup utility that has received a "95" rating from *MacGuide Magazine* (on a scale of 1-95) and is touted in the book *Macintosh Hard Disk Management*. This program has many useful features. Files are backed up in Macintosh format so that you can more easily restore and use single files. The program lets you split a large file to more than one floppy. It does incremental backups and will print reports that list backed up folders and files. But what's really exciting about the incremental backups is that they are done on your original complete backup set so that you use fewer disks than with other programs. The "Verify Writes" feature verifies that files are written correctly to disk. $74.95
SuperMac Technologies, Inc.
295 N. Bernardo Ave.
Mountain View, CA 94043
415/964-8884

Fastback Mac is a powerful, multi-featured, high-speed hard disk backup and restore software utility. The backup rate is more than one megabyte per minute and includes error detection and correction. You can fully customize your backup, which can include incremental backups. You can print labels for your backup set. $129.95
Fifth Generation Systems
1322 Bell Ave., Ste. 1A
Irvine, CA 92680
714/259-0541 or 800/225-2775

Hard Disk Backup is a full-featured utility that's easy to use. It was rated "95" by *MacGuide*. Features include disk formatting and verification; file specification or "filtering," that includes the use of wildcards; estimate of number of floppy disks needed for the backup; compressed file format; split files that are two large for one floppy; and backup on other media, such as another hard disk or a tape backup unit. $54.95
FWB Software, Inc.
2040 Polk St., Ste. 215
San Francisco, CA 94109
415/563-8381

HFS Backup provides a long list of features plus ease of use and reliability. This program lets you define a "Backup Set," which

specifies folders and files you back up most often and can serve as a template for future backups. Two copies of the Backup Directory are included automatically whenever you back up.
Useful features include backup customization; automatic disk formatting; and data verification. $49.95
Personal Computer Peripherals Corp.
6204 Benjamin Rd.
Tampa, FL 33634
800/622-2888 or 813/884-3092

SoftBackup works particularly well with tape media. This program lets you use multiple tapes for backup. You can set up an automatic backup schedule. You can pre-design different "scripts," or backup routines that back up different sets of files. $69.95
Diversified I/O, Inc.
1008 Stewart Dr.
Sunnyvale, CA 94086
408/730-2171

TAPE BACKUP DEVICE

Tecmar QT-Mac40 is a tape backup system that backs up automatically and unattended. $1,395
Tecmar, Inc.
6225 Cochran Rd.
Solon, OH 44139
216/349-1009

SPECIAL ORGANIZATIONAL UTILITY PROGRAMS

A number of specialized utility programs will help you correct specific file and data problems you may encounter on your computer. (See also the Chapter 6 resource guide.)

Data Access

Sonar is a text retrieval program that lets you search for key words and phrases in folders full of files, compare and analyze and create an index. $249.
Virginia Systems Software Services
5509 W. Bay Court
Midlothian, VA 23113
804/739-3200

Hard Disk Maintenance Utility

Disk Express is a disk defragmentation utility that will optimize your hard disk (as well as floppies). The program can verify your disk directory, making sure that what your directory says is on the disk, is actually there. *MacGuide Magazine* gave this program a rating of "95," on a scale of 1 to 100. $39.95
ALsoft, Inc.
PO Box 927
Spring, TX 77383
713/353-4090

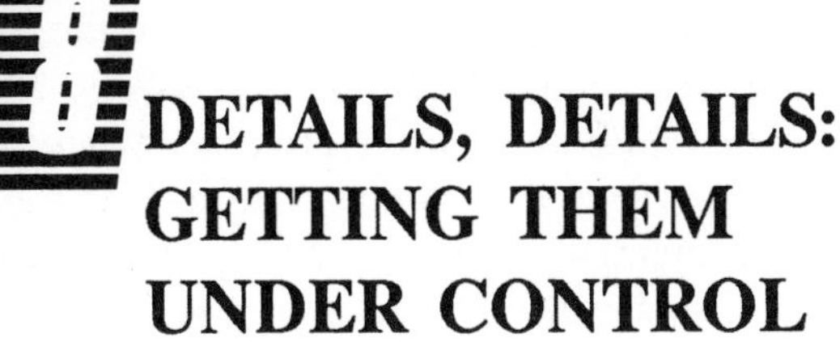

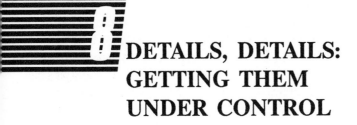

8 DETAILS, DETAILS: GETTING THEM UNDER CONTROL

Quick Scan: Discover specific tools and systems to keep track of the detailed information related to projects, assignments, people, resources and records. If just too many of your office details are slipping through the proverbial cracks, you could profit from a simple system or two. Here are some ideas that can help.

Let's face it. Life keeps getting more and more complicated each day. So many details to take care of and so much information to manage. How *do* you stay on top of it all?

Some people are lucky. They can delegate the details to someone else. But whether you can delegate or not, you need a **detail orientation** and **control over details.**

Why? If you're like most people, you probably do or supervise plenty of paperwork, record keeping and follow-up activities in your work, all of which generate many layers of information and details. When you manage details effectively, you're managing information and in doing so, you make a professional, lasting impression on people. It says you care about **quality** and **service**. It says you *care* enough to follow up and follow through–which is quite a feat in the midst of an ongoing information explosion.

Effective follow-up and follow-through require *systems* to organize details. Systems can be manual or computerized. Generally, it's best to start out using manual systems first (even if you have a computer). Complexity may necessitate a computerized system later on but start first with a manual one. The trick is to keep systems *simple*–as simple as possible.

Remember, too, a computer will not get you organized. Start planning logically and systematically on paper and then if necessary (and only if necessary) find a computer solution that conforms to you, not the other way around.

And should you happen to be fortunate enough to have an assistant, remember this: **when you have a good system in place, delegating is easy.**

WORK AND PROJECT MANAGEMENT SHORTCUTS

Where most people get into trouble is trying to remember everything in their head. And then they get upset with themselves when they forget something using the infallible "mental note system."

The other ploy that has equally bad results is relying on countless written slips of paper on your desk, in your wallet and on your wall. The problem with paper slips is that they create clutter and stress in your life. They also tend to "slip" through the cracks and get lost–which is probably why they're called "slips" in the first place.

TICKLER SYSTEMS

Almost all of us need to have our memories reminded or "tickled." That's where a **tickler system** comes in.

A calendar is the simplest tickler system just about everyone uses. But you need more than a calendar if you have many reminders or follow-ups.

CARD TICKLER SYSTEMS

Let's suppose you "prospect" or develop your market as part of your work. You'll probably want to set up a **card tickler system**, using ruled, colored index cards along with cardboard file guides printed with the days of the month and the months of the year. The cards come in different sizes–3-by-5, 4-by-6, 5-by-8. Decide what kind of data and how much you plan to write on each card.

I use a commercial card tickler system called **TIC-LA-DEX** that includes five, different colored, pre-printed 3-by-5 cards and three sets of pre-printed file guides–"1-31," "January to December" and "A-Z." Let me show you, step by step, how I use this card tickler system.

The mainstay for my marketing program, TIC-LA-DEX helps me to systematically develop new speaking engagements, promote my writing and stay in touch with clients. I use four colors to code my market into the following categories:

1. red–speaking/training prospects
2. blue–consulting clients
3. green–writing contacts
4. yellow–networking contacts.

Let me explain what I record on each card. See Figure 8-1 for a sample card.

I begin by writing the name of the organization or the name of the individual–whichever name I'm most likely to think of first. I then write the address and phone number and the key contacts and titles. I also make a point of listing names of secretaries, receptionists or other staff members to whom I speak.

I only write in an "action date" on the far left of the card for a *completed* action, e.g, actually talking to a key individual, not just leaving a message. The day I send out correspondence is an action date, too.

I keep a very brief summary of ongoing activity. For every attempted contact, I write a date on a line in the middle under "In Contact With." I also use my own codes and abbreviations. "TT" means "*t*elephone *t*o" and signifies I initiated the call. If I had to leave a message, TT is followed by "LM," which indicates I "*l*eft *m*essage." LM will be followed by the name of individual in parentheses with whom I spoke. A "K" inside a circle means we sent out an information *k*it to a prospect. "Fol" plus a specific date and often a time indicates the next phone call *fol*lowup or appointment.

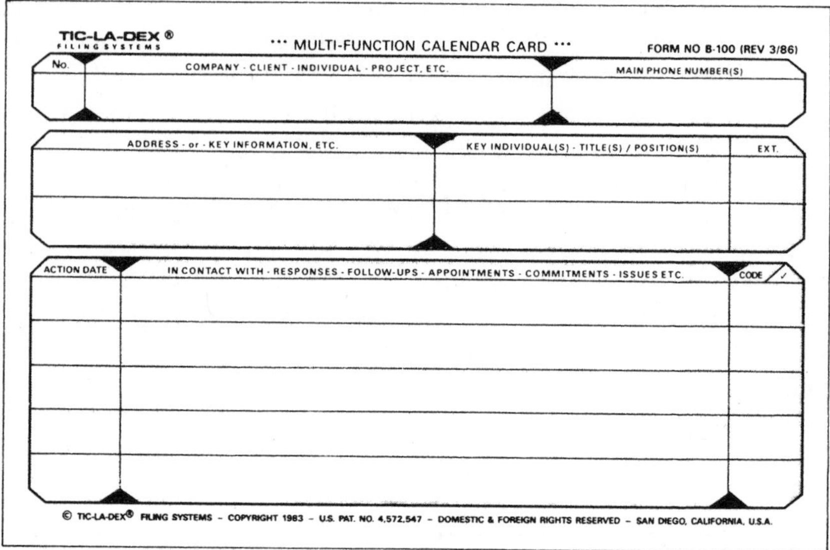

TIC-LA-DEX®
FILING SYSTEMS

*** MULTI-FUNCTION CALENDAR CARD ***

FORM NO B-100 (REV 3/86)

No. | COMPANY - CLIENT - INDIVIDUAL - PROJECT, ETC. | MAIN PHONE NUMBER(S)

ADDRESS - or - KEY INFORMATION, ETC. | KEY INDIVIDUAL(S) - TITLE(S) / POSITION(S) | EXT.

ACTION DATE | IN CONTACT WITH - RESPONSES - FOLLOW-UPS - APPOINTMENTS - COMMITMENTS - ISSUES ETC. | CODE ✓

© TIC-LA-DEX® FILING SYSTEMS - COPYRIGHT 1983 - U.S. PAT. NO. 4,572,547 - DOMESTIC & FOREIGN RIGHTS RESERVED - SAN DIEGO, CALIFORNIA, U.S.A.

Figure 8-1. A TIC-LA-DEX card has pre-printed sections on the front, which is shown here, as well as on the back.

When someone I've called isn't available, particularly someone I don't know well, I ask the receptionist or secretary to take down my name and company and indicate *I'll* call back, preferably at a specific time of day. I ask the receptionist or secretary when would be best. Then I'll jot down "IWCB," (*I* *W*ill *C*all *B*ack) on my card. IWCB lets me put my name before a new contact or prospect without making any demands on the person. It's also good marketing to give my name repeated exposure and hence some familiarity. No call is ever wasted. It's a good way to make cold calls warmer.

I use one other code mark on the card: a check mark in the top right-hand corner. Once a cold call becomes a warm prospect, my staff check marks the card after entering the name, address and phone number from the card into our computer data base.

The cards are filed in one of three places: behind a 1-31 card, a month card or an alphabetical card. If the next action on a card is to take place on a day of the current month, the card goes behind the correctly numbered day. If the next action should occur next month or later, the card goes behind the appropriate month. If the card has no known future followup but isn't ready to be removed from the system, the card is filed alphabetically by the name of the individual or organization.

The cards are small–3-by-5–but codes and abbreviations tell all of the action items at a glance. For more detailed information, I keep a **prospect notebook** that contains correspondence and notes that are stapled together, hole punched and filed behind alphabetical tab dividers. There they remain until the prospect becomes a client, whereupon the material goes into a client file folder. The prospect notebook is the longhand version of my marketing activity; the index card tickler system is the shorthand. And if prospects should call *before* the next followup date, I can quickly find their data because the prospect notebook has all of the key information.

DESK FILES OR SORTERS AND ACCORDION FILES

If you don't like having to hole punch papers for your prospect notebook, use an alphabetical **desk file** (also called a **sorter**) or an **accordion file**. The desk file (see Figure 8-2) opens like a book and has an expandable binding on the spine. The accordion file is enclosed on three sides and usually has a flap that folds over. Both the desk file and the accordion file come in either alphabetical (A-Z) or numerical (1-31) styles. One desk file that we've just begun using has 1-31 as well as January to December tabs and works as a handy tickler system.

FILE FOLDER TICKLER SYSTEMS

Some people prefer a **file folder tickler system** that has file folders labeled January to December and 1-31. A file folder tickler system can sit inside a desk drawer or in an upright rack or caddy on a nearby credenza, return or table.

There are many uses for such a system. One communications consultant I know uses a ruled sheet of paper in the front of each monthly folder to list followup calls for the month. He keeps corresponding notes for the calls inside an alphabetical notebook.

A file folder tickler system is also a great way to get reminder papers off your desk and into a chronological system. These are papers that require action on or by specific dates. They may include papers such as conference announcements, letters, memos, notes and even birthday cards. If you like visual, tangible reminders, instead of a note jotted down in your calendar or planner, this system could be ideal for you.

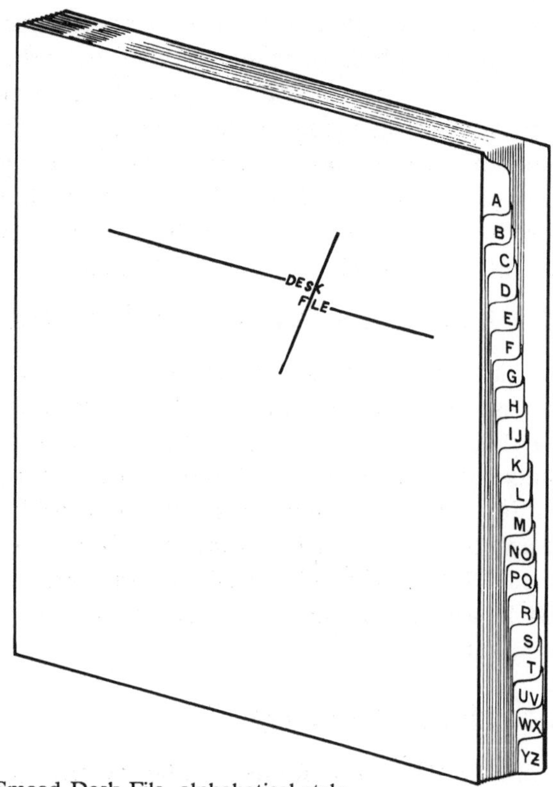

Figure 8-2. Smead Desk File, alphabetical style

Suppose you have some notes you'll need to use at a meeting on the ninth. Get those notes off your desk (or out of a generic, overflowing "pending file") and put them behind the "9" tab. A file folder tickler system is also handy for birthday cards filed on the day to be mailed or behind the appropriate month.

You can buy pre-printed file guides or Pendaflex hanging folder label inserts in 1-31, A-Z and Jan. to Dec. styles. Pendaflex also makes **Follow-up Tabs** that run lengthwise across a hanging folder and have a space for the file name plus two sliding signals that can be moved to indicate the month and the day of the month. Smead makes a Chan-L-Slide Follow-Up Folder. See Figure 8-3.

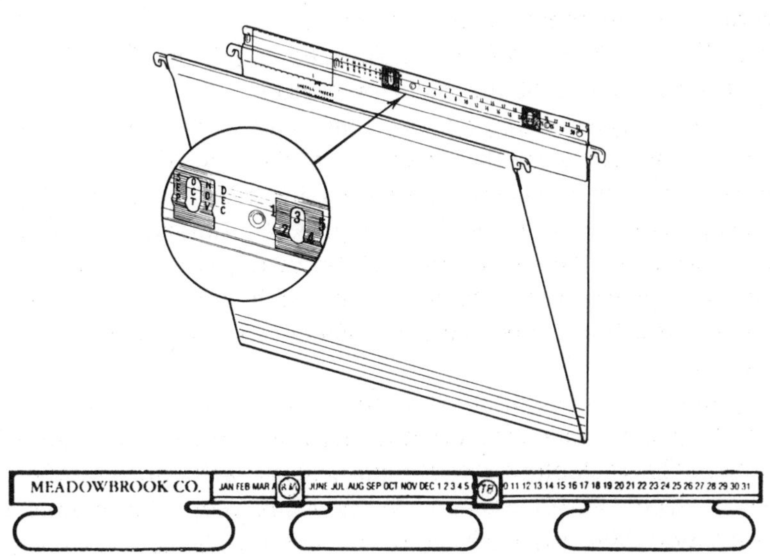

Figure 8-3. Smead Chan-L-Slide Follow-up Folder (top) and Pendaflex Follow-up Tab

TICKLER SLIP SYSTEM

If you have a very busy office in which you're responsible for many details and delegations, you may consider purchasing a **tickler slip system** such as Law Publications' **Tickler Record System.** Although designed for attorneys, the Tickler Record System also works great for other busy professionals with many deadlines.

The three-part, NCR (*n*o *c*arbon *r*equired), color-coded tickler forms are versatile. Don't let the legal terms throw you; let them stand for the kinds of work *you* do. A "case" could just as easily be a project or assignment and "attorney responsible" could be a staff member or colleague. See Figure 8-4 for a sample form.

The system is designed to be used with daily numerical and monthly card file guides along with alphabetical card file guides. The top white sheet is filed by the "Date of Event" or the final deadline or completion date. The middle yellow copy is filed by the first reminder date (there is room for three reminder dates). Having several different reminder dates helps prevent a form from getting lost in the system and a deadline from being missed. The pink copy is filed by the name of the client or project.

If you delegate to other people and want to keep track of their progress, consider using the system in another way. Give the original slip to your delegate, keep the yellow copy for yourself and file the pink copy alphabetically by client or project. You and your delegate should each file the slip by the date(s) action is necessary for you both. Perhaps for some people, you will only need to follow up on the due date; for others, such as trainees, you may need to follow up at each step.

If you work as part of an office team, you could adapt the Tickler Record System into a centralized tickler that is accessible to all team members. This adaptation works particularly well with sales teams. Each sales person, for example, writes a slip, keeps the original and files it inside their own deskside tickler system. The yellow copy goes into a central tickler system by date and the pink into a central alphabetical card file by client or project. One person monitors the central system and makes sure all follow-ups and deadlines are handled and reassigns activities if the responsible party is out of town or ill.

Two other tickler slip systems are also worthy of mention and are described and illustrated in the chapter resource guide under the "tickler systems" heading. They are SYCOM's **That Reminds Me** and Safeguard's **General Reminder/Assignment System.**

CUSTOMIZING YOUR OWN TICKLER SYSTEM

Consider designing your own tickler system. One accounting firm created the simple tickler form (in Figure 8-5) to be used in the office file folder tickler system.

Staff members complete the form, keep a copy and put the original in a centralized file folder tickler system arranged by the days of the month and the months of the year. One person in charge of the system makes sure that follow-through occurs.

If you do your planning by the week, it may make sense to use weekly tabs.

If you handle reoccurring tasks, projects or reports each month, consider using the tickler card system developed by **Judy Nowak,**

LP™ **TICKLER RECORD**
© **1977 by Law Publications,** A Division of All-state Legal Supply Co.
5910 Bowcroft St., Los Angeles, CA 90016
To reorder specify form E-120.

Client/ Case: Smith vs. Jones File No. 7785
Event: Motion to compel answers to interrogatories Dept. 5
Date of Event: 8/30/89 9 A.M.
Reminder Dates(s): 8/10/89
Attorney Responsible: Stephen Williams
Notes: See Rosen vs. Sparks for similar motion & points & authorities
☐ Done

Figure 8-4. Tickler Record System slip from Law Publications catalog

senior secretary at Rockwell International. Judy uses two sets of 1-31 cards for two months in a row. When she completes a task on a card as it comes up chronologically, she immediately files the card behind the appropriate number for the next month when the task will come up again. In this way she "files as she goes" and doesn't have to file a whole group of cards at the beginning of the next month. She's all set to go.

Nowak also makes sure she never misses a deadline because she has a reminder card that she files a few days before the actual card comes up in her system. She moves both the reminder card and the task card to the next month's 1-31 set when the task is complete.

COMPUTERIZED TICKLERS & TIME MANAGEMENT PROGRAMS

If you have a computer in your office that you use all the time, it may make sense to buy a time management program or a desktop management program that includes calendar tickler functions.

Some of these programs will even have alarms that will ring to remind you of appointments and deadlines. **Pop-Up DeskSet Plus**, for example, reminds your *computer* when to do things; for example, you can set the alarm clock so the computer dials a phone number at a certain time. In addition to an audible alarm, you could also have the reminder flash before your very eyes on your computer screen. If you find this feature too intrusive, you can turn it off. Computer analyst and writer Lawrence Magid jokingly calls programs with alarms and beeps "nudgeware."

Besides an alarm feature, look at the flexibility of the program. Can you schedule appointments only by hour- or half-hour-increments? Can you schedule 15-minute intervals? Can you schedule an appointment at a non-standard time, e.g., 3:20 p.m.? Does the program work on a 12- or 24-hour clock? Maybe you don't need this flexibility today, but perhaps you will down the road.

The program should let you make notes regarding your appointments or tasks. Some limit how long your notes can be–will it be enough for you?

If you manage or coordinate other people's activities, you may want to track their schedules. Select a program that lets you code the schedules of different people–a program such as **Metro** or **Homebase**.

One program humorously named **Shoebox** has a "pre-reminder" capability. With Shoebox, you can place a pre-reminder two to five days before your final deadline. The pre-reminder stays on the calendar. Shoebox can also schedule repetitive appointments for those meetings that meet on the third Wednesday or the last Thursday of the month, for example.

Besides the extensive variety of desktop management programs with calendar/tickler utilities, there are programs on the market now that are specifically designed to help you better manage your time. One such program, **Time Manager**, has been around since 1979 (which is almost ancient history when it comes to personal computers). This program is an electronic calendar that has a key word search feature. If you plan to call client Joe Smith, you can search for any entries that contain "Joe Smith." Time Manager lets you print out a hard copy of your schedule to keep on your desk or take with you.

Los Angeles attorney **Marty Weniz** is enthusiastic about **PrimeTime**, which he reviewed for *The UCLA PC Users Group Newsletter*. He particularly likes the way the program handles "tasks"–i.e., your to-do list. PrimeTime automatically moves uncompleted tasks to the next day. PrimeTime also lets you prioritize your to-do list. According to Weniz, the most outstanding feature "is the ability to tell PrimeTime *when a task is due* and then to watch as each day automatically 'counts down' until the due date is reached."

You can also specify your own time frames for task completion. Let's suppose you decide three projects should take one day, two weeks and three months, respectively. Just type in 1d, 2w and 3m and PrimeTime will automatically specify the exact date and day of the week. Says Weniz, "This feature alone is worth the price of the program."

There are appointment, assignment and address book features as well. The appointments feature lets you make ample notes, set alarms for reminders and easily change dates and times of appointments. The assignments feature lets you track delegations. An address book (referred to as "People/Phone), let's you track 150 people by listing names, addresses, phone numbers and comments.

The Reminder System is an easy-to-use system that can track entries through the year 1999. (Some systems are only based on the current calendar year.) The program is dubbed "the time management system that never lets you forget" (sounds like your mother, right?) The program allows for appointment scheduling, automatic scheduling for recurring events, project or report due dates, personnel reviews and sales-call follow-ups.

The Reminder System Plus includes a powerful but easy to use database that is tied directly to The Reminder System. Each main record you create can have up to 255 related records or reminders connected to it. You can search and sort your database in many different ways. A special calendar module lets you see a graphic representation of any week. You can generate telephone directories and print mailing labels. The program also comes with a calculator, an alarm and an automatic phone dialer. It's a very versatile and flexible program.

FORMS, CHECKLISTS AND CHARTS

It has been said one person's form is another person's red tape. But a *well-designed* form is a clear, concise and useful summary of information at a glance. And contrary to popular belief, forms can actually help you *reduce* paperwork.

A good form *consolidates* information that is repetitive or otherwise would be scattered in many different places in your office (or someone else's). A good form saves you time flipping through many pieces of paper (or through many different computer screens). Use forms to track such things as work flow, projects, responsibilities, schedules and personnel. Use forms to simplify communication.

Checklists and charts are specific examples of forms. Checklists are old standbys that insure you won't forget something and often can be kept and referred to repeatedly. I have travel and seminar checklists that I use year after year.

Charts provide the added dimension of a diagram or graph that shows relationships between different components. It is more of a visual picture of information, almost like a map.

Don't let forms, checklists or charts scare you. They aren't straitjackets; rather they're guideposts to help you work through the maze of details in your office and your head. Let's look at some examples and sources that may spark some ideas for you:

Project planning sheets help you pull together your thoughts and those slips of paper by organizing the main elements of projects. Use these commercial sheets either to plan a fairly simple project or to do the initial planning for a complex project.

The **Activity/Task Worksheet** by **Caddylak Systems** in Figure 8-6 is a handy form that helps you plan out activities, tasks, delegations and details related to a particular project.

Today's date ____________

FOLLOW-UP REMINDER

		FOLLOW-UP DATES
Re:	______________________	
Client:	______________________	____________
Client #	______________________	____________
Subject:	______________________	____________

Individual making request ______________________

Remarks: ______________________

____

____

____

____

____

____

Figure 8-5. Office tickler form used in an accounting office

Keeping track of written and verbal communications is easy with two forms from Day Runner, in Figure 8-7. Use the **Meeting** form to keep a concise summary of key points and decisions at meetings you attend or chair. The **Contacts** form is an ongoing "conversation log" that gives you a handy system to record communications.

Use forms to simplify and clarify reports. Sales manager **Steve Guentner** and his staff use the **Direct Sales Call Report** in Figure 8-8.

A simple, **confirmation memo form** by **San Diego State University** simplifies communications and prevents last minute misunderstandings and changes down the line (Figure 8-9).

A clever **form/response letter** in Figure 8-10 from the **Don Gambrell Insurance Agency** makes it easy for clients to respond.

A clean, well-designed form is not only pleasing to the eye but is more likely to insure a quicker response. Form-phobia really sets in only when clutter meets the eye. Figure 8-11 is a clean **invoice** created by industrial designer **Rob Splane.**

Use a standardized **checklist** to help you remember the repetitive tasks involved in similar projects. An aerospace company follows the checklist in Figure 8-12 for guests and visitors.

We use the **program tracking form** in Figure 8-13 to record important information and activities for each speaking engagement.

Create your own forms files in your file cabinet or on your computer. Collect samples of forms you like and those you frequently use.

We keep some forms and form letters on computer. Our WordPerfect word processing program lets us easily create a special form letter called a **merge letter.** We keep related letters together in the same file. Using a special WordPerfect feature called a "document comment," we created a mini table of contents for standard follow-up letters we use in our office. See Figure 8-14.

CHARTING IT OUT

The chart is a two-dimensional form that shows relationships visually and graphically. The chart maps out details and the big picture at the same time.

Let me share with you one of the greatest and *simplest* charts I use whenever I begin a project or a writing task. It's called a **mind map.** I first heard about it at a professional communications meeting on "writer's block."

The mind map is an effective way to free up your mind and let your ideas flow. Once you get the ideas out on paper, then you can add structure and sequence. It's a combination brainstorming and outlining tool where you can see your ideas and thought patterns more graphically. Figure 8-15 is a mind map for this chapter.

ACTIVITY/TASK WORKSHEET

DATE

PROJECT	PROJECT NO.	MGR.

ACTIVITY	TASK	DELEGATED TO	NOTES	✓	FOLLOW-UP

NOTES

Figure 8-6. Activity/Task Worksheet project planning form by Caddylak Systems

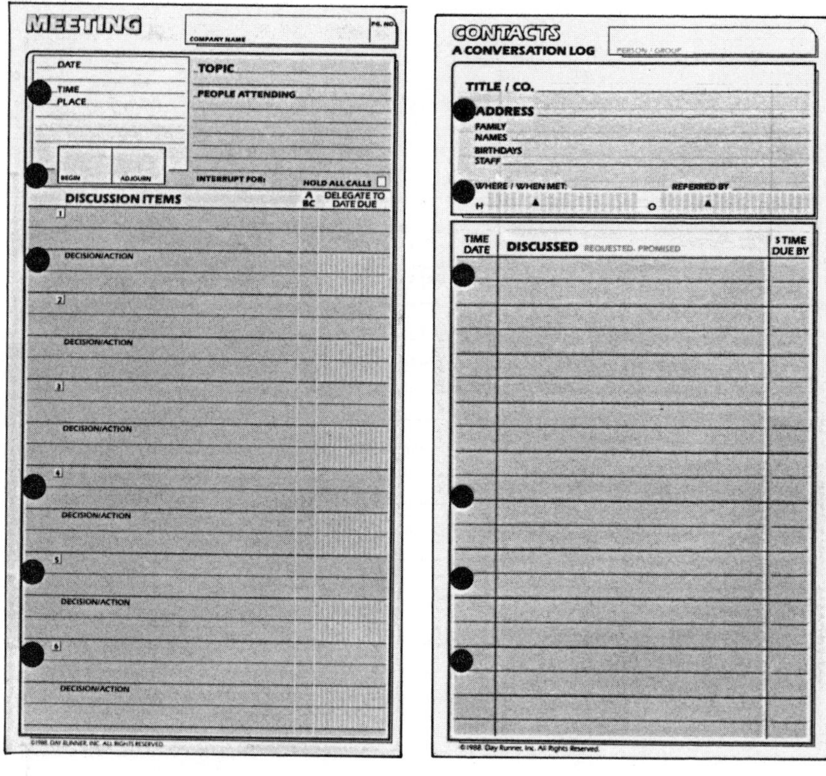

MEETING

COMPANY NAME PG. NO.

DATE

TIME

PLACE

TOPIC

PEOPLE ATTENDING

BEGIN ADJOURN

INTERRUPT FOR:

HOLD ALL CALLS ☐

DISCUSSION ITEMS A BC DELEGATE TO DATE DUE

1

DECISION/ACTION

2

DECISION/ACTION

3

DECISION/ACTION

4

DECISION/ACTION

5

DECISION/ACTION

6

DECISION/ACTION

CONTACTS

A CONVERSATION LOG PERSON / GROUP

TITLE / CO.

ADDRESS

FAMILY NAMES BIRTHDAYS STAFF

WHERE / WHEN MET: REFERRED BY

H O

TIME DATE DISCUSSED REQUESTED, PROMISED $ TIME DUE BY

©1988 Day Runner, Inc. All Rights Reserved

Figure 8-7. Handy Meeting and Contacts forms by Day Runner

DIRECT SALES CALL REPORT

COMPANY/DIVISION/LOCATION____

____

MAIN CONTACT(S) AND TITLE(S)_____________________________________

____

PROGRAMS____

____

NATURE OF APPLICATION____

____

____

____

PURPOSE OF SALES CALL____

____

____

____

RESULTS OF SALES CALL____

____

____

____

____

FOLLOW-UP ITEMS WITH DUE DATES___________________________________

____

____

____

____

____

NEXT CALL OBJECTIVES____

____

____

____

Figure 8-8. Direct sales call report form

EXTENSION AND SUMMER PROGRAMS
COLLEGE OF EXTENDED STUDIES
SAN DIEGO STATE UNIVERSITY
SAN DIEGO CA 92182

(619) 265-5152

SDSU EXTENDED STUDIES COURSE CONFIRMATION

FALL__________

WINTER__________

SPRING 1988

SUMMER__________

INSTRUCTOR: Silver

COURSE: Organized to Be the Best!

DATE(S): Saturday March 26

TIME: 9:30-12:30

LOCATION: CES Classrooms

If any of the information listed above is not correct, please contact Jan Wahl, SDSU Extension, 265-5152.

Figure 8-9. Confirmation memo form

THIS IS MY SIDE

Dear Friend:

You as a satisfied customer are our very best booster and most valuable asset.

We didn't get to renew your policy on the date shown above and frankly, we're concerned.

There is always a reason why a good insured lapses a policy, a reason we would like to know so we can remedy the difficulty if we have been at fault.

That's your side of the story, the side we want you to tell us.

Will you meet us halfway?

Will you fill in and mail us the other half of this letter in the enclosed envelope?

I will consider it a personal favor.

Sincerely,

P.S. If you've already paid this premium we don't expect a reply but will welcome a chance to hear from a friend anyway.

Figure 8-10. Form/response letter

DON GAMBRELL Insurance Agency
3620 Pacific Coast Hwy., Ste. 206
Torrance, California 90505
Bus: (213) 373-8426

Policy No. ______________________________

Lapse Date ______________________________

Amount Needed to Reinstate $______________

THIS IS YOUR SIDE

Dear Agent:

☐ Through an emergency you find us temporarily in financial straits.

☐ Everything is OK. As soon as I start using the car again I'll reinstate.

☐ I sold this vehicle and will let you know when I get a new one.

☐ I overlooked it. Reinstate! Payment enclosed.

☐ Your premium was too high, I'm presently with:
__________________ Insurance Company.

☐ Please call : __________________ AM PM

Date ______________________________

COMMENTS:

Signature ______________________________

Use other side for additional comments.

SD

SplaneDesignAssociates

10850 White Oak Ave.
Granada Hills, CA 91344

INVOICE

SOLD TO		
DATE BILLED	TERMS	DATE DUE
REGARDING		JOB #

DESCRIPTION	HOURS	PRICE	AMOUNT
	PAY THIS AMOUNT		

FOR YOUR RECORDS

DATE PAID	CHECK #	AMOUNT
NOTES		

Figure 8-11. Cleanly designed invoice form

PUBLIC AFFAIRS INTERNAL VISIT CHECKLIST

ACTIVITY	RESPONSIBILITY	DATE	DONE
Invitation			
Receipt of Acceptance			
Reserve Room			
Develop Agenda			
VA to Marketing			
Contact Briefers			
Arrange Tour Leaders			
Hand-out Materials			
Gifts			
Badges			
Parking			
Transportation			
Bump Caps & Glasses			
Food			
Photographer			
Arrange for Films/Slides			

Figure 8-12. Visitor checklist

Positively Organized!®

PROGRAM TRACKING FORM Today's Date:

Date/#__________ Time____________ Title__________________________________

Type of PO! Program________________ Type of Mtg_____________________#____

Fee/Contract Terms____

Name of **Organization**____

Key Contact/Title____
Off # Home #

Address____

Other Contacts/Numbers____

____

Location of Prog/Mtg_________________________________Mgr/#______________

Hotel Reservations at___________________________________By Org____GLA_____

Nearest Airport_____________________________Distance to Mtg/Hotel__________

Ground Transp.____

Travel: Drive/Fly Booked on_____________________________w/______________

Departure Date	From City to City	At	ETA	Airline	#
Departure Date	From City to City	At	ETA	Airline	#
Departure Date	From City to City	At	ETA	Airline	#

Deadline for Ticketing_________ Receive Tickets by___________ Fare $______

Program Checklist

Sent to Client

_____ Contract
_____ Photo
_____ Bio
_____ Blurb
_____ AV/Setup
_____ Handout for dup.
_____ PR
_____ Pre-program Ques.

_____ Intro
_____ Invoice
_____ TU Note

Requested from Client	**Date Rec'd**
_____ Signed Contract	_________
_____ Deposit of $_____	_________
_____ Hotel Confirmation	_________
_____ Mtg brochure/map	_________
_____ Mtg agenda	_________
_____ Trade pubs/bkg	_________
_____ Pre-program ques	_________
_____ Fee/reim	_________
_____ Letter of Rec.	_________
_____ Referral	

To Be Done **By Date** **Date Completed**

Write program____

Prepare handout____

Prepare/organize audio-visuals____

Confirm a-v, setup, handouts one week before______________________________

Contact introducer/confirm has intro______________________________________

Packout list/pack____________________**Wardrobe** __________________________

3420 Ocean Park Blvd., Suite 3060 Santa Monica, California 90405-3305 213/452-6332

Figure 8-13. Program tracking form

```
SPEAKING FORMS:

Page 1 & 2: Letter of Agreement
P. 3 & 4: Pre-program Questionnaire for a corporate seminar
P. 5: Program Logistics (part of pre-program questionnaire)
P. 6: Program Tracking Form
P. 7: AV/Handouts Letter

^D

^C

Dear ^C:

I am just delighted to be speaking ^C.  I'm looking forward to
working with you, ^C.

I have enclosed a "Pre-Program Questionnaire."  Thank you for
taking time to complete the questionnaire and for sending it back
to me by ^C along with previous conference brochures,
publications and anything else you think would be helpful to
increase my understanding of your ^C association, members,
products and challenges.
```

Figure 8-14. The beginning of our computerized speaking forms file showing our WordPerfect "document comment" summary and the start of our "merge" letter of agreement for speaking engagements

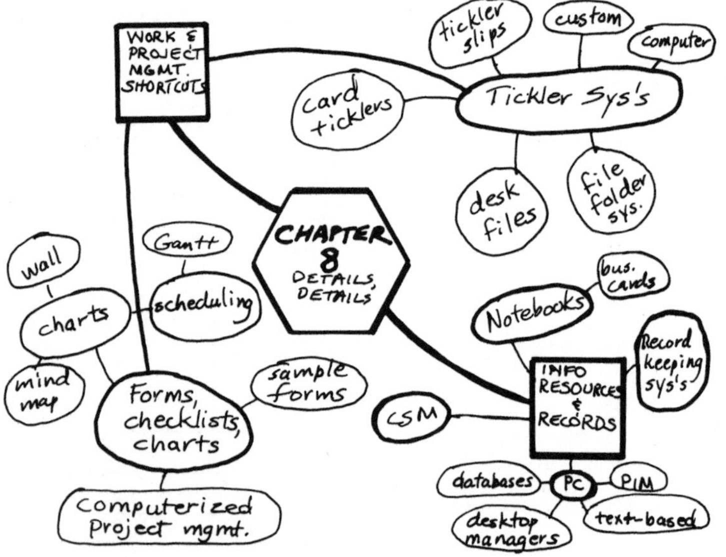

Figure 8-15. A "mind map" for this chapter

I like the **Personal Resource System Project** form in Figure 8-16 because it is well-designed and it incorporates the mind map, which is very useful in planning and connecting project details.

The **Personal Resource System Project Notes and Communications** form in Figure 8-17 is a simple and convenient way to keep on-going project information together.

Calendar or scheduling charts are a good way to show the relationship between periods of time and people, tasks or projects.

See Figures 8-18 and 8-19 for some typical ones.

Some scheduling charts, such as the one in Figure 8-19, list the months and weeks of the year. Such a chart can be easily turned into a **Gantt chart** or timeline that shows task start dates and deadlines and responsibilities. (Henry Gantt invented this useful chart while working for the government during World War I.)

Day-Timers (Figures 8-20 to 8-22) makes a variety of scheduling charts and forms that adapt elements from highly acclaimed project management tools such as Gantt charts, **PERT** charts (Performance Evaluation and Review Technique) and **CPM** (Critical Path Method). These tools show the steps and sequence that must occur for a project to be completed.

Charts, even simple, homemade ones, are great for quickly summarizing information at a glance. Figure 8-23 shows a simple **expense report** for the members of **IWOSC** (Independent Writers of

PROJECT

Title

Today's Date ____________ Proposed Completion Date ____________

Purpose of Project ____________

Goals for Project ____________

PLANNING/MIND MAP

SCHEDULING

#	Items to do	Date Due	Begin Date Sched-uled

No. 130

© 1980 Lee Berglund

Figure 8-16. Personal Resource System Project form, front (above) and back (next page)

PROJECT

Title ______________________________

#	Items to do	Date Due	Sched-uled

No. 130

PROJECT

Title

Notes and Communications

No. 140

Figure 8-17. Personal Resource System Project Notes and Communications form

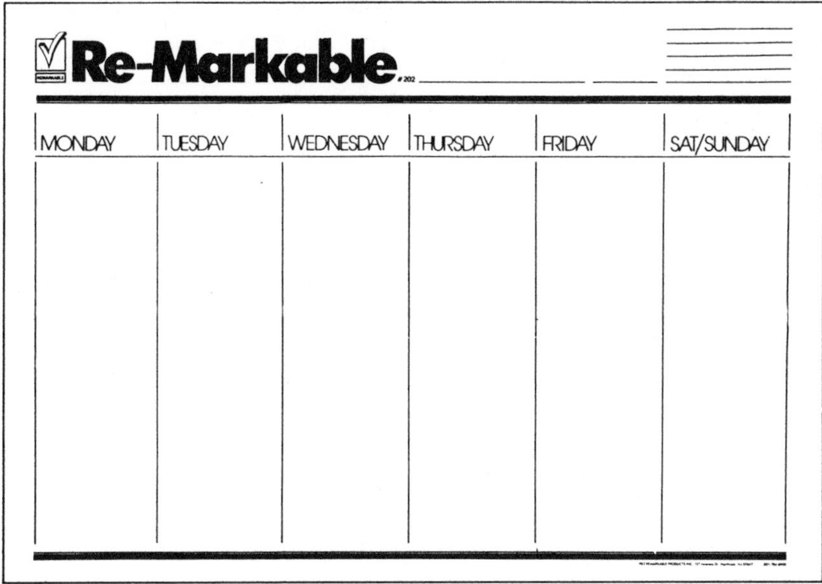

Figure 8-18. This weekly Re-Markable board features reusable sections to plan weekly schedules.

Southern California) who are reimbursed for expenses incurred throughout the year.

If you're comparing prices and features for products (such as computers) or services from suppliers (such as print shops) consider developing a simple chart so you can record the information as you go. It's a lot easier than whipping out all those notes later on. Your chart keeps you on track by reminding you to ask the same questions of everyone. Leave some blank spaces for additional questions that come up as you do your research.

Use **quadrille** or **graph paper** to make your own charts. The "non-repro blue" lines will not photocopy but they will guide you in drawing your own lines. They come in many different styles. See Figure 8-24 for some samples (check your office supply store or catalog for others).

WALL CHARTS

If you track projects or personnel visually in such a way where you and/or other people need to easily see the information, use **wall**

charts. Also called **scheduling** or **visual control boards**, wall charts provide visibility to keep you on target. They're not the most

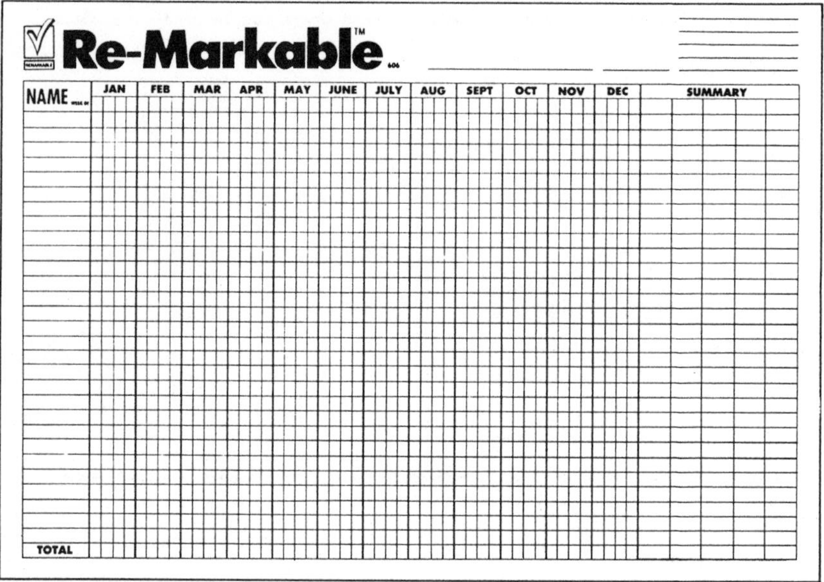

Figure 8-19. Project/Personnel Re-Markable board shows status of projects, assignments or personnel for the whole year on a weekly basis.

attractive things in the world but if you have a work room or don't have to impress anyone with aesthetics, they are very functional.

Wall charts have an advantage over other systems because they crystalize your ideas, intentions and plans and make them visible. A wall chart gives you a visible game plan and very little escape. It's staring you straight in the face.

Color coding works great for wall charts. You can code people, types of activities, progress and deadlines.

Use wall charts to track one complex project, several simultaneous projects, a production schedule, your master calendar, personnel schedules and marketing or fund-raising campaigns.

They come in many different sizes, styles, configurations and materials. **Magnetic** wall charts have different components that you can move around. See Figures 8-25 and 8-26.

Some people prefer the flexibility of a home-made chart such as the **action board** of nationally-known psychiatrist, author and talk show host, **Dr. David Viscott.** You create the action board by putting up six or seven index cards on a wall or bulletin board. Each card stands for a different project and includes a key contact. Under each project card you put another index card that lists the next step to be taken on the project. Each project relates directly to your most important life goals.

COMPUTERIZED PROJECT MANAGEMENT

If you need great control and flexibility over project planning and scheduling, consider **project management software programs** for the personal computer.

These programs combine charts and reports that let you see project information in a variety of ways. You can easily make changes such as automatically updating schedules. Reports are easy to generate and distribute. And it's easy to store completed projects and schedules for reference later on–which means less reinventing of the wheel down the road.

Look for these features when you select a project management program: ease of learning (does it take a Ph.D. in computer sciences to grasp it?); ease of use; a good manual that's just the right size (if it's too hefty, forget it); good reviews by experts and/or people you know; and an easy-to-use tutorial.

It's also a plus if the program can do both Gantt and PERT charts. Popular project management programs are listed in the chapter resource guide.

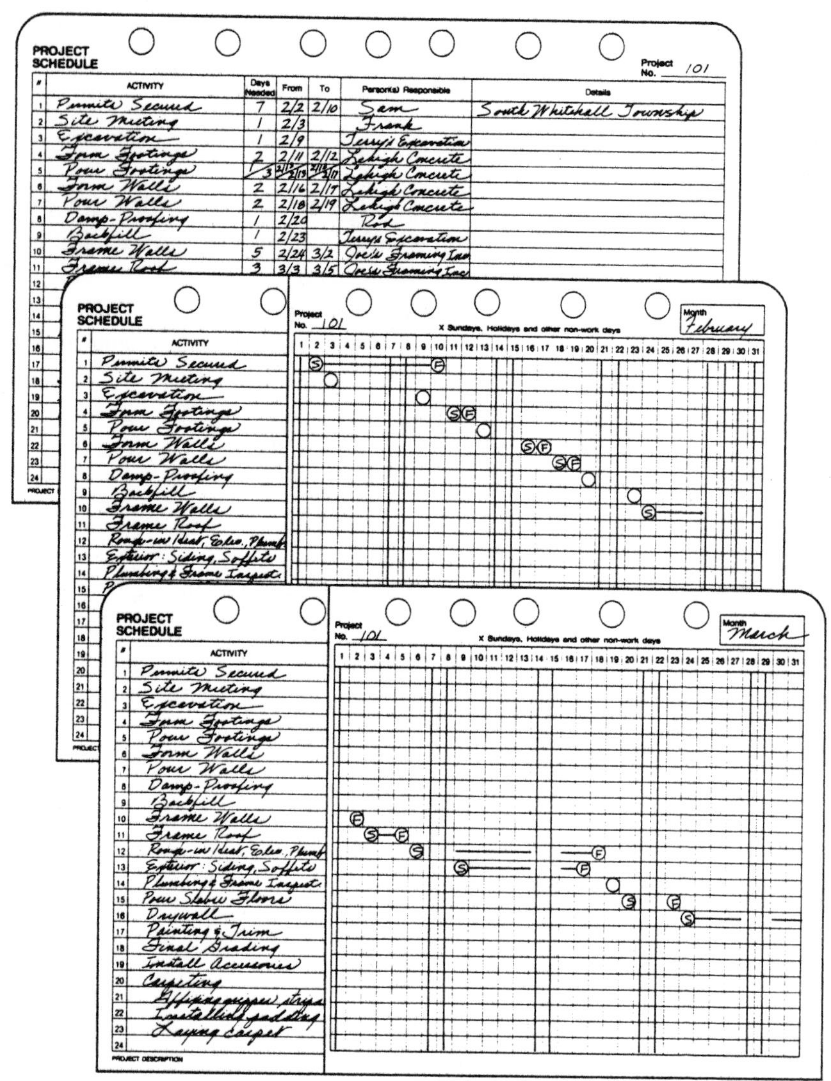

PROJECT SCHEDULE — Project No. 101

#	Activity	Days Needed	From	To	Person(s) Responsible	Details
1	Permits Secured	7	2/2	2/10	Sam	South Whitehall Township
2	Site Meeting	1	2/3		Frank	
3	Excavation	1	2/9		Terry's Excavation	
4	Form Footings	2	2/11	2/12	Lehigh Concrete	
5	Pour Footings	1 / 3	2/12 2/13	2/16 2/17	Lehigh Concrete	
6	Form Walls	2	2/16	2/17	Lehigh Concrete	
7	Pour Walls	2	2/18	2/19	Lehigh Concrete	
8	Damp-Proofing	1	2/20		Rod	
9	Backfill	1	2/23		Terry's Excavation	
10	Frame Walls	5	2/24	3/2	Joe's Framing Inc	
11	Frame Roof	3	3/3	3/5	Joe's Framing Inc	

PROJECT SCHEDULE — Project No. 101 — Month: February / March — X Sundays, Holidays and other non-work days

1. Permits Secured
2. Site Meeting
3. Excavation
4. Form Footings
5. Pour Footings
6. Form Walls
7. Pour Walls
8. Damp-Proofing
9. Backfill
10. Frame Walls
11. Frame Roof
12. Rough-in Heat, Elec., Plumb.
13. Exterior: Siding, Soffits
14. Plumbing & Frame Inspect.
15. Pour Slabs Floors
16. Drywall
17. Painting & Trim
18. Final Grading
19. Install Accessories
20. Carpeting
21. Affixing gripper strips
22. Installing padding
23. Laying carpet

Figure 8-20. Day-Timers PERT/CPM Sheets provide Project Schedule forms listing the steps for each project and monthly calendar overlays that establish logical sequences for scheduling. (Figures 8-20 to 8-22 are courtesy of Day-Timers, Inc., Allentown, PA 18195-1551.)

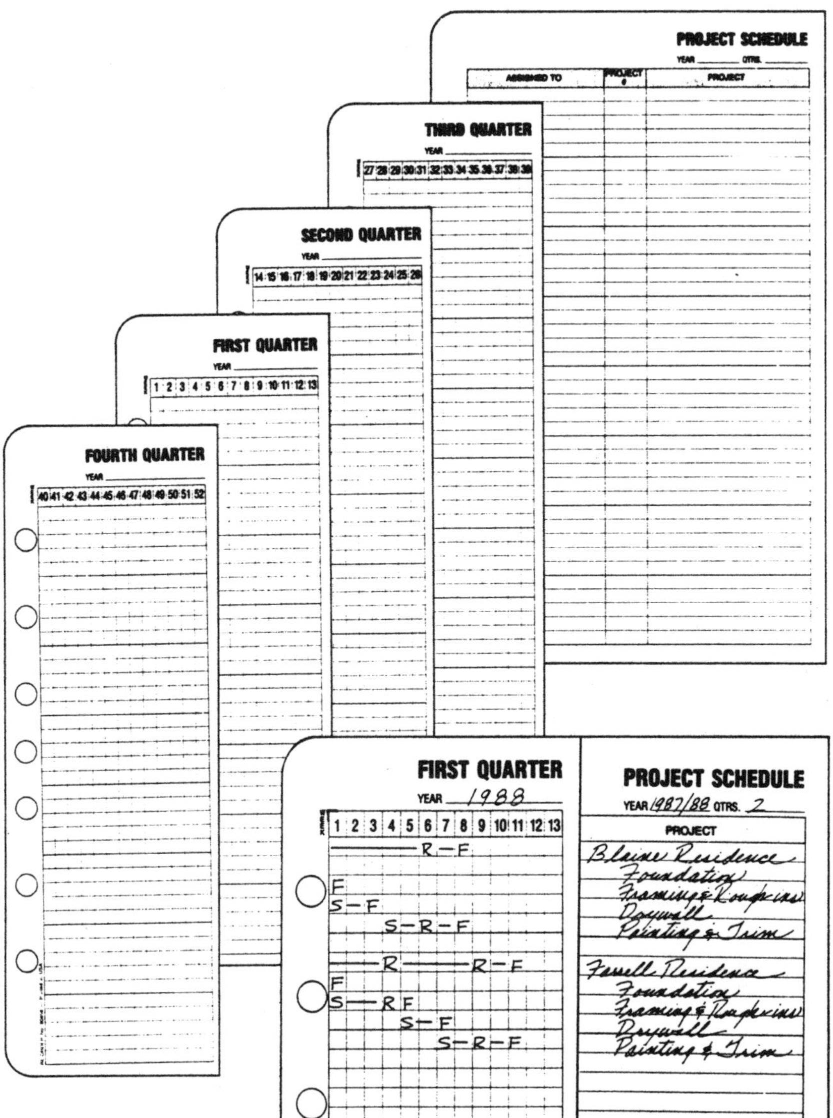

Figure 8-21. Day-Timers Quarterly Project Management Sheets

1988 YEARLY PROJECT SCHEDULE

(✓)	#	PROJECT		January				February				March					April			
		WK	0	1	2	3	4	5	6	7	8	9	10	11	12	13	14	15	16	17
	101	Smith Residence						S	—	—	—	—	—	R	—	—	—	—	—	R
		Foundation						S	—	—	F									
		Framing & Roughins									S	—	—	R	F					
		Drywall													S	—	F			
		Painting & Trim																S	—	R
	102	Jones Residence									S	—	—	—	—	—	R	—	—	—
		Foundation									S	—	—	F						
		Framing & Roughins												S	—	—	R	F		
		Drywall																S	—	F
		Painting & Trim																		
	103	Martin Residence													S	—	—	—	—	—
		Foundation													S	—	—	F		
		Framing & Rough-ins																S	—	—
		Drywall																		
		Painting & Trim																		
	104	Hamilton Residence																		
	105	Kite Residence																		
	106	Lanier Residence																		
	107	Blaine Residence																		
	108	Farell Residence																		

S = Start R = Review F = Finish

Notes ______________________

DAY-TIMERS RE-ORDER No 90684 — Printed in USA

JANUARY

WK	S	M	T	W	T	F	S
00						1	2
01	3	4	5	6	7	8	9
02	10	11	12	13	14	15	16
03	17	18	19	20	21	22	23
04	24	25	26	27	28	29	30
05	31						

FEBRUARY

WK	S	M	T	W	T	F	S
05		1	2	3	4	5	6
06	7	8	9	10	11	12	13
07	14	15	16	17	18	19	20
08	21	22	23	24	25	26	27
09	28	29					

MARCH

WK	S	M	T	W	T	F	S
09			1	2	3	4	5
10	6	7	8	9	10	11	12
11	13	14	15	16	17	18	19
12	20	21	22	23	24	25	26
13	27	28	29	30	31		

APRIL

WK	S	M	T	W	T	F	S
13						1	2
14	3	4	5	6	7	8	9
15	10	11	12	13	14	15	16
16	17	18	19	20	21	22	23
17	24	25	26	27	28	29	30

Figure 8-22. A portion of Day-Timers Yearly Project Schedule

85-01

IWOSC EXPENSE REPORT

date: ________________

name: ____________________ position held: ________________

address: ____________________ budget category(ies): ____________

____________________ ____________________

phone: ____________________ PLEASE TOTAL YOUR EXPENSES IN EACH BUDGET CATEGORY AND LIST IN APPROPRIATE BOX BELOW

month of expenditure:

item:	Jan	Feb	Mar	Apr	May	Jun	Jul	Aug	Sep	Oct	Nov	Dec
phone												
prof. fees & services												
room rental												
printing & duplicating												
postage & mail serv.												
office supplies												
entertain-ment												
advertising & publicity												
t-shirt manufac.												
publications												
bank charges												
other												

total submitted: ________________

COMMENTS: ____

____

____
signature

ATTACH **ALL** RECEIPTS!

Figure 8-23. Simple expense report

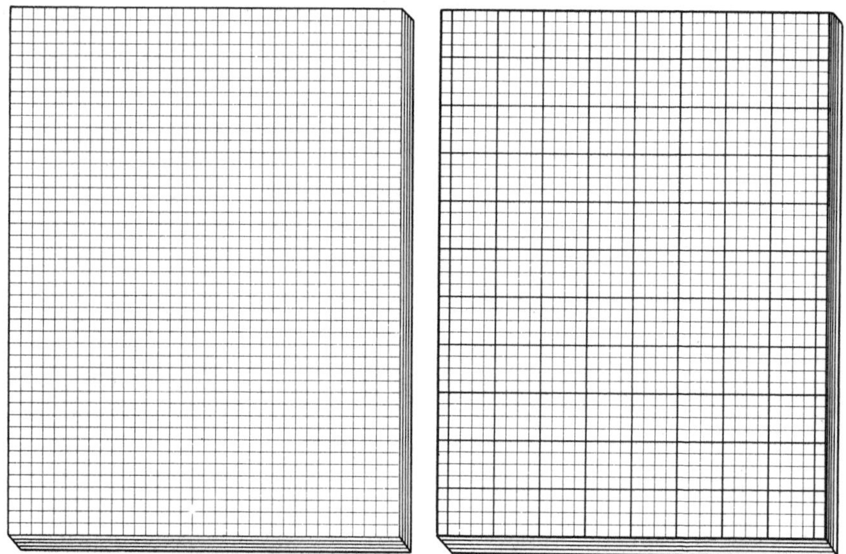

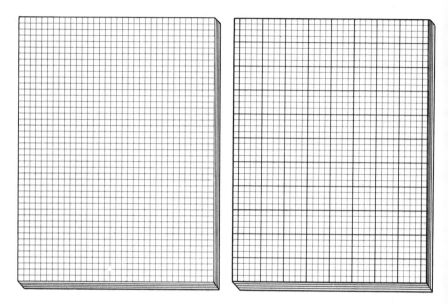

Figure 8-24. Ampad quadrille and cross-section graph pads

Figure 8-25. Magna Visual Work/Plan Visual Organizer Kit

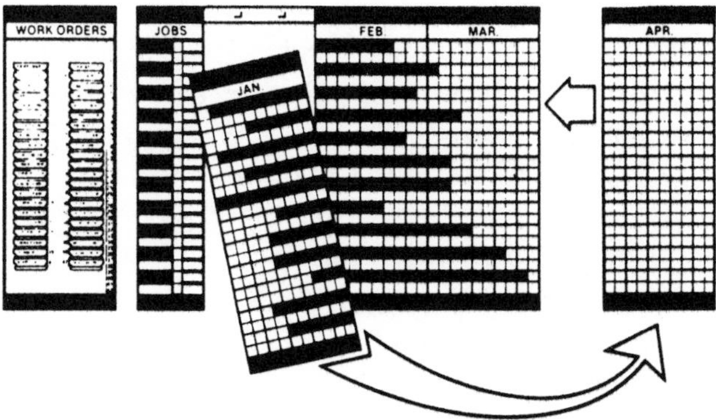

Figure 8-26. Abbot Office Systems Join-A-Panel lets you update your schedule by rotating panels.

TOP TOOLS AND SYSTEMS TO MANAGE INFORMATION RESOURCES AND RECORDS

Each day as you're bombarded with more and more bits and pieces of information, it becomes a real challenge to organize all this information. Fortunately, you have many options.

NOTEBOOKS AND ACCESSORIES

The notebook (the three-ring binder) in all its different sizes is still one of the best organizational and storage devices around for paper resources and records *referred to frequently*. Sure, it's easier to throw something in a file, but when you go to find it, the notebook wins hands down.

You say you hate hole punching? Then buy the three-hole pre-punched plastic sleeves with a margin that allow you to store 8½-by-11 papers without additional punching. See Figure 8-27.

Use notebooks to store articles and clippings, updates, product literature, samples, ideas, active client summary sheets, the latest professional or trade information–the list is endless.

As a professional speaker and writer, I keep an **anecdote notebook** with alphabetical tabbed dividers. Under each letter of the alphabet, I have key subject words that begin with that letter. For example, under the letter "I" are the subjects, "Information Management," "Inspiration" and "Insurance." Blank sheets of white paper are labeled with the key words. Short clippings are cut and pasted onto the appropriate page. Articles I want to keep are labeled with key words and are either hole punched or placed in plastic sleeves.

Author and publisher **Dan Poynter** suggests that authors use a notebook to store resource material for each chapter of their book. It's a great idea, one which I used for this book, in fact–thanks, Dan!

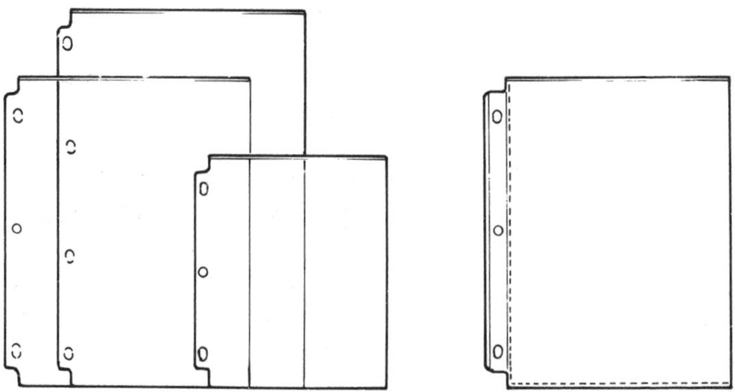

Figure 8-27. 20th Century Plastics Sheet Protectors allow you to store 8½-by-11-inch papers in protective sleeves that are sealed on three sides and large enough so you don't have to hole-punch the papers.

BUSINESS CARD ACCESSORIES

If you attend many meetings and you want a more organized way to keep business cards, start a **business card notebook** with plastic business card sleeves that are tabbed. Label the tabs with either letters of the alphabet or names of organizations and associations. Before you go to a meeting, scan the cards and any notes you made on them.

Izer International makes a **Cardwear Hardware** business card organizer that fits right into a 5½-by-8½-inch, three-ring, daily planner or organizer. It comes with two, side-by-side filers with 50-card capacity, plus blank tabbed dividers and labels to create a customized portable filing system for key contacts and clients. See Figure 8-28.

Day Runner Inc. has just come out with a loose-leaf business card accessory called **Cardfiler Plus** that fits right inside your organizer. As shown in Figure 8-29, Cardfiler Plus uses a business card as is, without having to recopy the information. Just put a glue strip on the special page and press the business card in place. There's pre-printed space for notes, additional information and follow-up details. Organize the card sheets by category and you have a very useful manual database that's portable, too. Cardfiler Plus comes in two sizes: 5½ by 8½ inches and 3¾ by 6¾ inches.

THE CRAWFORD SLIP METHOD

This is a special project management system that is particularly useful for putting together employee and procedures manuals. Designed by Dr. C. C. Crawford, professor emeritus at the USC School of Productivity, the Crawford Slip Method (CSM) has a distinct methodology that is described in two booklets, both available from USC. CSM is an idea generator and organizer.

For anyone who loves slips of paper, this may be the system for you! (This is also one of the few paper slip systems of which I approve!) But not just any slip of paper will do: CSM specifies the precise *size* of paper you can use and just how and what you can write on each slip.

The slips, along with specially designed index cards, are used with custom cardboard trays with organizing slots. You can purchase the trays from USC for a minimal price ($5 each) and you can have the slips and cards cut to size by a print shop.

Briefly, here's how the system works. One person acts as the facilitator for the members of a group, department or company who are guided in generating ideas for a manual. Each idea is written down on paper slips measuring 2¾ -by-4¼. The facilitator sorts and organizes the collected slips and puts them in the cardboard tray

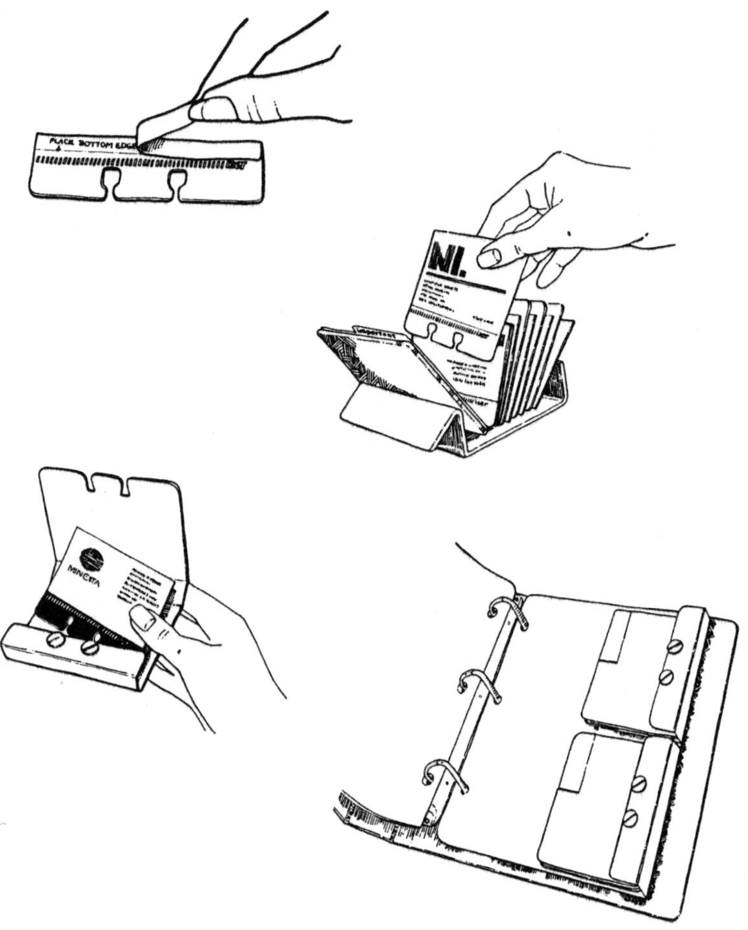

Figure 8-28. Cardwear Hardware business card management accessories: Cardwear Strip that affixes instantly to business cards; Cardwear Case, a pocket-sized card file; Cardwear Organizer for daily planners

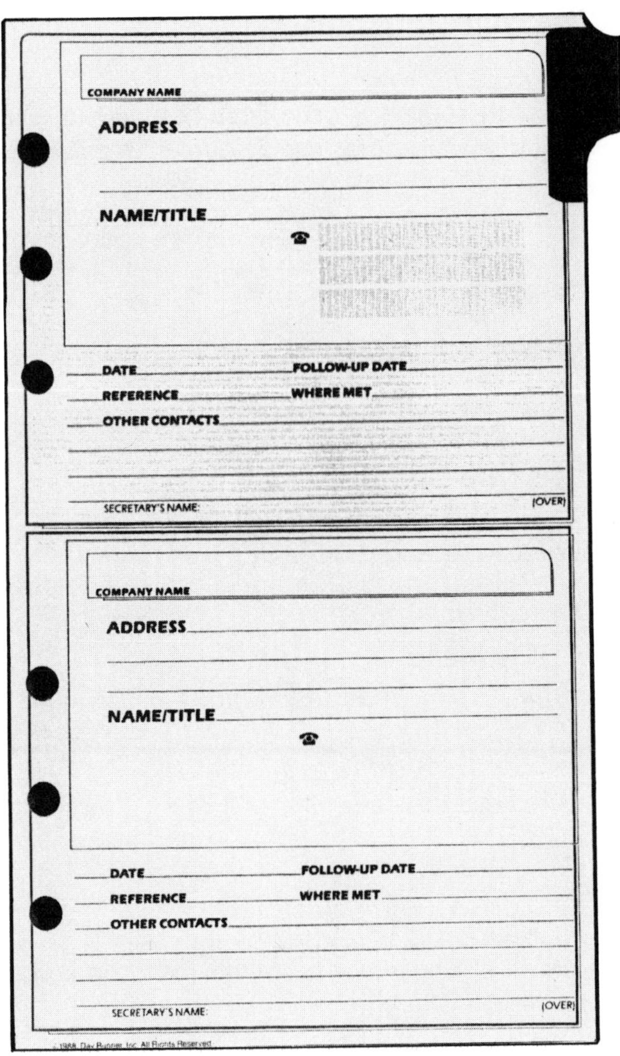

COMPANY NAME

ADDRESS

NAME/TITLE

☎

DATE FOLLOW-UP DATE

REFERENCE WHERE MET

OTHER CONTACTS

SECRETARY'S NAME: (OVER)

COMPANY NAME

ADDRESS

NAME/TITLE

☎

DATE FOLLOW-UP DATE

REFERENCE WHERE MET

OTHER CONTACTS

SECRETARY'S NAME: (OVER)

Figure 8-29. Day Runner Cardfiler Plus is a database for business cards that fits right in your organizer.

slots. Slips are further categorized by colored, specially-cut index cards that serve as guides. Once all the information has been collected and organized, it's a fairly simple task to transform the information into a written manual. See Figure 8-30.

PERSONAL COMPUTER OPTIONS

Databases

A computerized **database** is one of the best ways to gain control over and access to many records and resources. A database program

Figure 8-30. The Crawford Slip Method includes the "Think Tank," brainstorming specific, topic-centered ideas on paper slips and then sorting and organizing slips in a logical order.

lets you not only store but *sort* and call up information based on criteria that you select. It's the sorting capability of a computerized database that provides real information power.

There are different types and names for database management programs. The two simplest programs are called **file managers** or **file management programs**, not to be confused with utility programs bearing the same names described in chapters 5 and 6. (I think it's awful that these terms are used interchangeably.)

Such programs have these names because they generally manage one file at a time. One file, however, can contain hundreds or even thousands of **records**. Each record is an entry consisting of different items or **fields** of information. Let's suppose you create a file of all your clients. Each client would be a different record in the file. The client's name, address, phone number are three different fields in the record. A computer record is a form with different blank fields that are completed for each record. This form is called a **data-entry form**, because you use it to *enter* the *data* or information for each record.

The simplest file managers are **mailing list programs**, which basically store names and addresses and print mailing labels, and **mail merge facilities** that come with many of today's word processing programs, which let you print labels and form letters. If you need more features but you'll be storing less than 100 names, one of the desktop managers or organizers in the next section may be suitable.

The most sophisticated database management programs are the **relational databases**. Most of them are difficult to learn, some require a programmer and they tend to be expensive. What sets them apart besides these negatives, however, is their ability to work with more than one file at the same time. Relational data bases can share related information between two or more files, keeping files up to date. Relational databases are great for inventory control and billing, for example.

Many file managers are starting to adopt some of the more sophisticated features of "high-end" relational data base programs, while still maintaining ease in learning and use.

Desktop Managers or Organizers

Sometimes also called "desktop utilities," these programs typically take items from your desk, such as a calendar, calculator, appointment book and business card file and computerize them. These programs often can do file management functions, too, such as naming, renaming, deleting or moving computer files.

Text Based Programs

When the resource information you want to store on computer isn't as structured as database records, you may prefer to use a **text based management system** or a **text based program.** Such a program is much more *free-form* in nature, generally without pre-defined fields and records.

Text based programs give you more flexibility, although frequently much less speed. You don't have to make your information conform to a database configuration. Search features are varied; some programs have you search on key words, others can search for "strings" of words or phrases.

As an organizer, I generally believe it's better to have some kind of structure, rather than a completely free form database, particularly when there are common elements among the data you will enter. If all your data is free form, it may be slower to sort and retrieve your data. It may also be more difficult to clean out your floppies and hard disk later on as your free form data accumulates. Restricted to special situations, however, such as speech writing, a text-based program could be just what you need. Just don't use it in place of a structured database because it's easier to use.

Personal Information Managers

This is a new genre of software that combines elements of database programs, desktop managers and text-based programs. Personal information managers (called PIMs) let you store and arrange random bits of information such as notes, ideas, plans and activities in freeform style, linked loosely by categories that you create.

PIMs let you enter information as it occurs and then let you organize it later. They also provide speedy text retrieval capabilities. PIMs are not designed for people who need to do traditional, formal reports; rather they are for those who create and manage ideas.

The term "personal information manager" was first coined by Lotus who used it in conjunction with their "Agenda" program.

Often, however, you'll see the term applied to other programs, such as desktop organizers, which manage "personal information" such as an address book or a daily schedule. *Personally,* I think it's all very confusing and yet, at the same time, very exciting as we explore ways to make information more and more accessible–no matter what we call information management programs.

RECORD KEEPING SYSTEMS

Beyond the programs and products we've already discussed, a couple of other systems can help you track record keeping details. Let me tell you about a few of my favorites.

If you work with different clients or projects, the Law Publications catalog has an easy manual system to keep track of billable time or expenses for clients or projects. No longer will you have to spend hours searching through your files, calendar, receipts and notes at billing time. (Although designed for attorneys, this system easily adapts to other professionals, such as consultants and writers.)

The system comes in two styles: a time and service record system called **Time Record** and a system that tracks costs and expenses called **Expense Record**. Both are "one-write" systems that are designed to be used "as you go" (which is the ideal way to use a system anyway).

Let's see how the Expense Record works. You chronologically record expenses as they occur on the two-part Expense Record form, shown in Figure 8-31. As you write on the top sheet, a piece of carbon paper transfers your records to the second sheet.

The pre-printed top sheet is die-cut into 15 self-adhesive labels. When the sheet is full, each of these labels can be peeled off and attached to their respective project, case or client sheets known as "Client/Case Costs Record" forms. Bills or statements can be produced from these record forms (which you can keep in a handy notebook filed either alphabetically or chronologically). Your carbon copy remains as your chronological backup copy.

The Time Record works the same way as the Expense Record. Some of my clients have selected one or the other, depending upon the type of records they need to keep the most. Some people like keeping all the information together and then separating expense and time labels on the record form. Others like having the two different systems.

Builder/contractor **Greg Bravard** uses the Time Record to keep track of time and materials on building job sites. The Time Record form is attached to his clipboard, making for a convenient and portable system that's with him all the time.

Another "one-write" record keeping system that I recommend to clients is the **Safeguard bookkeeping system** (available in many different formats). This is a simple-to-use, manual system that is great for an entrepreneur or professional in private practice. We use it in our office. It actually makes bookkeeping *fun!*

The system comes with a "pegboard" or accounting board, imprinted checks in duplicate, journal sheets and sometimes special ledger sheets (depending on the style of system you select). First you set up your journal sheet (which is similar to an itemized check register). See Figure 8-32 for a sample journal sheet with some typical categories.

When you write a check, the information is automatically transferred in one-write fashion to the duplicate check as well as the journal underneath. (A permanent carbon strip is on the back.) Then you simply write the amount of the check under the appropriate column. At the end of a monthly cycle (or when the journal fills up) use a calculator with a tape to add up all the columns vertically and horizontally to make sure you're in balance.

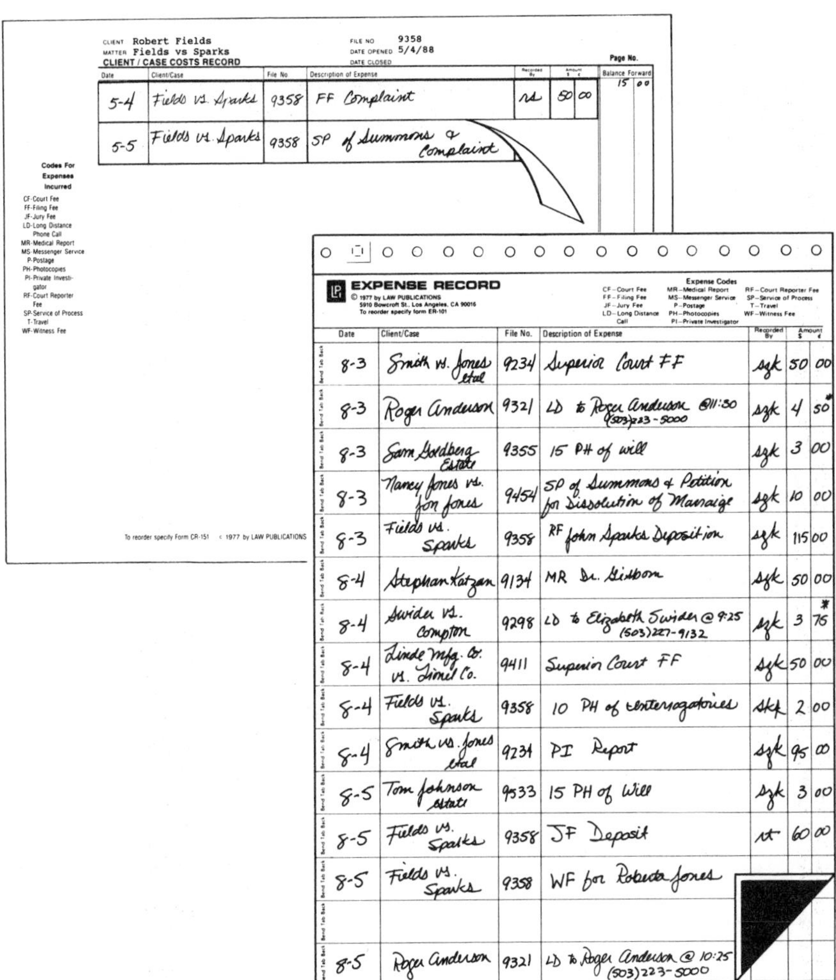

CLIENT Robert Fields
MATTER Fields vs Sparks
CLIENT / CASE COSTS RECORD

FILE NO 9358
DATE OPENED 5/4/88
DATE CLOSED

Page No.

Date	Client/Case	File No	Description of Expense	Recorded By	Amount $	¢	Balance Forward	
							15	00
5-4	Fields vs. Sparks	9358	FF Complaint	rs	50	00		
5-5	Fields vs. Sparks	9358	SP of Summons & Complaint					

Codes For Expenses Incurred
CF-Court Fee
FF-Filing Fee
JF-Jury Fee
LD-Long Distance Phone Call
MR-Medical Report
MS-Messenger Service
P-Postage
PH-Photocopies
PI-Private Investigator
RF-Court Reporter Fee
SP-Service of Process
T-Travel
WF-Witness Fee

To reorder specify Form CR-151 © 1977 by LAW PUBLICATIONS

EXPENSE RECORD
© 1977 by LAW PUBLICATIONS
5910 Bowcroft St., Los Angeles, CA 90016
To reorder specify form ER-101

Expense Codes
CF–Court Fee
FF–Filing Fee
JF–Jury Fee
LD–Long Distance Call
MR–Medical Report
MS–Messenger Service
P–Postage
PH–Photocopies
PI–Private Investigator
RF–Court Reporter Fee
SP–Service of Process
T–Travel
WF–Witness Fee

Date	Client/Case	File No.	Description of Expense	Recorded By	Amount $	¢
8-3	Smith vs. Jones et al	9234	Superior Court FF	sgk	50	00
8-3	Roger Anderson	9321	LD to Roger Anderson @11:30 (503)223-5000	sgk	4	50*
8-3	Sam Goldberg Estate	9355	15 PH of will	sgk	3	00
8-3	Nancy Jones vs. Jon Jones	9454	SP of Summons & Petition for Dissolution of Marriage	sgk	10	00
8-3	Fields vs. Sparks	9358	RF John Sparks Deposition	sgk	115	00
8-4	Stephan Katzan	9134	MR Dr. Gibbon	sgk	50	00
8-4	Swider vs. Compton	9298	LD to Elizabeth Swider @ 9:25 (503)227-9132	sgk	3	75*
8-4	Linde Mfg. Co. vs. Limel Co.	9411	Superior Court FF	sgk	50	00
8-4	Fields vs. Sparks	9358	10 PH of Interrogatories	skf	2	00
8-4	Smith vs. Jones et al	9234	PI Report	sgk	95	00
8-5	Tom Johnson Estate	9533	15 PH of Will	sgk	3	00
8-5	Fields vs. Sparks	9358	JF Deposit	rs	60	00
8-5	Fields vs. Sparks	9358	WF for Roberta Jones			
8-5	Roger Anderson	9321	LD to Roger Anderson @ 10:25 (503)223-5000			

Figure 8-31. Law Publications Expense Record System

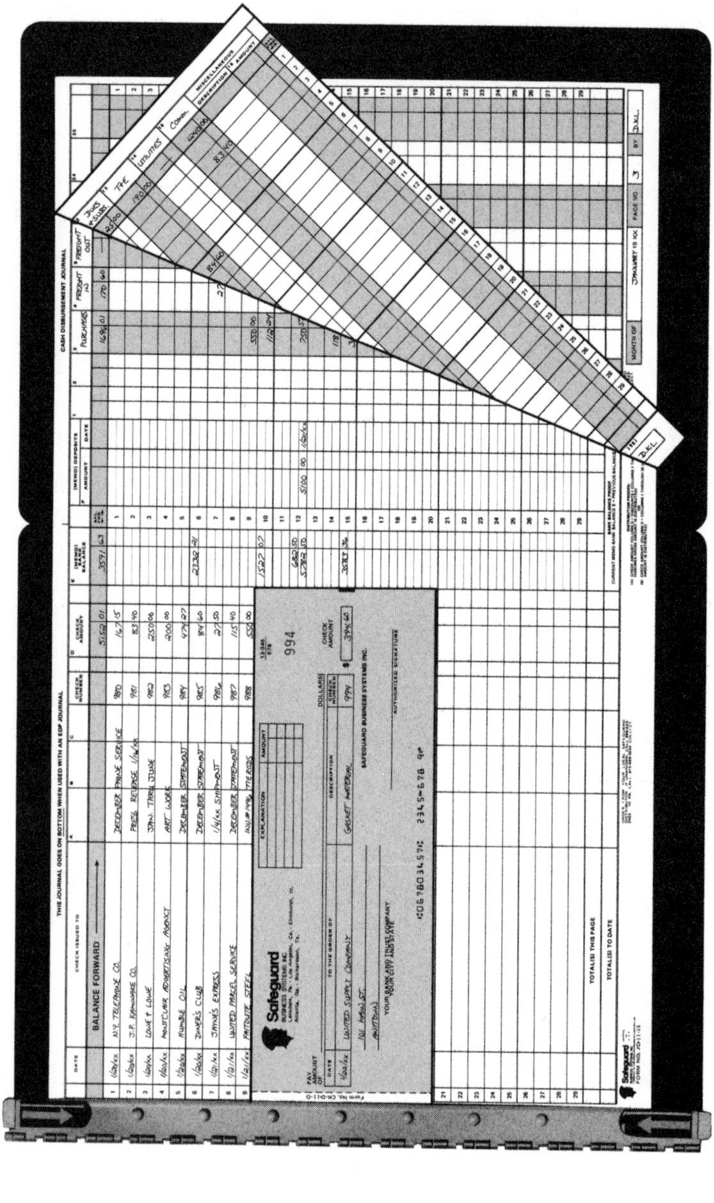

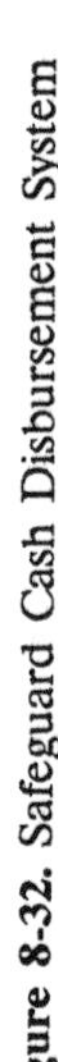

Figure 8-32. Safeguard Cash Disbursement System

RESOURCE GUIDE

WORK AND PROJECT MANAGEMENT

TICKLER SYSTEMS

Manual

Desk Files/Sorters are work organizers for sorting and storing paperwork that you refer to frequently. The 1-31 style and the 1-31 plus Jan.-Dec. format work great as ticklers. The durable, plastic tabs are indexed front and back. The desk file opens like a book and with the accordion gusset spine, there is a large storage capacity. $11.00 for the 1-31 style and $15.00 for the 1-31 and Jan.-Dec. desk file. Available in a good office supply catalog or store. Popular brands are Oxford, Smead and Wilson Jones.

General Reminder/Assignment System by Safeguard is an easy-to-use method for organizing responsibilities, deadlines, delegations and appointments. This system is ideal for a wide variety of business and professional applications, including sales follow-ups, preventive maintenance schedules, job scheduling, tracking assignments and long range planning. Components include Assignment Slips, Writing Board, Indexes (daily, monthly and alphabetical ones available), File Trays and Cross File Tray. See Figure 8-33.
Safeguard Business Systems, Inc.
PO Box 7501
Fort Washington, PA 19034
800/523-2422 (for the name of your local Safeguard consultant)

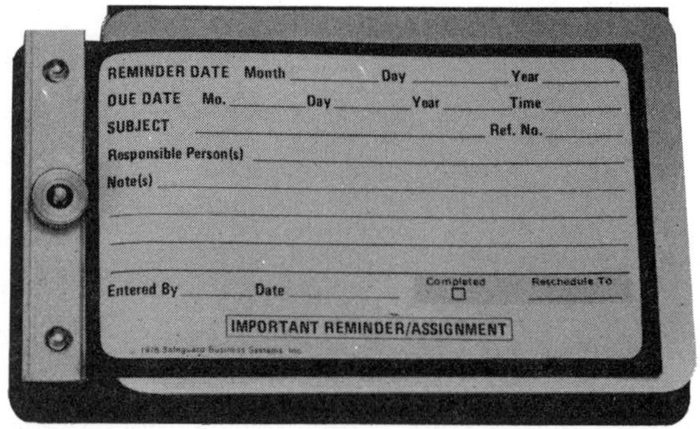

Figure 8-33. Safeguard General Reminder/Assignment System slip

Memofile is a combination 3-by-5 tickler card and planning system in one. The 365 daily cards are dated and tabbed. There are also 100 client/customer cards, 12 monthly tab cards, 52 weekly expense cards, an A-Z telephone index, A-Z guides, 100 blank record cards, a storage box and a 3-by-5 carrying case. You can carry up to two weeks of daily cards in the right side of the case and selected client/customer cards, telephone index and weekly expense cards on the left side. $31.95 to $39.95, depending on the leather case.
Memindex
149 Carter Street
Rochester, NY 14601
800/828-5885 or in New York, 716/342-7890

Pendaflex Follow-up Tabs and **Label Inserts** are useful supplies to help you create your own hanging file tickler system. The follow-up tabs run lengthwise across a hanging folder and have a space for the file name plus two sliding signals that can be moved to indicate the month and the day of the month. Pre-printed file guides or Pendaflex hanging folder label inserts come in 1-31, A-Z and Jan. to Dec. styles. These supplies are available from a good office supply store or catalog. Incidentally, you'll often see the names **Oxford Pendaflex** together when you're trying to find Pendaflex filing supplies in a catalog. To make matters even more confusing, the manufacturer's name is **Esselte Pendaflex** (located in Garden City, New York).

That Reminds Me (Figures 8-34 and 8-35) is an organized tickler system designed to help tickle upcoming deadlines, appointments and delegations. The system is based on a rotating three month daily breakdown. It also allows planning as far ahead as 12 years. The system uses carbonless "reminder/assignment slips" (you can make as many duplicates as you need). Each kit contains three sets of 1-31 3-by-5 cards; January to December cards; 12 blank, tabbed index cards; one Rubbermaid, black file box; 200 Reminder/Assignment Slips; and one writing board for the slips. $49.95 for the kit; components can also be purchased separately. This product is featured in SYCOM's Professional Office catalog, along with many other useful products. SYCOM also has a forms and supplies catalog for attorneys.

SYCOM, Inc.
PO Box 7947
Madison, WI 53707-7947
800/356-8141

REMINDER DATE Month ____________ **Day** ____________ **Year** ______

DUE DATE Mo. __________ Day __________ Year ______ Time ______

Subject ____

Contact Person ____

Correspondence To _____________________________________

Note ____

____

____

Prepare by ________________
Date
Due Date ________________
Entered by ____________________

Completed	Reschedule To
☐	________

IMPORTANT REMINDER/PROJECT

Figure 8-34. That Reminds Me reminder/assignment slip (a product of SYCOM, Inc., Madison, WI, 1/800/356-8141, in Wisconsin, 1/800-356-9152)

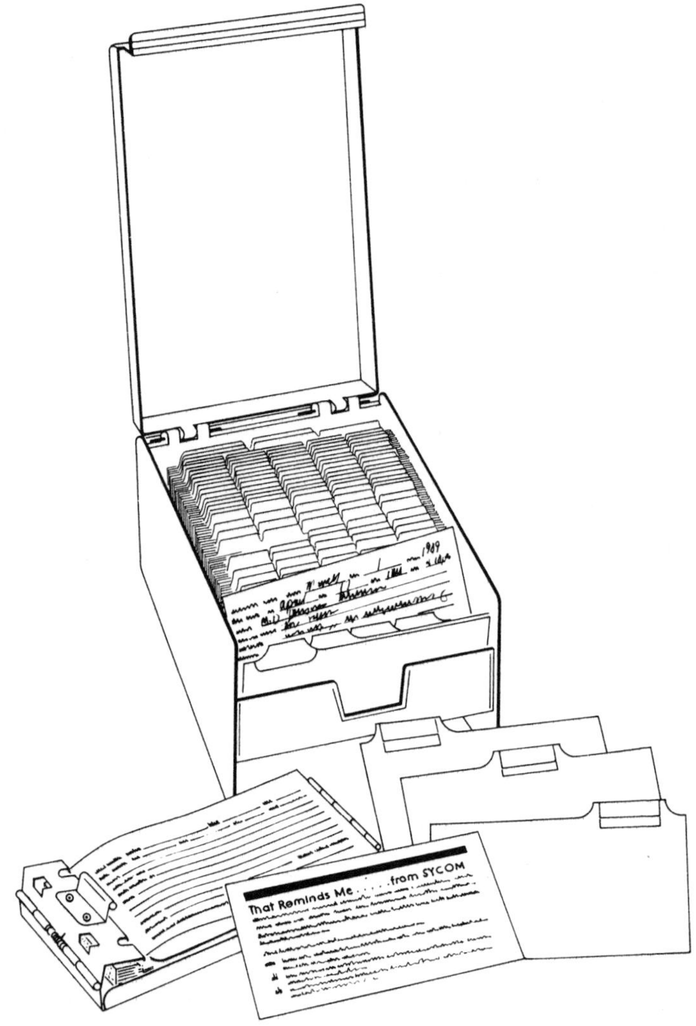

Figure 8-35 That Reminds Me slip tickler system by SYCOM

Tickler Record System is a three-part, NCR paper slip tickler system useful for a heavy load of deadlines and delegations involving other people. Designed for law offices, this system is applicable to many professions and offices. $45.95 for the "starter set."
Law Publications
5910 Bowcroft Street
Los Angeles, CA 90016
800/421-3173; in California, 800/858-7474; in Los Angeles, 213/558-3933

TIC-LA-DEX is a pre-printed, color-coded file card system that lets you systematically follow-up on prospects, clients or projects. $24.95
Tic-La-Dex Business Systems
3443 Camino Del Rio South, Suite 326
San Diego, CA 92108
619/281-7242

Computerized Ticklers & Time Management Programs

CPA Tickler is used with Lotus 1-2-3 to monitor deadlines and commitments in a CPA office.
Front Row Systems
PO Box 550346
8 Piedmont Center, Suite 520
Atlanta, GA 30355
404/231-0349

Homebase 2.5 is a full-featured, desktop management program that lets you track numerous calendars and schedules as well as to-do lists and time-and-expense logs. $89.95 plus $5 shipping
Brown Bag Software
2155 S. Bascom Ave.
Campbell, CA 95008
408/559-4545

Metro, a desktop management program that replaces Spotlight, has a complete and flexible calendar function with many features. Reminder alarms will ring even if the program isn't loaded. Notes can be attached to the calendar and appointments can be made any time of the day (or night). The program handles several calendars and schedules on a daily, weekly or monthly basis. A mini time-and-

billing program with a built-in timer will track time for 100 clients, projects or activities. $85
Lotus Development Corp.
55 Cambridge Parkway
Cambridge, MA 02142
800/345-1043

PrimeTime 1.2 is a well-designed time management program that helps you set goals, organize and prioritize tasks on your to-do lists, keep a chronological record of your accomplishments and remember delegations and deadlines. $99.95
Wiseware, Inc.
3176 Pullman Street, Suite 106
Costa Mesa, CA 92626
714/556-6523

The Reminder System lets you schedule appointments, due dates and follow-ups. A special feature allows for automatic rescheduling of repetitive events or activities. $99 **The Reminder System Plus** comes with its own database program plus many other special features discussed in this chapter. $299
Campbell Services, Inc.
Software Division
21700 Northwestern Hwy., Suite 1070
Southfield, MI 48075
800/521-9314 or 313/559-5955

Shoebox has a "pre-minder" feature that reminds you of deadlines *before* they occur.
Techland Systems, Inc.
40 Waterside Plaza
New York, NY
800/832-4526; 212/684-7788

Smart Alarms for the Macintosh is a personal reminder system that comes with **Appointment Diary**, a calendar program that keeps track of all your appointments clear through 2039! Smart Alarms can store up to 1,600 reminders, which can be set to remind you with alarms and on-screen displays. $49.95
Imagine Software
19 Bolinas Rd.

Fairfax, CA 94930
415/453-3944

FORMS, CHECKLISTS AND CHARTS

Abbot Office Systems distributes scheduling kits, boards and systems for projects and production.
Abbot Office Systems
Asbury Ave.
Farmingdale, NJ 07727
800/631-2233

Caddylak Systems distributes wall planning charts and boards and has a wide array of planning and project forms. You may want to request all of their catalogs.
Caddylak Systems, Inc.
201 Montrose Road
Westbury, NY 11590
516/333-8221

Day Runner Inc. has time and information management forms that can be purchased together with or separately from their versatile personal organizers at department and stationery stores.
Day Runner, Inc.
3562 Eastham Drive
Culver City, CA 90230
800/232-9786 or 213/837-6900

Day-Timers, planners and work organizers in many different sizes and formats, have a wide range of time, information and project management forms. See these forms in the free mail order catalog.
Day-Timers, Inc.
PO Box 2368
Allentown, PA 18001
215/395-5884

FormsFile is a software program that gives you access to hundreds of business forms in such categories as Memo & Office, Sales and Personnel/Payroll. An illustrated booklet catalogs and helps you select forms. You'll find Daily Planners, Weekly Reminders,

Purchase Orders, Employment Applications, Packing Slips, to name a few. You can edit or create your own.
Power Up!
PO Box 7600
San Mateo, CA 94403
800/851-2917 or in California, 800/223-1479

FormWorx is a software program that lets you create forms from scratch or modify one of the supplied forms. *PC Magazine, PC Week* and *The Wall Street Journal* had good things to say about this program. $95. FormWorx with Fill & File (which lets you fill out the same form again and again) $149.
FormWorx Corp.
Reservoir Place, 1601 Trapelo Rd.
Waltham, MA 02154
800/992-0085; in Massachusetts, 617/890-4499

The Instant Business Forms Book by Roger Pring has more than 150 clearly-designed forms printed on perforated sheets for easy removal and photo copying with room to affix your business card for customization. $12.98
Addison-Wesley, Reading, MA

Magna Chart is a magnetic visual control board system that comes in different styles.
Magna Visual, Inc.
1200 N. Rock Hill Road
St. Louis, MO 63124
314/962-9804

Overdrive helps WordPerfect users easily generate merged files by providing 50 general business forms and letters, including personnel forms, business letters, legal agreements, contracts and 20 forms for shipping (e.g., Federal Express, labels, etc.). Additional editions of the program are planned for Microsoft Word, WordStar, Multimate as well as special editions for General Business, Legal, Real Estate, Medical, Banking and Government applications. $99.95
TurboSoft
2135 112th Ave., NE Ste. 101
Bellevue, WA 98004
206/454-7675

Re-Markable boards are versatile, write-on-wipe off wall charts.
Remarkable Products, Inc.
157 Veterans Drive
Northvale, NJ 07647
201/784-0900

Word Guide templates take the guesswork and tedium out of mapping forms when you're using a program such as FormScribe on your computer. It's also a good design tool for manually produced forms, layouts and reports. $15.95 (or $9.95 when you purchase FormScribe at the same time).
Power Up!
PO Box 7600
San Mateo, CA 94403
800/851-2917 or in California, 800/223-1479

PROJECT MANAGEMENT SOFTWARE

Instaplan is a simple, project manager for novices or for those without heavy project management needs. $149 (includes "Tracker Option")
Instaplan Corp.
655 Redwood Highway, Suite 311
Mill Valley, CA 94941
415/389-1414

Microsoft Project is a useful program particularly if you're more interested in doing Gantt than PERT charts. Easy to use, Microsoft Project is more for small and medium-sized projects.
$395
Microsoft Corp.
16011 NE 36 Way
Box 97200
Redmond, WA 98073
206/882-8080

PC Manager is a "goal-oriented management software" program useful for managing people, projects, goals and deadlines. It goes a step beyond other programs in two regards. First, there is a password protection system for privacy and security. Second, the program is "intelligent," offering suggestions and comments from time to time.

For example, if you have entered only negative items related to an employee, PC Manager will suggest you enter something positive once in a while. The program also provides reminders of appointments.
Sterling Castle
702 Washington Street, Suite 174
Marina Del Rey, CA 90292

Superproject Plus was rated "first-rate" by **InfoWorld**. It has many powerful features, excellent documentation, speed and ease in learning. It will do both Gantt and PERT charts and has extensive reporting capabilities. You can use this program at one of three levels of expertise–beginner, intermediate or expert. $495
Computer Associates International, Inc.
2195 Fortune Drive
San Jose, CA 95131
408/942-1727

Time Line 3.0 is a complete project manager for planning and tracking large projects. It continues to get rave reviews (including "Editor's Choice" by *PC Magazine*). It's a powerful program with excellent documentation, a built-in tickler "alarm clock" and on-line tutorials that help reduce the learning curve. It's easy to learn and use and is inexpensive as project managers go. $495.
Breakthrough Software
505-B San Marin Drive
Novato, CA 94947
415/898-1919

ViewPoint is a powerful program that has no limitations with regard to project size. It was selected as a *PC Magazine* "Editor's Choice." $1,995
Computer Aided Management
24 Professional Center Pkwy.
San Rafael, CA 94903
415/472-5120

OTHER WORK MANAGEMENT TOOLS

Crawford Slip Method (CSM) is a booklet that describes a manual idea generator and organizer that is great for people who like to physically manipulate, categorize and arrange ideas on slips of paper. CSM is particularly useful for assembling employee and procedure handbooks and manuals and can be used with groups of people whose ideas you want to tap. The booklet is $3; the sorting box and the sorting tray are $5 each.
University of Southern California
School of Public Administration
University Park MC 0041
Los Angeles, CA 90089-0041
213/743-7152 (The School of Public Administration Business Office)

Executive Scan Card Organizer is a card/notebook system that lets you track major activities related to projects with color-coded cards. The notebook comes with a Month-at-a-Glance Planner, telephone index, business card holder, letter size pad, inside storage pockets, pen loops and calculator. The system will show 12 project cards in full view and will hold up to 60. $54.95
Memindex
149 Carter Street
Rochester, NY 14601
800/828-5885 or in New York, 716/342-7890

For Comment is a highly rated software program that allows up to 16 reviewers to revise or annotate a document. The program allows you to report or add reviewers' changes or comments in a variety of ways. $195 for one author; $995 (for networks and 16 authors)
Broderbund Software Inc.
17 Paul Drive
San Rafael, CA 94903
415/479-1170

Planmaster Information Control System is a card/notebook organizer for managing time, projects, personnel and other priorities. You write information once and then move the PlanCards to various positions within the system, without having to rewrite information. Pre-printed, color-coded cards are labeled "General Purpose,"

"Expense," "Memo," "Things-To-Do" and "Phone Message." You can organize these cards under header cards such as the days of the week, "Next Week," etc. on three panels that fit inside a notebook. A pocket wallet for travel lets you condense the system. The system holds 306 cards but can be expanded to 510 cards. $89.95
Memindex
149 Carter Street
Rochester, NY 14601
800/828-5885 or in New York, 716/342-7890

RPMS (Rep Profit Management System) is a data management system designed for the manufacturer's rep. RPMS will track orders from quote to factory commission statement. Modules and features include invoice and commission tracking, order tracking, product tracking, direct mail, commission reconciliation and sales forecasting. $995 for Module I (Invoice and Commission Tracking), $700 for Module II (Order Tracking) and $275 to $375 each for other features.
Creative Software Systems, Inc.
Box 11008
Kansas City, MO 64119-0008
800/762-3377, Ext. 200; in Missouri, 816/561-0141, Ext. 200

WordPerfect, 5.0 is the word processor we use. It's considered state-of-the-art and I highly recommend it for heavy-duty word processing needs. $495
WordPerfect Corp.
1555 N. Technology Way
Orem, UT 84057
800/321-4566 or 801/227-4433

RESOURCES AND RECORDS
PERSONAL COMPUTER OPTIONS–IBM

Database Software

Don't be fooled by the term "database software." Many of these database programs are extremely flexible and combine features such as built-in ticklers and word processors, too.

ArtFile enables you to create your own database of literature references. It's like having your own card catalog on computer. It's a single purpose database that is easy to use. $75
Mail order item available from the following company, which offers free telephone support:
Selective Software
903 Pacific Avenue, Suite 301
Santa Cruz, CA 95060
800/423-3556 (in California, 800/872-6656)

Congressional Toolkit is a specialized database that provides the names and stats of current members of Congress, including committees on which they serve. A built-in word processor lets you do mail-merge form letters. The program comes with the federal database or a single state database. $49. $39 for each additional state database.
BJ Toolkit
Alexander Lane
Croton-on-Hudson, New York
914/271-8271

Dac-Easy Base is touted as an easy-to-learn relational database program that provides on-screen help and an affordable price. $49.95
dac software, inc.
4801 Spring Valley Road, Bldg 110-B
Dallas, TX 75244
214/458-0038

PC-File:db is the database program we use in our office. It has many useful features, including word processing capabilities that enable you to do form letters and mail merges. The program will find, list or delete duplicate records.
ButtonWare, Inc.
PO Box 96058
Bellevue, WA 98009
800/JBUTTON (orders only); 206/454-0479

Q&A is a full-featured, powerful database program. Although not relational, it includes a state-of-the-art natural language called "Intelligent Assistant" that lets you easily do reports and other functions. It works with many popular application programs, such

as WordPerfect and Lotus 1-2-3 and has its own word processing capabilities. $349
Symantec Corporation
10201 Torre Avenue
Cupertino, CA 95014
408/973-9597

Desktop Managers/Organizers and Personal Information Managers

The following programs go by a variety of different names. They're difficult to classify because they do such a variety of useful functions. These are among the best:

Agenda lets you organize and view your thoughts and ideas in creative ways. Bill Howard, of *PC Magazine*, describes it as "natural for anyone whose job involves managing ideas." $399
Lotus Development Corp.
55 Cambridge Parkway
Cambridge, MA 02142
617/577-8500

GrandView brings together word processing, outlining and database functions, letting you freely track information about people and projects. $295
Symantec Corporation
10201 Torre Avenue
Cupertino, CA 95014
408/973-9597

SideKick Plus is the latest upgrade to a popular favorite. SideKick Plus offers a file manager, notepad, calculator, time planner, outliner, communications module, a good manual and many, many features. Unlimited free technical support is included with this versatile program. $199
Borland International
4585 Scotts Valley Dr.
Scotts Valley, CA 95066-9987
408/438-8400

Sales, Telemarketing Programs

These programs are ideal for anyone who is managing a client database and/or is marketing products or services and wants to track these marketing efforts. Many of these programs combine features from other software such as database management, word processing, telecommunications and built-in follow-up. Consider these programs if you're in real estate, insurance, inside or outside sales, consulting, purchasing, financial services, association management, direct mail marketing, to name a few areas. You don't have to be in sales; you just need to deal with a large number of contacts on a regular basis.

CMS Software is designed for insurance agents and offices and offers a core program called CMS One as well as special modules for commission tracking, commission accounting, underwriting, letter writing and report writing and comes with a tickler system. A versatile, easy-to-use system, CMS adapts to a variety of different needs and number of users. CMS provides such features as instant policy information, an "action date" log for appointments and renewal dates, full password protection, built-in telephone dialer, free-form pages for notes and exciting reporting capabilities. The latest upgrades, Junior Partner and Senior Partner, include an advanced telemarketing and tickler prompt feature as well as a "Letter Writer" module which prints mail merge letters, mailing labels, cards for your rotary card files and envelopes right from the client screen. You can call up appointments within any date range, specify when telephone calls are to be made and see which letters have been sent to clients in the past. Junior Partner, $229.95; Senior Partner, $575.95; network versions and separate program modules vary in price.
CMS Software Systems
753 Salem, 2nd Floor
Glendale, CA 91203
818/500-1555

The Maximizer is ideal for sales people, especially those who work in real estate offices. This program offers a fast and flexible database. Since records are not "fixed" in size, you can add as many notes as you want. The program includes tickler and scheduling time management functions. A simple built-in word processor lets you do

form letters (the program comes with typical business letters or you can create your own). You can print labels and envelopes. The program can perform calculations such as payment schedules, particularly those that relate to real estate. (The publisher has been doing programs for the real estate industry since 1983.) The program is easy to learn and use. $295
Pinetree Software, Inc.
8100 Granville Ave., 9th Floor
Richmond, B.C. V6Y 1P3
Canada
800/663-0375

RPMS (Rep Profit Management System) is a data management system designed for the manufacturer's rep. RPMS will track orders from quote to factory commission statement. Modules and features include invoice and commission tracking, order tracking, product tracking, direct mail, commission reconciliation and sales forecasting. $995 for Module I (Invoice and Commission Tracking), $700 for Module II (Order Tracking) and $275 to $375 each for other features.
Creative Software Systems, Inc.
Box 11008
Kansas City, MO 64119-0008
800/762-3377, Ext. 200; in Missouri, 816/561-0141, Ext. 200

SaleMaker, a *PC Magazine* "Editor's Choice," is a client management and telemarketing software system that continues to get rave reviews by reviewer and end user alike. Pop-up windows and well-designed screens make this an easy-to-use program. Features include an "Active Call List Window" that lists clients to call today in the order to call them; "History Windows" provide a concise summary of the last ten times you had contact with each client, including who made the call, date, time, length, objectives, results, scheduled follow-up and notes; "Literature & Form Letter Window" asking you which letter to send and what is to be enclosed; "Script Windows" display successful sales pitches, product specs and the like; and "Memo Pad Windows" store several pages of freeform notes. SaleMaker will work on a Novell network. A 20MB hard drive will hold about 6,000 client records. $495.

Software of the Future
Box 531650
Grand Prairie, TX 75053
800/433-5355 or 214/264-2626

SpaceBase is a "vertical market" program for people in advertising sales. SpaceBase has different databases for advertisers, agencies, people, ads, call reports and form letters. The program provides tracking of ad orders over time. A built-in word processor generates letters, envelopes, labels and mass mailings. It will also produce mail-merge files from *WordStar, WordPerfect, New Word* and *XyWrite*. $695 for Level I, a single salesperson; $1,795 for Level II for up to 26 users (not a network version).
Stadis Corp.
15716 Wing Point
Dallas, TX 75248
214/991-0010

TeleMagic is an easy-to-use program that features database management (holding up to one billion records per file) and "instant retrieval" on two ID's; tickler file; order entry, invoicing, history; form and mail merge letters, labels, envelopes; electronic mail; sales scripting function; auto-dialer, clock, alarm, calculator; on-screen display of telephone call duration; up to 32,000 character "notepad" for each contact. $95 for the "personal" version; $295 for the "professional" version; $795 for the "network" version.
RemoteControl
1320 Ocean Avenue, Bldg. E
Del Mar, CA 92014
619/481-8577

Text-Based Programs

IZE can search, link and generate outlines and can search extremely fast for data. $445
Persoft Inc.
465 Science Dr.
Madison, WI 53711
608/273-6000

SmartNotes, Version 2 is an "annotation program" that permits you to attach notes to files in different applications, including those for

word processing, spreadsheet and text database. This program was selected as a *PC Magazine* "Editor's Choice." $79.95
Personics Corp.
2352 Main St., Bldg. 2
Concord, MA 01742
800/445-3311 or in Massachusetts, 800/447-1196

Tornado is a freeform text database that lets you make miscellaneous notes on computer (instead of on paper slips) and search for them instantaneously. If you keep lots of miscellaneous notes or ideas that are unrelated to each other or to particular projects or people, this could be a handy program. $99.95
Micro Logic Corp.
PO Box 174
Hackensack, NJ 07602
800/342-5930 or 201/342-6518

Reading Up On Software

Public Domain Software, Untapped Resources for the Business User, by Rusel DeMaria and George R. Fontaine, is a good book if you're all tapped out in terms of computer expenditures. In this book you'll discover hundreds of free or low-cost programs that rival the commercial programs. You will, however, need a modem to download these programs. $19.95
M&T Publishing Inc.
Redwood City, CA

PERSONAL COMPUTER OPTIONS–MAC

Client/Customer, Sales, Telemarketing Management

Market Master is a sales and marketing program that tracks people and helps you design sales programs complete with designated follow-up, form letters and sales scripts. This program received a "95" in *MacGuide*. $275
Breakthrough Productions
10659 Caminito Cascara
San Diego, CA 92108
619/281-6174

Databases, Desktop Organizers and Other Information Managers

Business Filevision is a pictorial database management system that lets you store and work with information in pictures as well as numbers and text. This program is particularly useful for engineers, planners and architects. $395
Marvelin Corp.
3420 Ocean Park Blvd., Ste. 3020
Santa Monica, CA 90405
213/450-6813

C.A.T., which stands for "Contacts/Activities/Time," is an easy-to-learn and -use relational database management program. It will help you manage all of your contacts, whether they be clients, prospects, colleagues or personal friends, as well as the tasks and activities you're doing. C.A.T. is a flexible program that works in ways you like to work, linking related information together. *MacGuide* gave this program a "96" rating. $395
Chang Laboratories, Inc.
5300 Stevens Creek Blvd.
San Jose, CA 95129
800/972-8800, 800/831-8080, 408/246-8020

FileMaker Plus is an easy-to-use, non-relational database that has special form design features. You can create your own data entry forms as well as customized business forms. Sorting and searching are very quick with this program, which has many useful database management features. $395
Nashoba Systems, Inc.
1157 Triton Dr.
Foster City, Ca 94404
800/274-0610 or 415/578-1970

HyperCard is a powerful, yet easy to use program that lets you create your own information management programs. It lets you link information by association, more like how the mind naturally works. $49; comes bundled with all new Macs.
Apple Computer, Inc.
20525 Mariani Ave.
Cupertino, CA 95014
408/996-1010

HyperEASY is a 5.5-hour training program designed to make HyperCard even easier. Aimed at the novice, the program offers four modules that each come with a disk, audio cassette and a booklet. (Personal Training Systems also produces tutorial products for Microsoft's Excel, Works, and Word; Symantec's More; and Aldus' PageMaker.) "Using HyperCard" is $39; the other three modules, "Creating Cards and Stacks," "Basic Scripting" and "Advanced Scripting" are $49 each.
Personal Training Systems
PO Box 54240
San Jose, CA 95154
408/559-8635

Idealiner is a low-cost, easy-to-learn (there's an on-line tutorial) outliner designed for writers, attorneys and others who write. $40
Jimmy Mac Software
PO Box 957
Murfreesboro, TN 37133
615/895-6427

MORE is an idea processor/outliner that helps in organizing and developing ideas for projects and presentations. $295
Symantec Corporation
10201 Torre Avenue
Cupertino, CA 95014
408/973-9597

QuickDEX is a text database that uses a friendly file card/Rolodex style approach for keeping track of personal information such as names and addresses. It's a desk accessory that retrieves text strings very quickly. It comes with an auto-dialer. The program will load up to eight "card decks" or databases at a time. $35
Greene, Inc.
15 Via Chualar
Monterey, CA 93940
408/375-0910

RecordHolderPlus is an easy-to-use, inexpensive, multi-featured database program good for simple database management such as maintaining mailing lists. It offers excellent report and search capabilities. It received a "93" in *MacGuide*. $69.95

Software Discoveries, Inc.
137 Krawski Dr.
South Windsor, CT 06074
203/872-1024

SideKick is a desktop organizer that has a calendar ("CalendarBook"), a phone book ("MacDialer"), a mini-word processor ("Notepad+"), a calculator, "Area Code Look-up," a telecommunications program ("MacTerm"), an outliner ("Outlook") and a simple spreadsheet ("MaxPlan"). $99.95
Borland International
4585 Scotts Valley Dr.
Scotts Valley, CA 95066-9987
408/438-8400

RECORD KEEPING SYSTEMS

Manual Record Keeping Systems

Cardwear Hardware provides practical solutions to business card management. Accessories can be used in the office or on the go.
Izer International
8467 Melrose Place
Los Angeles, CA 90069
213/655-3868

Expense Record and **Time Record** allow for easy, as-you-go record keeping related to time and billing. Even though these systems are designed for attorneys, they are easily adaptable to a variety of professions.
Law Publications
5910 Bowcroft Street
Los Angeles, CA 90016
800/421-3173; in California, 800/858-7474; in Los Angeles, 213/558-3933

Safeguard's One-Write Bookkeeping System is great for a private practice or a small office. You keep a check journal and your tax records as you go. We've used this system for years.
Safeguard Business Systems, Inc.
400 Maryland Drive

PO Box 6000
Ft. Washington, PA 19034
800/523-2422

20th Century Plastics Sheet Protectors let you store papers in three-ring binders without hole-punching. 20th Century also makes **Century-Safe Paperwork Arrangers** to keep related paperwork together in plastic jackets, sealed on two sides, with clear front and brightly colored back.
20th Century Plastics
3628 Crenshaw Blvd.
Los Angeles, CA 90016
800/421-4662 or 213/731-0900

Record Keeping Software–IBM

The Little Black Book lets you store and print out your most important names and addresses. The program comes with extra address book covers to make up books for home, office or travel.
Pocket Address Book prints address books, cards, labels and envelopes and manages mail lists. You can print directories by category (you can designate up to 10 categories). Pocket Address Book handles up to 2,000 names per file and comes with special paper (that is ruled on the back to allow for hand entries), three spiral bindings, a calendar, pen and a black leather cover. The book fits the DayTimers Senior Book and similar organizers. $69
Power Up!
PO Box 7600
San Mateo, CA 94403
800/851-2917 or in California, 800/223-1479

Project Billing is a time billing program for ad agencies, graphic designers and print shops. It tracks billable time and expenses, prints reports and prepares invoices.
Satori Software
2815 Second Avenue, Suite 590
Seattle, WA 98121
206/443-0765

Timeslips III provides time and billing for 3,400 clients and 250 activity codes. $199.95
North Edge Software Corporation

239 Western Ave.
Essex, MA 01929
617/468-7358

Record Keeping Software–Mac

MacInUse keeps track of your Macintosh usage for your tax records (particularly if you use your Mac at home for business). The program runs in the background but can also be automatically called up to add extra information. The program received a "95" in *MacGuide*. $79
Softview, Inc.
4820 Adohr Lane, Ste. F
Camarillo, CA 93010
805/388-2626

Shopkeeper is a simple point-of-sale, invoicing, inventory, accounts receivable and billing program for shop owners and other small business owners, including some consultants. $159
ShopKeeper Software Inc.
PO Box 38160
Tallahassee, FL 32315
904/222-8808

Timeslips III for the Macintosh is a time and billing system for service professionals. $199.95
North Edge Software Corporation
239 Western Ave.
Essex, MA 01929
617/468-7358

OTHER RECORD KEEPING

The **Pro-8 Client Timekeeping System** is designed for attorneys and others who keep track of billable time. This system will track up to eight accounts or clients through "accumulators." Each accumulator can store and display up to 99 hours, 59 minutes. At billing time you can see the accumulated totals. I'd recommend using this device to keep track of individual blocks of time as you go, as a timer, and then immediately transferring those numbers along with a written description of services rendered on computer or a manual system such as the Time Record. At billing time check totals only as a backup.

Time Mark Corp.
11440 East Pine Street
Tulsa, OK 74116
918/438-1220

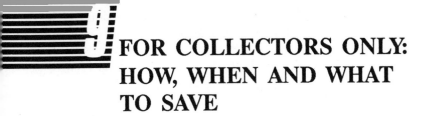

9 FOR COLLECTORS ONLY: HOW, WHEN AND WHAT TO SAVE

Quick Scan: If you're an inveterate collector or you're in a profession that simply requires you to save many records, documents or resources, this chapter is for you. Here are some guidelines that will help you save only the essentials.

I'm convinced the world is divided into two groups of people–those who save and those who don't. And there has to be a Murphy's Law somewhere that says, "If you're a collector, you're probably living or working with someone who isn't."

I admit it. I'm a collector. Not only do I have many interests and avocations (I suffer from the "Da Vinci Syndrome"), but I have chosen occupations that attract collectors. I have been a school teacher, an editor and a manager. Today I am a professional speaker, writer and consultant and I continue to maintain well-organized resource material.

I am not against collecting. Certain professions demand it. But collecting requires strict guidelines and routines if you ever hope to stay in control.

Consider the degree your collecting habit is taking control over *you*. Recognize that it can be tamed and turned into a constructive resource that will give you a professional edge.

TYPES OF COLLECTORS

Sometimes it's helpful to see the different kinds of collecting traps we fall into. People who love the printed word are "information junkies." These are people who love to learn, read, write, improve themselves and find out what the experts have to say.

People with a "possession obsession" like to buy new things and add to their growing collection. And once something enters their environment, it remains for the duration.

"Chipmunk collectors" don't go out of their way to purchase new possessions. Instead, they squirrel away everything for the winter–*every* winter. "Waste not, want not" is their motto. Chipmunks were taught to hold onto everything for dear life. Beware of thoughts like these: "I might need this someday" or "Somebody else might need this" or "This could really come in handy."

If you can relate to any of these collecting habits (and most of us can), you'll want to keep reading. Any of these habits can become nightmares in short order if you don't put a lid on them. The way you do that is by learning to *make decisions* about paper and possessions. But as we discussed in chapters 1 and 2, decisions aren't made in a vacuum.

MAKING DECISIONS ABOUT 'COLLECTIBLES'

The secret to making decisions and controlling paper and possessions is simple: know your goals and values. Know what's important to you and what's really worth your time and energy. According to Roy Disney, Walt Disney's brother, "Decisions are easy when values are clear."

Once you're clear about your values and goals, you're ready to establish some stick-to-'em criteria. The problem people have when they're going through papers and possessions is that they aren't using the right criteria. As a result, every item requires a major decision from scratch.

Start by recognizing that there are only three basic decisions you will need to make: 1) what to **save**, 2) how to **sort** it and 3) where to **store** it.

TO SAVE OR NOT TO SAVE... THAT IS THE QUESTION!

If you're suffering from "Discard Dilemmas," the following two general guidelines can help you with troublesome papers:

1. When in doubt, save tax, legal or business items.
2. When in doubt, **toss** resource information, especially information you seldom, if ever, use.

When you're in a discard mode (or should we say discard *mood*) use these simple guidelines along with the following criteria:

Nine Questions to Toss Out When Deciding What to Save

1. Do you need the item now?
2. Was it used last year? More than once?
3. Will you use it more than once next year? (How likely will you *ever* need it?)
4. Would it be difficult or expensive to replace? Could you get it from someone else?
5. Is it current (and for how long?)
6. Should it be kept for legal or financial reasons?
7. Could someone else use it *now*? (Or could someone else wrestle with this decision instead of you?!)
8. Does it significantly enhance your work or life?
9. Is it worth the time and energy to save?

Go back and star any that you could use. Keep them right in front of you as you make your discard decisions. Here's some space to add any others that specifically fit your situation:

Or follow the "cardinal office rule" of well-known Los Angeles attorney and philanthropist **Richard Riordan** who advises, "Don't keep it in *your* file if someone else can keep it in *theirs*."

THE SORTING PROCESS

Now that you've established your criteria for saving (or tossing), you're ready to begin the actual process of sorting your collectibles. Your best bet is to make it a game with definite time limits. You can spread out your game over a period of time, doing a little this week and a little next week. Or maybe you prefer to dig right in and work for a few days straight, such as a weekend. Or instead, try this one on for size: pretend you have to move your office in less than 24 hours to a space that is half the size. ('Got your adrenalin flowing yet?)

Whichever is your style, choose blocks of time without interruptions as this is real mental work that requires concentration. Block out at least a few hours. Have on hand the necessary supplies–a trash basket (or barrel), a pencil, a timer, empty cardboard boxes (Fellowes Bankers Boxes or other cardboard file boxes with lids are great) and space to work.

Tackle a small area at a time–one pile on your desk, a file drawer, a section of a file drawer, etc. Begin where the need is greatest. If your file cabinets are packed to the gills, start there. If you haven't seen your desk in years, there's no better place to begin. It's best to choose something small and be able to work through it. Set your timer to establish a reasonable time limit (an hour or less).

Begin by sorting through the designated area, deciding what to save, what to toss and what should be stored elsewhere. As you decide which items to save, sort them in categories based on *types* of items (e.g., books, files, supplies, personal items to take home), as well as *how often* you intend to use them (e.g., daily, several times a week, once a month). **Only things you use or refer to regularly during your working hours should be in your office.**

The process is not simply willpower, of sitting down and forcing yourself to go through your stuff (although a little willpower won't hurt). What you need is a **plan of action**, particularly if you have "long-term buildup." (Chapter 12 will help you design a simple plan of action–you may wish to read that chapter before attempting to tackle long-term buildup.)

Write as you sort. It's helpful to list your criteria and your sorting categories as you do the process. This list, along with a written plan of action, will help you tremendously. Carefully number and label boxes and drawers *as you go*. Keep a written record of any items going into storage.

I use my computer to keep a record of boxes that are stored off-site. It's easy to update my word processing document, which is named "Files." I also keep a printout of "Files" in my manual filing system. My boxes are labeled alphabetically (I'll double up on letters should I ever get to "Z," heaven forbid!) I share an off-site storage room with my husband whose system uses numbered boxes.

An attorney who is a solo practitioner keeps track of open and closed client files with two index card boxes–one for "Open" and another for "Closed" files. Each card has the name of a client, the number and location of files for the client and when those files were opened or closed. The cards are filed alphabetically in the appropriate box.

What if you inherited somebody else's clutter? I received a letter from **Sharon Lawrence**, a student of mine who ran into this problem several months after taking two of my seminars. She had just accepted a position as a financial management analyst in a California county administrative office. She writes:

> I have a new job and a new challenge to being organized. I left my organized office for a complete disaster area. I couldn't believe my new office; when I walked in, my mouth fell open. There were three inches thick of papers strewn over the entire surface of the desk, a bookcase filled with a year's worth of obsolete computer printouts and two file cabinets filled with five-year-old data which belonged to other analysts.
>
> I informed my boss that I couldn't function until I had gotten organized. It was hard to know where to begin. By

> the end of the second day, I had thrown away four trash cans full of obsolete reports and duplicate copies of letters and reports. I had also managed to clear the desktop. I was still faced with four piles of paper which had been sorted into broad categories.
>
> Working a little each day for two weeks, I have now managed to organize the piles of information into file folders. I have also given away two file cabinets and distributed their contents to the appropriate analysts.
>
> People now walk by my office and say things like, "Wow, what a difference!" I tell them about your classes and how this is the new me.

This is great, you say, if you know what you're going to need on the new job. But what if the job isn't second nature to you? When **Nancy Schlegel** became a systems engineer for IBM she waited a year before she tossed out information. "After a year, I knew what I needed and what I didn't and I was in a better position to set up a filing system."

WHERE TO STORE IT

Deciding where to store your records and resources depends on four factors:

1. Up-to-date sorting and purging
2. Frequency of use
3. Size, shape and quantity of materials
4. Proximity to related items.

First, have you completed the sorting and purging process *before* you buy that extra filing cabinet or bookcase? Where to house something should only be considered after you decide *if* you should keep it.

Second, the more frequently you use an item, the more accessible it should be. Identify *prime* work areas in your office–those areas that are most accessible. If your desk top and a deskside file drawer are the most accessible areas, do they contain items that you use most often in your office?

Third, the size, shape and quantity of your resources will suggest the types of containers, accessories or pieces of furniture you select to hold those resources. If you have 12 inches of file folders you probably won't be choosing a five-drawer lateral file cabinet. If you're a graphic designer or a printer you may need special cabinets to hold large, oversized art boards.

Fourth, things that go together should generally stay together. Group similar types of books, files and supplies together. 'Sound like common sense? You'd be amazed to see how many items that are unrelated to each other end up together–sometimes for years.

HOW TO PREVENT LONG-TERM BUILDUP

Having a philosophy about paper helps Revlon's **Kathy Meyer-Poppe**, Corporate Fleet director. She says, "File a paper or toss it out–it's either important enough to be filed right then and there or it's not that important. So throw it away."

Bill Butler, president of Butler Consulting Group in Indianapolis, makes it a point to clean one file a day. Butler says, "One file you can manage. As a result, you have fewer files, which means fewer places to lose things."

There are no rules to maintenance. You may like to adopt Butler's "one file a day" or Poppe's "file or toss" routine. On the other hand, once a week or once every six months may work better for you. Or perhaps you want to wait until the need arises–bulging file cabinets or an impending move. Some people tell me the only way they can get organized is by moving–so they actually plan a move every few years!

It can be thrilling to "clear a path" as one client described making headway on her collection. It's also thrilling for me to get letters like the following from **Coleen Melton,** a California art teacher:

> I'm writing to report to you that my goal is accomplished: 20 years of art placed into retrievable order thanks to your "Positively Organized!" class and your notes of support. I even have my husband wanting to organize his filing cabinet, and that is a miracle in itself.

Even lifelong collectors can learn and use the art of organization.

RESOURCE GUIDE

(Addresses and phone numbers are included for mail order items and generally *not* for products that are widely available through office supply catalogs and stores.)

ART WORK, BLUEPRINTS, AND PHOTOGRAPHIC MATERIALS

ARTIST AND DOCUMENT STORAGE FILES

Artists portfolios, art folios, art cases, presentation cases are all different names of portable containers for storing, transporting or displaying art work. Check out good office supply or art stores and catalogs.

For storage rather than show consider the following items available in most office supply catalogs:

For Flat Storage

The Art Rack by Safco (Figure 9-1) is a modular, vertical filing system with eight large compartments. It's 29"H x 24 1/8"D x 36"W and $139.95. This and other Safco products in this book are available nationwide through office products dealers, industrial supply dealers and art and engineering dealers. For a catalog or more information, contact a local dealer or write:

Safco Products Company
9300 West Research Center Road
New Hope, MN 55428

Fellowes Art-Folio, Safco Portable Art and Drawing Portfolio or **Smead Artist Portfolio** are low-cost, durable files with handles useful for transporting art work, film, drawings and large documents. See Figure 9-2. From $3.85 to $20

Fellowes Portable Storage Case is used for carrying, shipping or storing large documents flat. It includes a handle. See Figure 9-3. $23 to $27 each.

Safco 5-Drawer Corrugated Fiberboard Flat Files and **Safco 12-Drawer Budget Flat File** are economical alternatives to expensive

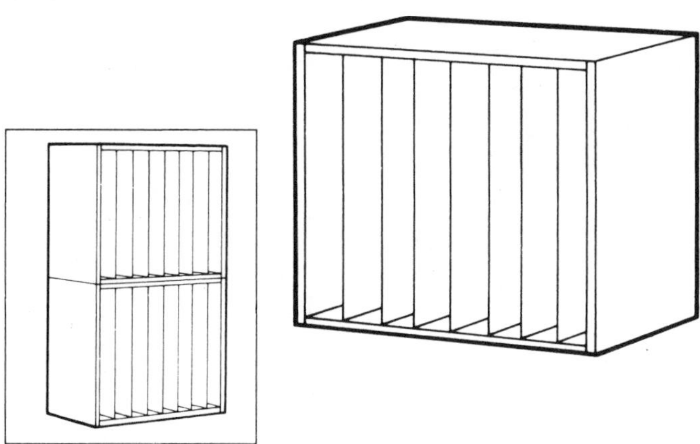

Figure 9-1. The Art Rack by Safco can be stacked vertically, used side-by-side or alone.

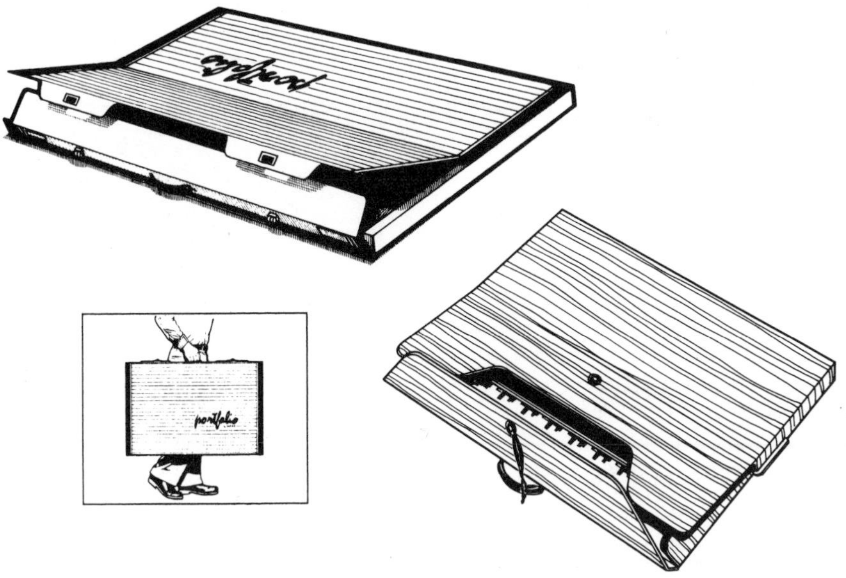

Figure 9-2. Safco Portable Art and Drawing Portfolio (left) and Smead Artist Portfolio

metal files for art boards, blueprints, film, drawings, drafting paper and other oversized documents you want to store flat. See Figure 9-4.

Figure 9-3. Fellowes Portable Storage Case

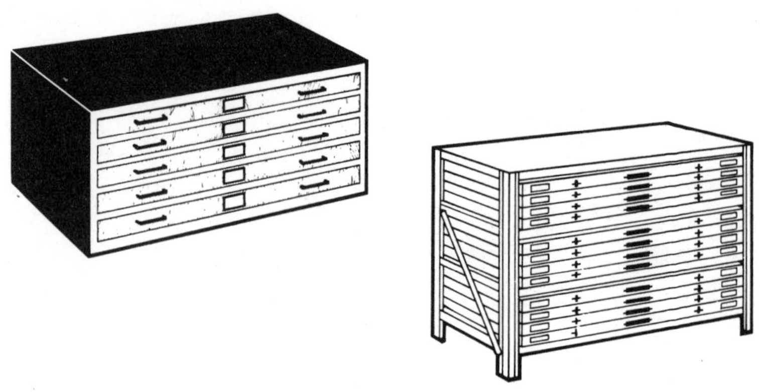

Figure 9-4. Safco 5-Drawer Corrugated Fiberboard Flat Files (left) and Safco 12-Drawer Budget Flat File

Safco 5-, 7-, and 10-Drawer Steel Flat Files come with or without open or closed bases. See Figure 9-5. From $479 to $1,150.

Safco Vertical Filing Systems offer efficient systems for keeping large sheet materials well protected, yet organized and easily accessible. Hanging Clamps form the basic unit and hold up to 100 sheets each. Choose from three systems shown in Figure 9-6: the Drop/Lift Wall Rack, $28; the Pivot Wall Rack, $125; or the Mobile Stand, $274.

Figure 9-5. Safco 5-, 7-, and 10-Drawer Steel Flat Files

For Rolled Storage

Safco Corrugated Fiberboard Roll Files are an economical way to organize and store large materials. The roll file comes in three different tube lengths. See Figure 9-7.

Fellowes Roll/Stor Stands, Perma Products Vertical Roll Organizers and **Safco Upright Roll Files** in Figure 9-8 are good choices for deskside filing of rolled documents. They come with four rubber feet to raise the units off the ground. Choose 12 or 20 compartments. From $33 to $37.95

Fellowes Roll/Stor Files (in Figure 9-9) feature a space saving tambour sliding door for easy access and a neater appearance. Units can be stacked and interlocked to form a storage center for rolled blueprints, drawings, charts, etc. From $70 to $89.

Safco Tube-Stor KD Roll Files (in Figure 9-10) is an ideal low-cost system for active or inactive storage. There are two convenient label areas on the inside and the outside to list rolls and locations. Units come with 18 or 32 tube spaces. Built-in tube length adjusters let you customize tube length. $39 to $52.

Safco Mobile Roll Files (in Figure 9-11) are good for active rolled materials. The units themselves can be "rolled" to areas where they're being used. From 12 to 50 compartments.

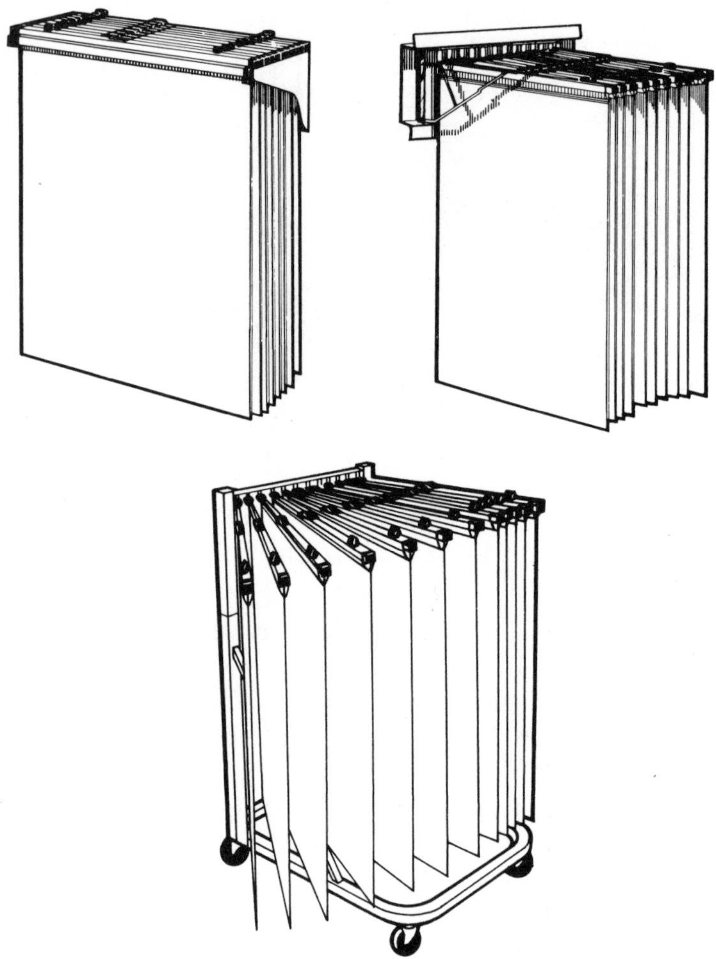

Figure 9-6. Safco Vertical Filing Systems Drop/Lift Wall Rack (left), Pivot Wall Rack (right) and Mobile Stand (bottom)

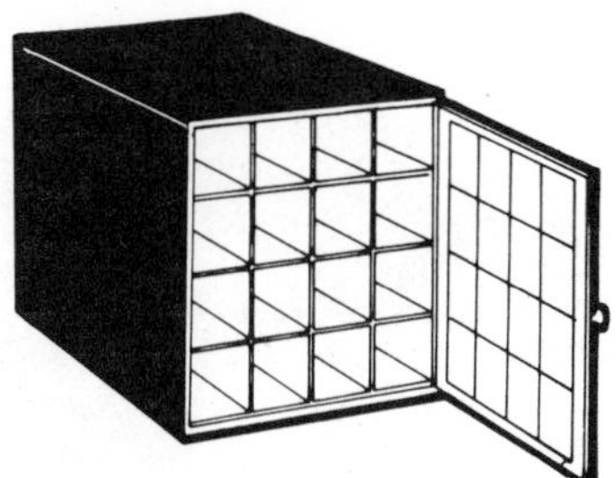

Figure 9-7. Safco Corrugated Fiberboard Roll File

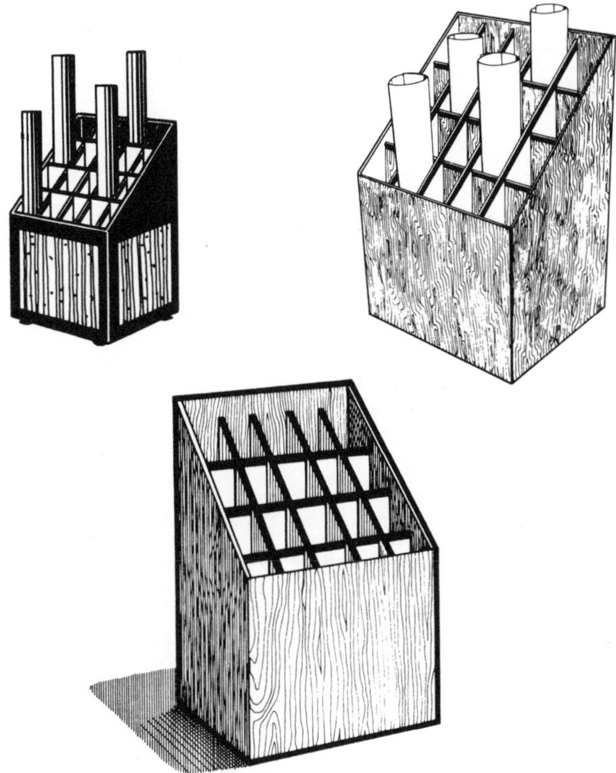

Figure 9-8. Fellowes Roll/Stor Stand (left), Perma Products Vertical Roll Organizer (right) and Safco Upright Roll File (bottom)

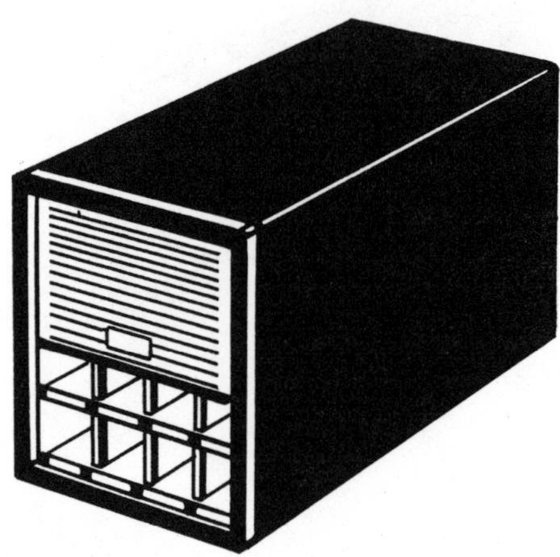

Figure 9-9. Fellowes Roll/Stor File

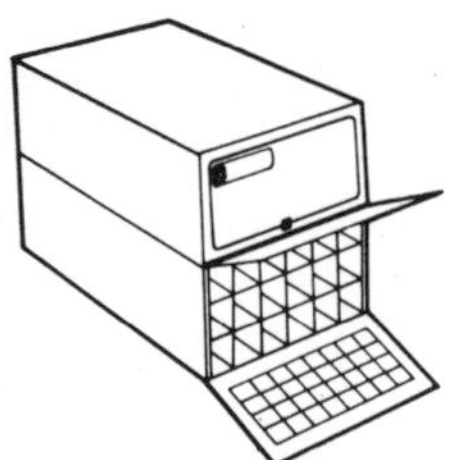

Figure 9-10. Safco Tube-Stor KD Roll File

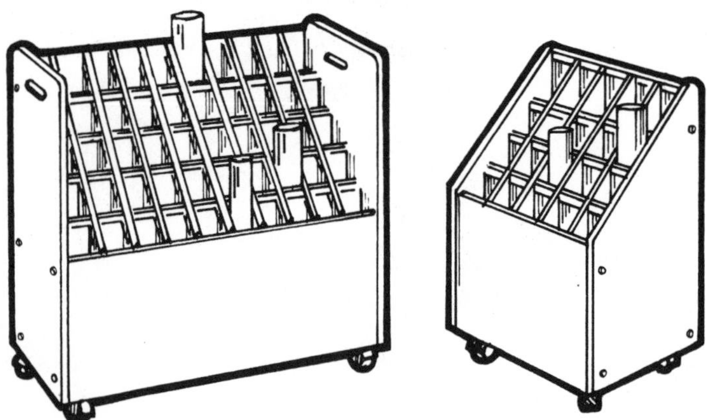

Figure 9-11. Safco Mobile Roll Files

Photographic Storage–Slides and Prints

Light Impressions is a photographic and fine art storage and presentation catalog featuring archival supplies and equipment. A sampling of their products is included in this chapter. To get their catalogs contact them at:
431 Monroe Avenue
Rochester, NY 14607-3717
800/828-6216 (or in New York, 800/828-9629)

The following Light Impressions items are of special interest to photographers:

Nega*Guard System preserves and indexes hundreds of negatives. (Figure 9-12.)

PrintFile in Figure 9-13 is a complete negative filing and storage system providing rapid access to negatives that consists of transparent, polyethylene protectors in a wide range of styles and formats. Many can be filed in binders.

Simple **slide boxes** to metal **slide cabinets** will hold hundreds or thousands of slides. Light Impressions carries many of the Neumade metal cabinets. For the full line of cabinets contact:

Neumade Products Corp.
PO Box 5001
Norwalk, CT 06856
203/866-7600

20th Century Plastics is an excellent source for photo, slide and negative pages and albums. To get their catalog contact them at:
PO Box 30022
Los Angeles, CA 90030
800/421-4662

FILES AND RECORDS

When you have inactive records, look in your office supply catalog or store under the category "storage files." There you'll find boxes made of corrugated fiberboard that come in a variety of sizes, with attached or separate lids and with places to label contents. Popular

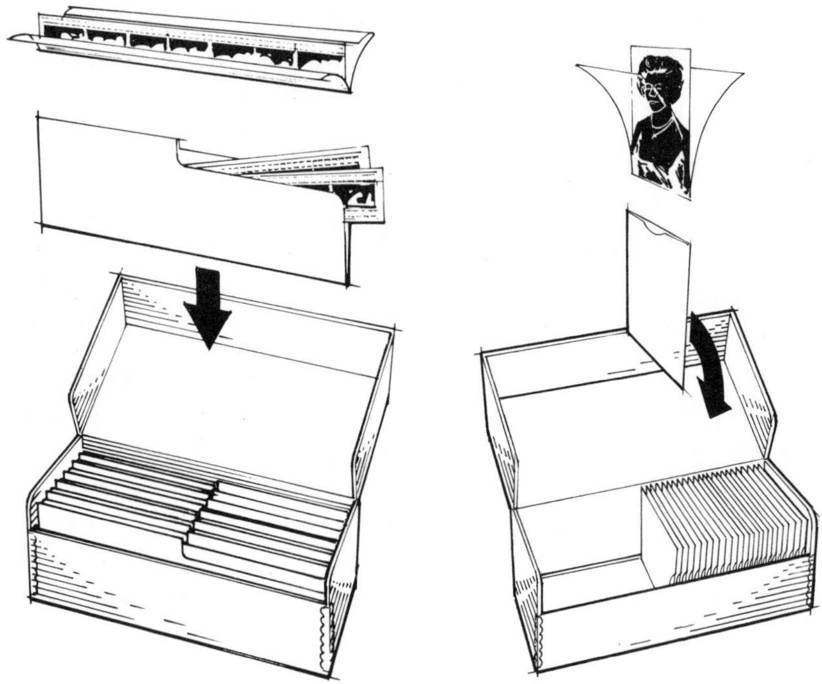

Figure 9-12. Nega*Guard System

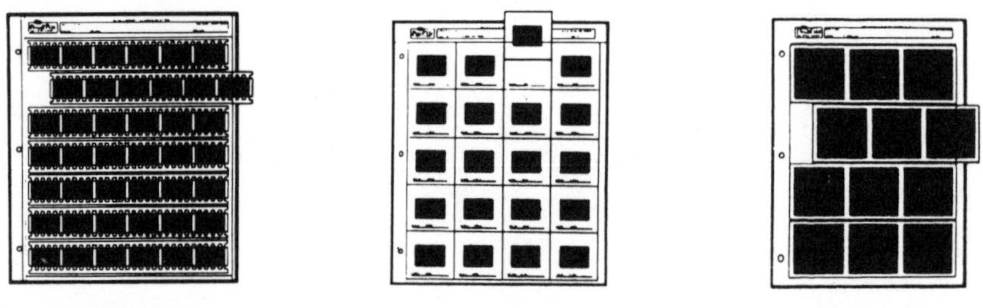

Figure 9-13. PrintFile Archival Preservers come in a wide range of formats for storing negatives and slides. Shown here are sleeves for 35mm negatives, 35mm mounted slides and 120 film negatives.

brands include **Perma Products Perma Pak** and **Fellowes Bankers Box** in Figure 9-14.

Figure 9-14. Perma Products Perma Pak and Fellowes Bankers Box (both lines feature boxes with separate or attached lids)

If you have many, many boxes you want to store off-site look in the Yellow Pages under headings such as "Business Records Storage" and "Offsite Records Storage." See also Chapter 4 for more information on filing.

LITERATURE ORGANIZERS

Magazine files or **holders** sit right on a shelf or table and are great for storing magazines, catalogs, manuals or reports. The **Oxford DecoFile** is made of high-impact plastic and comes in eight colors (which you could use for color coding different types of literature). Made of corrugated fiberboard, the **Fellowes Magazine File** costs less but will still do the job. (See Figure 9-15.)

Literature sorters and **organizers** come in many different styles and sizes and are great for catalog sheets, brochures and forms that you use frequently or that need to be assembled into kits. See Figure 9-16.

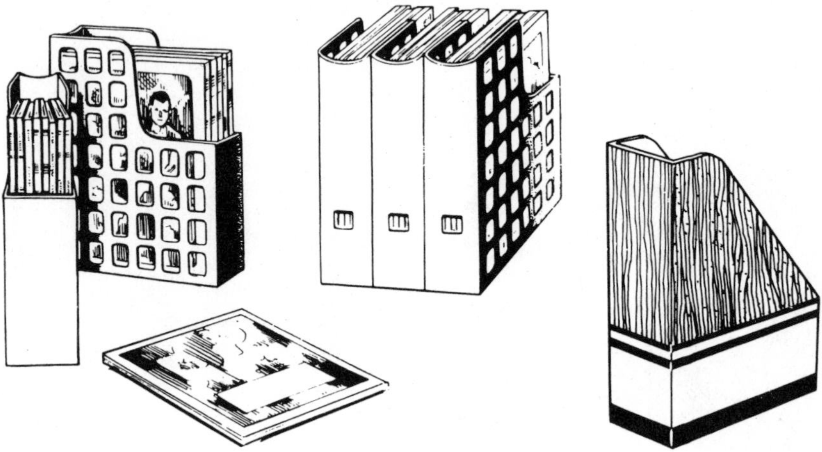

Figure 9-15. The Oxford DecoFile (left and middle) and Fellowes Magazine File

Figure 9-16. Fellowes Premier Line Mail/Literature Center (top left), Fellowes Literature Organizer, Fellowes Literature Sorter (bottom left) and Safco All Steel E-Z Stor Literature Organizer

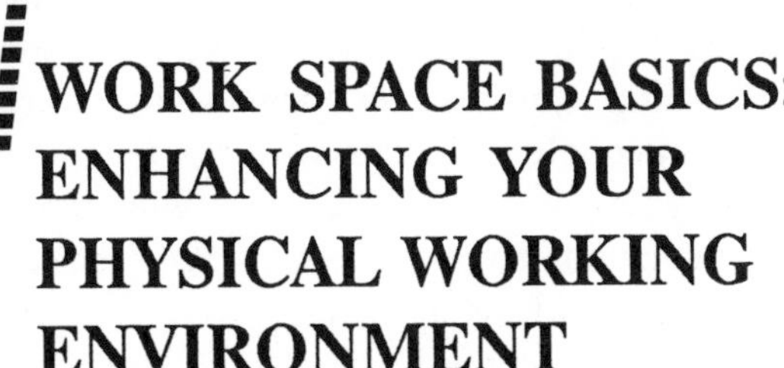

10 WORK SPACE BASICS: ENHANCING YOUR PHYSICAL WORKING ENVIRONMENT

Quick Scan: Whether you're planning a move or you just have a sneaking suspicion your office design is missing the mark, this chapter will reveal the physical features your office should have to be a more productive, comfortable environment. Many of these features are inexpensive and easy to implement. You'll be amazed to see how the little things can make a big difference.

Do you feel like everything in your office has been put in place with CrazyGlue?

Once you get used to an office, it usually feels pretty permanent. Everything seems as if it's always been there (and always will be.) But when you become too used to your environment, you don't see the possibilities. Or if you do, you figure you can't do anything about them anyway.

I love the story that stockbroker **Alan Harding** shared at one of my seminars many years ago. Harding had wanted a window office. As he saw it, though, he didn't need to change offices–he just needed to install a window in a wall that faced the outside. So

Harding asked his boss to have a window installed but his boss refused. For most people that would have been the end of it.

Not for Harding. You see, he spent a good part of every day in that enclosed office. He had been with the company awhile and was planning on staying a good while longer. Since he really wanted that window, he decided to spend his *own* money to have one installed–to which his boss agreed.

But that's not the end of the story. After seeing how serious Harding was about the window, his boss then decided to chip in and split the cost. What's more, when Harding came in on a Saturday to physically do the installation, his boss ended up helping. Harding says, "The whole thing wound up as a cooperative effort." It's amazing what can happen when you keep open the "windows of your mind."

There are three types of physical factors related to your office over which you have some control: your physical space, your furnishings and your total environment.

MAXIMIZING YOUR PHYSICAL SPACE

Look at where and how your work space is organized. Two space factors come into play.

LOCATION, LOCATION, LOCATION

Where is your office located? 'Sounds like a simple enough question. But you probably could provide many answers.

For example, any of the following could be truthful responses: near the freeway, 40 miles from home, next to the water cooler, on the fifth floor, far away from clients or close to the marketing department.

The last time you probably thought about your location was when you changed jobs or moved to a different office. But so often we just forget about location factors. We may even experience some irritation and not realize that that irritation is directly related to our location.

So just take a moment to think about the location of your work space, to see if there are some aspects that really bother you. Take this little survey. Next to each item, write "O" for Outstanding, "S" for Satisfactory, "N" for Needs Improvement or "NA" for Not Applicable (or not important).

1. Commuting distance
2. Proximity to colleagues
3. Proximity to vendors or suppliers
4. Proximity to your market–clients, customers or patients
5. Traffic flow in or near your office
6. Privacy
7. Noise
8. Lighting
9. Proximity to equipment and supplies
10. Proximity to personal or professional services–e.g., restaurants, shops, attorney

Take a look at any "N's" you've marked. Are there any ways you could change or modify undesirable locations? Don't just accept things the way they are, especially if your performance and productivity are really suffering. Be creative–like Alan Harding.

LATITUDE IN YOUR LAYOUT

Now take a look at your **layout**–the location and arrangement of the furniture and equipment within your own office space. There are two essentials of every good office layout: adequate **work space** and **storage space**. Sometimes it's hard to tell, however, if work and storage spaces are adequate, especially if a desktop hasn't been seen in years, filing is less than routine and a move hasn't occurred in more than a decade.

Differentiate between work and storage space. Unfortunately, in far too many offices, the distinction is nonexistent. Work and storage spaces are all lumped (and I do mean lumped) together. You'll be making great headway if you can separate these two basic spaces.

The biggest problem comes when your desktop becomes more a storage space than a work space. Too often the desk becomes a place where things are *waiting to happen*; make it instead a place for *action*. Think of your desk as an airport runway. If you were a pilot, you wouldn't find spare parts in the middle of the runway. They would be in the hangar. So, remove the obstacles from your work surface and **clear your desk for action!** Get out of the habit of keeping *everything* at your fingertips.

ELIMINATING THAT CLOSED IN FEELING

How do you break the keep-the-clutter-close habit? First, set up appropriate systems for paperwork and projects (see Chapter 3 on desktop management, Chapter 4 on paper files and Chapter 8 on managing details).

Second, put only those items you *use most frequently*–be they accessories, supplies, furniture or equipment–closest to you.

Third, make sure you have enough work space! I generally recommend at least **two surfaces plus adequate, accessible storage space** for most people. The surface right in front of you should be your primary work surface and ideally should contain only things you use every day. This is the area where you would be doing your most common work activities. A secondary surface off to the side or behind you could be used as a work area for a particular activity, such as telephoning or typing. This secondary area could also provide storage for items you use frequently such as your daily paperwork system, telephone/address directory and stapler.

An **L-shape** layout uses two surfaces–a primary one such as a desk and another one off to the left or right side, which when attached is called a **return**. A return is a small, narrow extension of a desk that is designed to hold a typewriter (or can be adapted to hold a computer terminal). See a desk with a return in Figure 10-1. You can order a desk with either a right or left return.

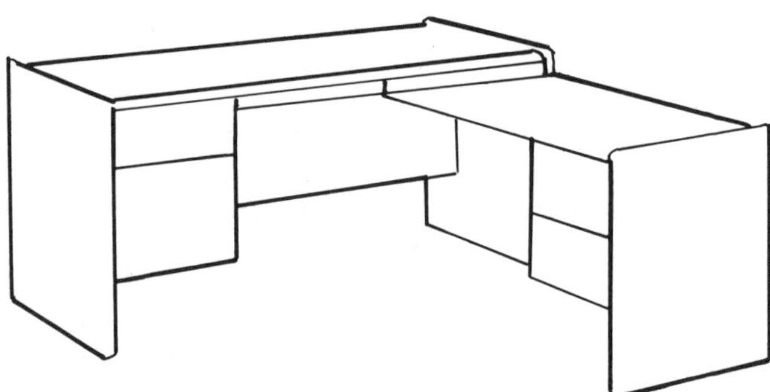

Figure 10-1. Desk with right return

You can see in Figure 10-2 how to easily create an L-shape layout by putting a table alongside your desk. Or if you don't like using a desk at all, try two tables at right angles shown in Figure 10-3.

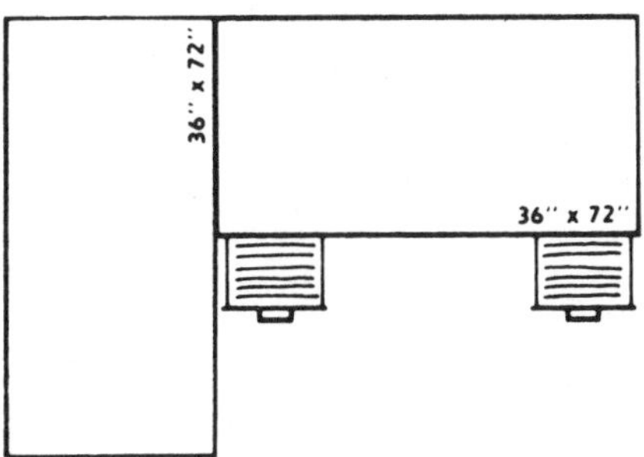

Figure 10-2. L-shape layout with table alongside desk

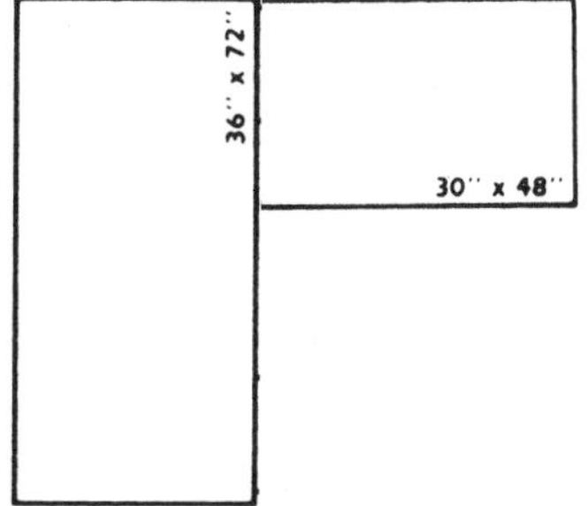

Figure 10-3. L-shape layout with two tables at right angles

A **U-shape** layout, as in Figure 10-4, gives you more work surface and usually more accessible storage. I use a modified U-shape in my office–I call it a **J-shape**. I have combined modular computer furniture with two two-drawer filing cabinets and a three-shelf bookcase to provide additional work surfaces and storage space. Figure 10-5 shows my office layout.

The **triangular** layout in Figure 10-6 takes advantage of a corner, makes good use of angles and plays up the importance of the desk as a focal point.

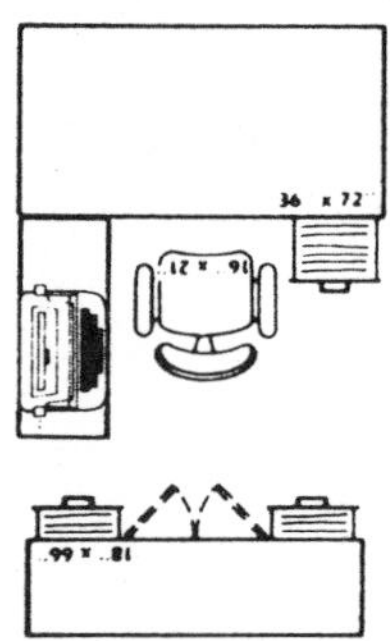

Figure 10-4. U-shape layout

A **parallel** layout, shown in Figure 10-7, places the main work surface, such as a desk, parallel to and in front of a storage unit (a credenza or lateral file cabinet, for example) or another work surface, such as a table.

DESIGN YOUR OWN LAYOUT

Get objective about an existing or proposed office layout. Make a quick, little sketch of your layout. Or better yet, particularly if you're planning a move, buy some graph or engineering paper (quadrille pads work great) and draw your office and make paper cutouts of your furniture to scale. Cutouts work great if you have a small office space and your furniture is going to be a tight fit. Also it's a lot easier moving cutouts around on paper than moving the real things. I've yet to see anyone throw out their back moving around cutouts. Another option is to buy a Stanley Tools Plan-A-Flex Office Designer kit to help you with your space planning. The kit, as shown in Figure 10-8, comes with a grid sheet and hundreds of reusable, peel-and-stick office furniture and equipment symbols pre-drafted by an architect. Just press the symbols on the grid sheet to design your layout. (The kit is listed in the chapter resource guide.)

Even if you're not moving, remember you're allowed to move things around. I consulted with a public relations executive who had one of the most beautifully designed and equipped offices I had ever seen. But she had been designed into a corner.

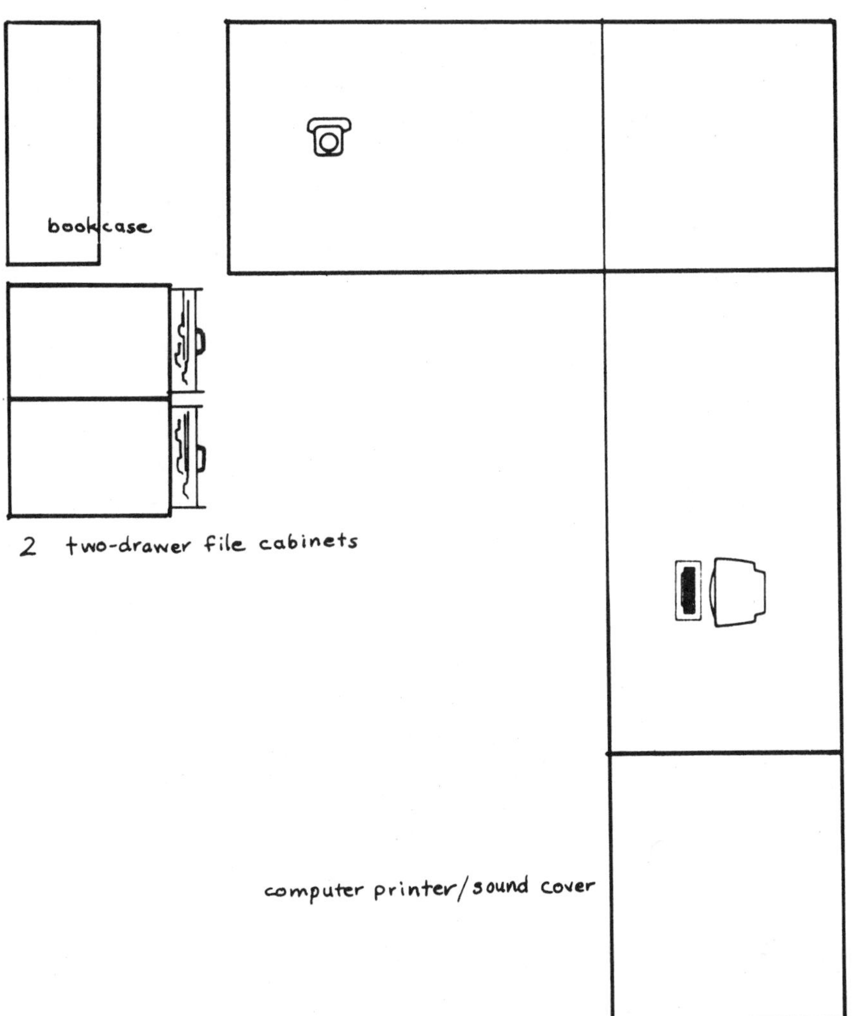

Figure 10-5. My office configuration uses a J-shape layout.

She had a huge pedestal desk, with a large, cumbersome chair. Behind her was a custom-built, corner credenza with all kinds of shelves and drawers, which she never used. Instead the surfaces of her desk and credenza were piled high with papers.

Why didn't she use the credenza? Simple–she didn't have enough space to easily move the chair and access the credenza. My solution:

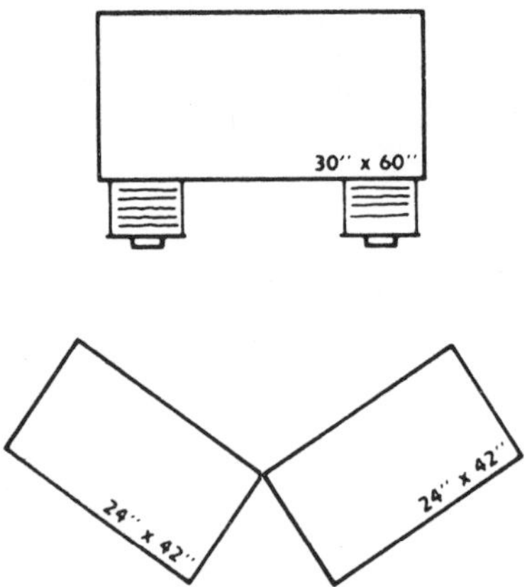

Figure 10-6. Triangular layout

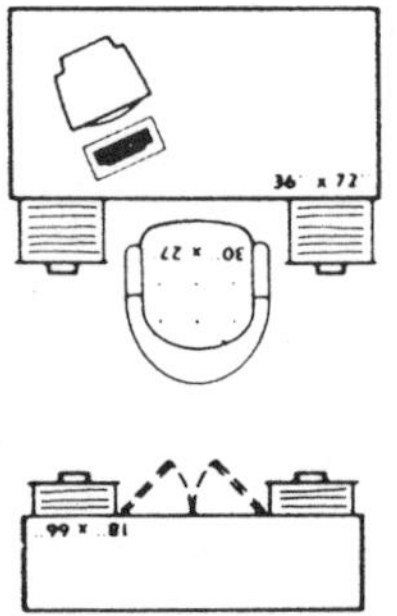

Figure 10-7. Parallel layout with a desk and credenza

move the desk farther out from the credenza! Why hadn't she thought of moving the desk? Probably because the designer had indicated where the furniture was to go and there it remained. Also the desk top was a heavy piece of glass. These factors suggested real *permanence.*

Once people are in their offices, the thought of changing a layout simply doesn't occur. Here's a chance to check out your layout. Quickly sketch out the main elements of your office space–furniture, equipment, walls, windows, light sources, plants. Don't worry about scale at this point.

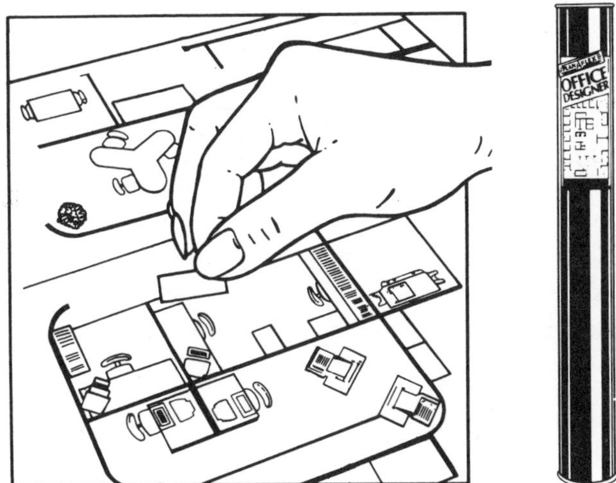

Figure 10-8. Stanley Tools Plan-A-Flex Office Designer kit (many of the figures for this chapter were done using this handy kit)

Ask yourself these questions:

- Is your layout convenient?
- Are the things you use most often close at hand?
- Do you have enough storage and work space?
- Do you have enough space for your equipment, especially your computer equipment?
- Do you like the way your office is configured to meet with others–co-workers, clients or customers?
- Does your layout invite irritating distractions? (For example, do you always catch someone's eye as he or she walks by?)
- Do you have different areas in your office for different types of work or activity–e.g., telephoning, computer work, meeting with clients? How and where do you like to do various kinds of work?

All of these factors may enter into the kind of office layout you can live with. Some of these factors are very subtle but their subtlety shouldn't diminish their importance.

PROXEMICS

One subtle factor concerns **proxemics**–the study of spatial configurations and interpersonal relations. Did you know that the seating arrangements in your office influence the relationships you have with your colleagues as well as your clients? Your seating arrangements make subtle statements. If, for example, in Figure 10-9, you are "A," sitting behind your desk, and you're meeting with "B," you are in a distinctly authoritarian, power position. This configuration may be totally appropriate when meeting with a client but if you're meeting with a colleague, perhaps the side by side configuration in Figure 10-10 would be more effective.

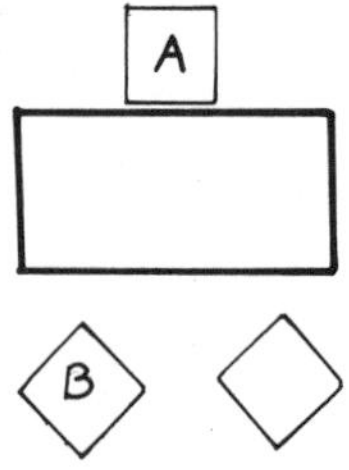

Figure 10-9. Authoritarian configuration with "A" having the advantage

If you have meetings in your office and you tend to run meetings in which you assert your authority, you would select a rectangular table, as shown in Figure 10-11, and sit at the head. If, however, you tend to meet informally and you're trying to foster that "good ol' team spirit," select a round table.

Of course space considerations as well as purpose will affect your final layout decisions.

THE DOORWAY

Decide, too, where to place your desk in relation to the doorway. If you're facing the doorway (or the opening of your cubicle) and you're in a high people traffic zone, you may find interruption is your constant companion. Turning your back to the doorway may appear too severe or even anti-social. You may prefer instead to angle your desk so as not to catch everyone's eye but to remain responsive.

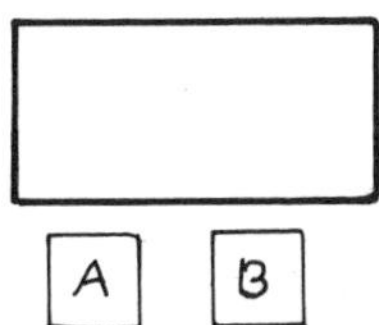

Figure 10-10. Side by side configuration

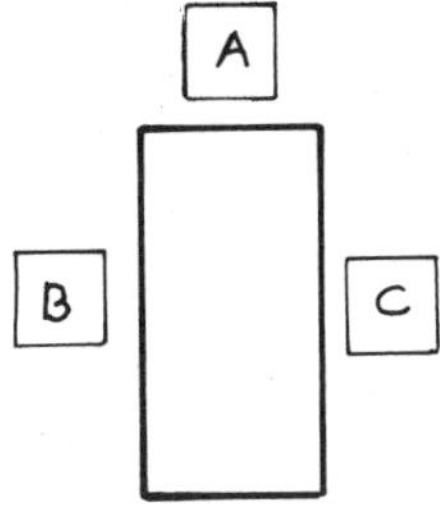

Figure 10-11. Meeting at a rectangular table with "A" in charge at the head of the table

When **Kim Villeneuve** was a divisional vice president for The Broadway department store in Southern California, she changed her position toward the doorway depending on the type of work she was doing. Since she needed to remain open to staff most of the day, she generally sat facing the door. But when she used the telephone and didn't want interruptions, she would swing her chair around to the credenza behind her. Her telephone sat on the credenza and there she did her phone work without inviting interruption. The credenza became an area designated for important telephone work, without interruptions of people as well as any distracting paperwork on her desk.

YOUR WORK STYLE

Finally, consider how you like to work when you design your layout.

Dr. David Snyder, a physician in Fresno, California, prefers just a desk in his private office. He uses the desk to process patient files and other paperwork quickly and efficiently. He says, "I will never have a credenza again–that's where I put stuff I didn't have time to do."

FURNISHINGS THAT FIT

Walk into your office as if you were walking into it for the first time. Pretend you've just arrived from Mars (some days don't we all feel that way!) Look at your office with fresh eyes and notice all your furnishings–your furniture, equipment, accessories and supplies.

Are they all well-organized, in good repair and well placed? Are they as functional as they should be? Do you have enough storage space?

FURNITURE AND EQUIPMENT

With today's changing technology, *flexibility* is a key word to apply to your choice of furniture and equipment. **Modular** furniture with interchangeable components works great, particularly in automated offices.

I searched long and hard to find modular furniture that met my computer equipment needs. I found it in a line called **Biotec**, made by Hamilton Sorter. Biotec is a versatile, attractive, quality line that comes in a variety of different sized components.

What I like about Biotec is the superb engineering and design that combines flexibility and functionality. Those qualities are particularly important if you'll ever be moving your office. Since buying my Biotec furniture, I have moved once. Each of my offices required a different configuration. Figure 10-12 shows how I was able to take my original configuration from my old office and simply reverse the components to fit my current office requirements.

Biotec could also accommodate my letter-quality printer with its cut-sheet feeder. Biotec makes a large, roll-top sound cover and stand (Figure 10-13) that match the other components. I highly recommend a sound cover if the sound from your printer is disturbing to you or co-workers or can be heard during telephone calls. Remember, too, to check that your sound cover and stand have slots in the right places for feeding paper to and from your printer.

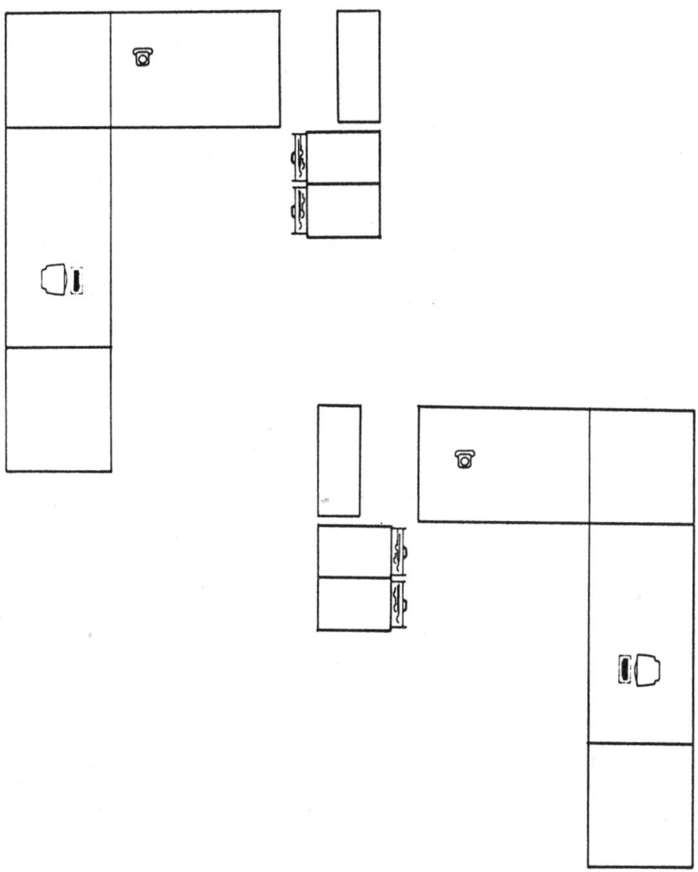

Figure 10-12. I was able to take my old layout (top) and easily reverse it (bottom) to fit my new office because I have modular furniture.

Your sound cover should also come equipped with an automatic cooling fan. Make sure the switch for the fan is conveniently located.

Figure 10-14 shows a three-dimensional view of a typical Biotec work station. Without drawers there is completely unobstructed legroom. (My own Biotec work station has shelves under each work table for storage.) The Biotec recessed panels ensure you don't

Figure 10-13. Biotec roll-top, printer sound cover and stand

Figure 10-14. This Biotec work station features an adjustable keyboard base unit built into a free standing return. The computer terminal is sitting on an adjustable platform.

wrack up your knees as you swivel to different areas. If you have to have drawers, consider getting a pedestal with or without casters (Figure 10-15).

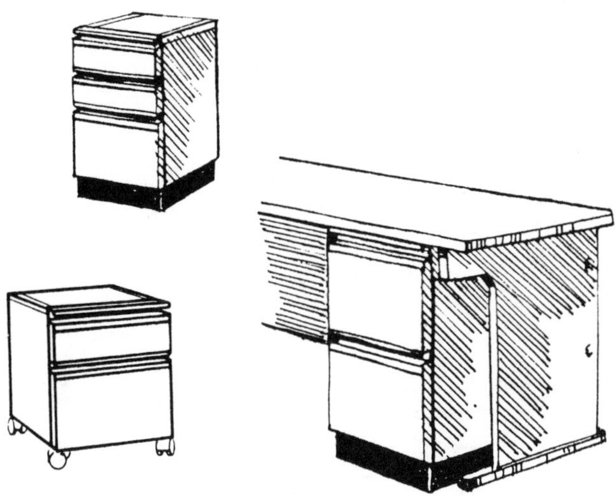

Figure 10-15. Biotec Undertable Pedestals

ERGONOMICS

Biotec is a fine example of applying **ergonomics** in office furniture design. Ergonomics is the science of making the work environment compatible with people so they can work more comfortably and productively. Ergonomics looks at the dimensions of work tables, desks and chairs and matches them to the wide range of body sizes and shapes according to certain recommended standards that are illustrated in Figure 10-16.

When you pay close attention to these standards you can avoid such symptoms as fatigue, eyestrain, blurred vision, headaches, stiff muscles, irritability and loss of feeling in fingers and wrists. The longer you work at a desk or computer, the more you need to consider the importance of correct angles of eyes, arms, hands, legs and feet.

Use a good **ergonomic chair** whose back and seat are adjustable. A good chair is more than a piece of furniture; it's a necessity for long hours of computer work. A bad one is literally a pain in the back.

Apply ergonomics from head to toe. A **footrest** not only supports the feet, but the angle is beneficial for the back and circulation. Putting an **anti-glare filter** on your computer screen reduces glare

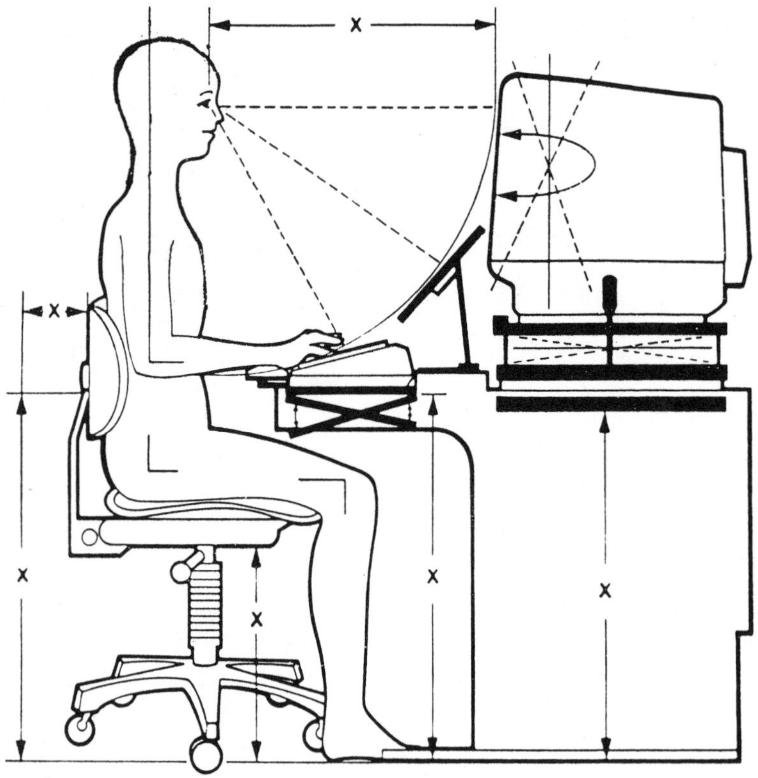

Figure 10-16. Ergonomics-The Human Factors (adapted from Biotec chart)

and eyestrain.

Remember, too, that good ergonomic *work habits* will make a big difference. Take the **20-20 rule** as described in Peter Lewis' article, "Using a Computer Need Not Be a Strain." The 20-20 rule says to keep your face at least 20 inches from the screen and to pause every 20 minutes or so to look away from the screen and to change your close-up focus by looking at distant objects. The 20-20 rule can help you prevent eyestrain.

Positioning and **placement** of equipment is an ergonomic factor that relates to left- or right-handedness. At my Positively Organized!

Office seminars I ask participants whether their telephone should go on the right or left side of the desk if they are right-handed. Answers are usually evenly divided between "left" and "right." The correct answer is "left." If you're right-handed you'll be writing with your right hand. So place the phone on the left so that the phone doesn't get in the way. You'll want to hold the phone with your left hand to your left ear, leaving your right hand free to write.

Consider, too, how you like to turn your body in relation to equipment. Do you prefer a typewriter or computer on a left or right hand return? Where do you want to place the copy stand and materials–on the left or right side of your typewriter or computer? Most people just don't stop and think about the things that they use every day.

The **accessibility principle** should influence your decisions about equipment placement, too. Even a work surface has areas that are more convenient than others. Angle your computer, for example, off to the side for occasional use; place it right in front of you for frequent or constant use.

One last tip on equipment: avoid the "$12,000 paper clip." It's the little things that count as one man found out after losing two $12,000 copiers because of paper clips that somehow became lodged inside. This man now uses a $3 magnet attached to a piece of velcro on his copier to hold paper clips.

ACCESSORIES AND SUPPLIES

In my consulting work I notice that clients either have too few or too many accessories for their paperwork, telephone and computer. Those who have too few generally lump their work all together on the desk, on tables, on shelves, in drawers and on the floor. Those with too many (if one pencil holder is good, six are better) collect accessories along with good intentions. They buy a new accessory every time they're inspired to "get organized." Soon the accessory becomes just another catchall rather than a clearly defined tool. The original purpose is too soon forgotten.

Any time you add a new accessory to your environment, define its purpose and *get in the habit of using it.* And from time to time, check to see if it's doing its job. If it has outlived its usefulness, *get rid of it!* Let's look at some of the most useful work space accessories (and see also chapters 2, 3, 4 and 9).

PAPERWORK ACCESSORIES

One of the most versatile paperwork accessories is the **expanding collator**. It comes in plastic or aluminum with 12, 18 or 24 slots. If you're a CPA or an attorney, use it for large, bulky *active* client files that you're referring to daily or several times a week. (While it's always safer to put client files away each night in filing cabinets, using the collator is a good intermediate step for anyone who is still piling files on couches and floors.)

Use the collator near your copier or computer printer to store large quantities (up to 500 sheets) of different types of paper. I use a twelve-slot collator that sits atop my computer printer sound cover.

You can always use the collator for its original purpose, too–collating! It's great for assembling or sorting literature and handouts.

The **stationery holder** is a wonderful accessory to hold letterhead, envelopes, forms and note paper. Some stationery holders are designed to fit inside a desk drawer; others sit on top of furniture or on a shelf. Place a stationery holder where you'll be using it.

Magazine files or **holders** are indispensable boxes for storing catalogs, directories as well as magazines. They're usually made out of plastic, acrylic or corrugated fiberboard. **Fellowes** makes several inexpensive, "knock-down," corrugated fiberboard versions that are easy to assemble and easy to store flat when not in use. **Eldon**, **Oxford** (**Esselte Pendaflex**) and **Rubbermaid** make plastic magazine files and holders that come in a variety of colors and designs.

If you use a typewriter or computer you should have a **copy stand** with a movable marker. There are many different types for the computer; some even sit between the screen and keyboard. But it's better to look for one that can be placed at the same eye distance as the screen. It's hard on the eyes when you have to keep refocusing to accommodate different focal lengths.

If you have wall partitions, consider installing one of the **wall unit paper management systems** now available. As office space decreases into more flexible, partitioned "cubicles," using vertical wall space for accessories makes sense. Wall systems help you get paper off your desk and yet make it accessible and organized.

TELEPHONE ACCESSORIES AND FEATURES

Selecting a basic telephone today has become a major decision given all the different features and accessories that are available. Look for these features:

- speaker phone with on-hook dialing
- automatic on-hook re-dialing
- automatic memory dial
- compatibility with your headset, telephone answering machine or other telecommunications equipment.

If you're on the phone a lot (at least one to two hours) or you have any neck or shoulder trouble, a **telephone headset** is the answer. Besides being more comfortable, a headset frees up your hands to take notes, handle paperwork or operate a keyboard. I always use a headset whenever I do interviews for articles or seminars or when I know I'll need to write or type during the call.

Make sure your headset is compatible with your phone equipment. Some headsets will not work with *electronic* phones. If your phone has any of the typical bells and whistles–redial, speaker phone, memory dial–it's probably electronic. I discovered my first headset would only operate with a *mechanical, modular* phone, the traditional kind of phone with a removable handset (the part you hold in your hand). So in addition to purchasing the headset, I also purchased a standard, mechanical phone that I only used with the headset. Standard phones, however, have become harder and harder to find because very few are still being made.

Where do you buy a headset? Radio Shack has headsets, as do many stores that sell telephones and other electronic equipment. Look for headsets in mail order catalogs, too, such as **The Sharper Image** from San Francisco. Office machine dealers may have them, too. Again, I can't emphasize enough the importance of compatibility. Very often sales people will not be aware of compatibility problems so either bring your phone to the store to check it out or if you order a headset, make sure it is completely refundable.

I recently discovered a company that distributes headsets that are compatible with *any* phone. The company is called **Plantronics** (800/662-3902) and their headsets start at $59.95.

A **telephone answering machine** is a must in our office. There are many on the market today with a variety of features from which to choose. Here are some features that are nice to have:

- ability to pick up messages off-site, preferably without having to carry a special remote control unit
- ability to change outgoing messages off-site
- built-in phone with a two-line option.

You may use a **Rolodex card file**, but are you aware you can turn it into more of a resource database? There are special Rolodex plastic divider tabs you can insert to divide up your Rolodex into different categories. Use an alphabetical system within those categories instead of throughout the entire Rolodex. With several different subject categories, it's often easier to look up listings, rather than trying to remember the names. Colored cards and colored plastic card protectors are also available with the system.

If you find the standard 2¼-by-4-inch Rolodex size too small, consider using the 3-by-5 size. The cards are large enough to hold stapled business cards (without having to recopy the information). There's also room for brief notes. Some people prefer the smoked Rolodex box to keep dust and light from ruining the cards.

While the most common brand name, Rolodex is not the only brand of card file. There are many brands as well as styles from which to choose. Compare card files made by Bates, Eldon and Rubbermaid (available in office supply stores and catalogs). Cardwear Hardware, as discussed in Chapter 8, is a good alternative, too.

And to maximize your telephone time, use a **clock** placed strategically in front of you. Or if you frequently place calls to another time zone use a second clock with say, Eastern Standard Time, for example. A **countdown timer** (available at Radio Shack) will help you consciously choose how much time you want to spend on each call.

COMPUTER ACCESSORIES

Protect your eyes. Make sure your screen has an **anti-glare filter** (as mentioned earlier) or a protective coating. Purchase an anti-glare filter at your local computer store or through one of the catalogs listed at the end of the chapter. Or if you're buying a monitor, consider one such as the Amdek brand that comes with a protective mesh coating on the glass screen. (If you buy such a monitor, however, realize you can't touch the screen with your fingers or clean the screen with a cloth; the only way to clean it is with a mini-vacuum for computers or with a can of compressed air from a camera store.)

Set your monitor on a **tilt stand** if you need to adjust the proper angle of the screen to your eyes.

Protect your ears. Enclose your noisy letter quality or dot matrix printer in a **sound cover.**

Protect your floppy diskettes. Buy **plastic diskette boxes** with divider tabs to store programs, files and backups on disks.

Guard against electrical power disturbances wiping out data by using a **surge protector**, also called a **surge suppressor**. (Figure 10-17.)

Figure 10-17. WilsonJones six-receptacle surge suppressor for computers and peripherals

Adapt a desk return that's too shallow with a **keyboard extender** as shown in Figure 10-18 that conveniently pulls out your keyboard

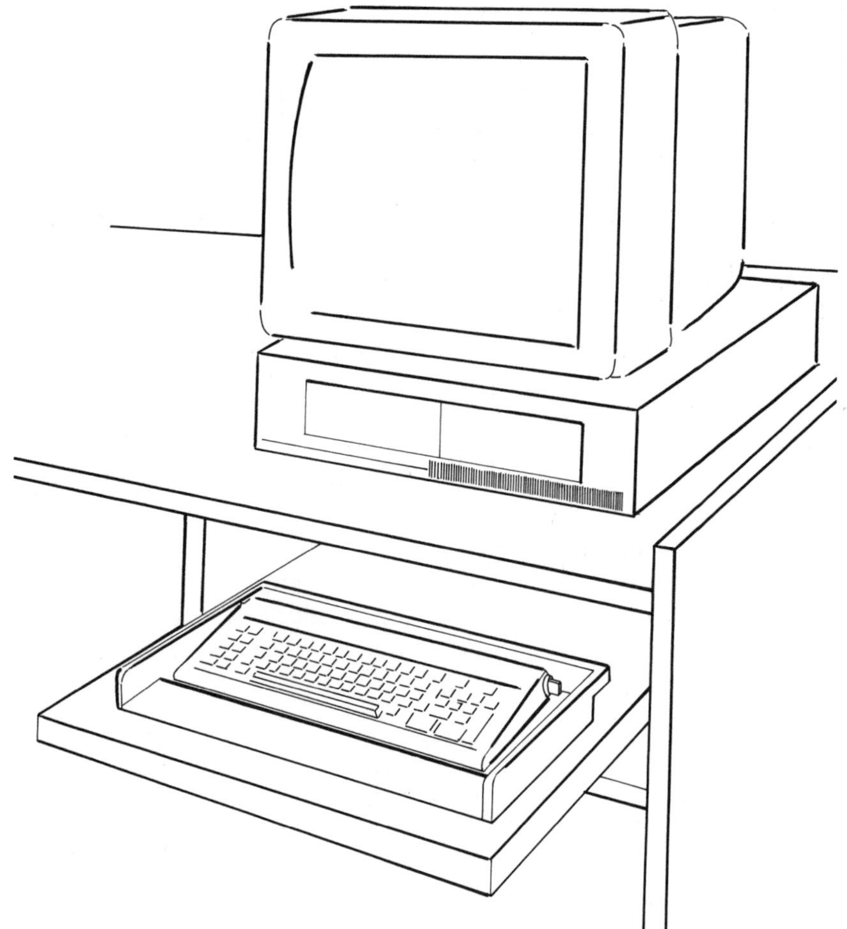

Figure 10-18. Keyboard extender (line art courtesy of Moore Business Products)

and hides it under the cpu (central processing unit) and monitor when not in use.

YOUR SUPPLIES

Keeping your supplies organized requires a systematic approach. The following will help:

- Organize your supplies for easy access, keeping the most frequently used most accessible.
- Group supplies by type as well as by frequency of use.
- Label supply shelves, drawers or cabinets and/or use color coding.
- Replenish supplies regularly and systematically and have one person in charge of the ordering process.
- Use a re-order chart near supplies for people to indicate whenever a supply is getting low.
- Use re-order slips placed strategically near the end of pencils, pads, etc.; whoever gets a slip turns it in to the person who orders supplies.
- Prepare a "frequently ordered items" form for each vendor you use, listing items and stock or catalog numbers; refer to these forms to speed up the ordering process.

YOUR TOTAL ENVIRONMENT

How do you feel about your office space? Do you feel comfortable there? Is it *you*? Is there something about it that rubs you the wrong way (or the right way)?

There are five important environmental factors that affect just how you feel about your office space. See to what degree any of these environmental factors influence your feelings.

AESTHETICS

If you spend at least one third of every week day in your office–that's at least eight hours a day–you deserve to have a working environment that's aesthetically pleasing.

COLOR

Many studies have revealed the "psychology of color," showing the affect of color on our emotions and state of mind. They have found, for example, that red excites us; in fact, when red is used in restaurants it is supposed to make us salivate! But used in moderation, red can be a great accent color, particularly for a sales or marketing office where you want an upbeat atmosphere.

Blue is perhaps the most universally pleasing color and is generally a calm color, depending on the shade, of course. Grays, browns and other neutrals are even more subdued. All three can work well in professional offices.

Burgundy and deep forest green are rich colors that can work well together or separately in professional offices, too. They can be used as main or accent colors.

Use of "trendy colors" can give a more contemporary feeling, which may be important for your type of office. You do run the risk, however, of having those colors go out of style more quickly. Use of more traditional colors and color schemes avoids this problem and may convey a more permanent, solid business environment. Base color decisions on the nature of your business, who comes into your office and your own particular preferences.

Choose light and dark colors to enhance your space. Lighter colors tend to open up space and work well in smaller offices. Darker colors make rooms feel smaller, cozier and more intimate. They work well in large office spaces that could otherwise appear too intimidating or sterile.

Don't ignore the impact of color. The question to ask is, What are the right colors for you?

PERSONALIZATION

Color alone is not enough. Your office is not just a place to work. It should be a reflection of you. It needs to be personalized with objects you love.

Why not have objects you love around you–such as plants, art, photos? Just remember they should complement not clutter your work space.

If you've become bored with your office, consider moving personalized objects to different places. We all need variety; just moving things around or changing objects from time to time can make a big difference.

AIR

What can you do about the air you breathe? First of all, be aware of it. Second, see if you can change any unpleasant atmospheric conditions or adapt to them.

AIRBORNE TOXINS

The most obvious toxin in the air is cigarette smoke. Some studies have shown that cigarette smoke is more harmful to someone nearby inhaling "secondary" smoke than the smoke inhaled by the actual smoker. If smoke is a problem for you, stay away from it!

Many cities and companies now specify that smokers go outside or to other specially designated areas to smoke. If your city or company doesn't have such requirements, consider working toward establishing them. Sure it'll take some of your precious time, but isn't your health precious enough? At the very least, make sure that smokers have an air cleaner or purifier unit on their desk to remove at least some of the smoke.

As far as other toxic substances, such as asbestos, read your newspaper to stay current on new discoveries and legislation. Notice, too, if you experience certain symptoms such as nausea and dizziness only in your office environment. Invisible toxic substances pose a real problem in detection and in identification but we're bound to see more research in the future.

TEMPERATURE

Here's one of those factors that is far easier to adapt to than to change. I can't tell you how often I have complained to facilities managers about the temperature, which for me is almost always too cold in modern buildings, where you are at the mercy of a thermostat that either isn't working or is adjusted to somebody else's body!

I used to work for a major aerospace corporation. Our department was on the same thermostat as a computer room. It was always "freeeezing" in the office. I kept a little portable heater on under my desk.

My office today doesn't usually get cold enough for a heater, but I keep an extra sweater in the office at all times, particularly during the summer when the air conditioning tends toward the cool side. I also close off most of the vents in my office in the summertime when the air conditioning is running fast and furiously. If your office is too hot, just about your only option is to keep complaining or work at home. But recognize temperature is a factor in your productivity and your attitude toward your work place.

COMFORT AND SAFETY

Fifty percent of disabling office accidents are the result of slips or falls–most of which could have been prevented.

Keep floors clear of cords, cables and other objects. Even a rubber band on the floor can be a hazard. One office worker slipped on a rubber band, breaking his arm in two places and crushing his elbow. He lost six weeks of work.

Our discussion of ergonomics in this chapter certainly relates to comfort and safety. Check out your chair and your equipment according to the ergonomics chart and criteria we discussed earlier.

LIGHTING

Lighting is related to comfort and safety, as well as aesthetics. Select the right **amount**, the right **kinds** and the right **direction** to make lighting work best for you.

Make sure you have enough light. Some offices are too dark and depressing. Interior offices usually need additional lighting. That one panel in the ceiling just won't do it.

Make sure you don't have too much of the wrong kind of lighting in the wrong places. If you're using a computer terminal, all those overhead fluorescent lights could be causing irritating glare. Better to use a lower level of overhead lighting combined with **task lighting**, localized sources of lighting for specific tasks or areas. An example of task lighting is a desk lamp that sheds light on desktop paperwork only and stays off the computer screen.

Balance fluorescent lighting with either a natural light source (a window) or incandescent lighting. Fluorescent lighting by itself is very hard on the eyes.

In addition, some research studies indicate fluorescent lighting may be emitting harmful ultraviolet rays that cause such symptoms as fatigue and dizziness. Some retail stores are putting **ultraviolet shields** on their fluorescent lights. You may also consider replacing your fluorescent lighting with **full spectrum lights**, also called **health lights** or **Durolights.**

PRIVACY

The last environmental factor concerns the need for privacy in your office. Privacy usually comes from some sense of *enclosure*, which can include visual as well as sound barriers. Having some barriers, be they walls, movable panels, plants or file cabinets, is important for most people.

For one thing, effective communication needs privacy. Studies have shown that employees who sit in an open, "bull pen" environment tend to communicate less freely. On the other hand, employees who have some measure of enclosure and privacy tend to communicate more freely and openly.

Privacy also can improve productivity. Most people need to have their own space to focus, concentrate and shut out some of the distractions. A smaller, more controlled environment is also less stressful for most people.

RESOURCE GUIDE

FURNITURE AND EQUIPMENT

Whenever possible, see furniture and equipment "in person." At the very least, get color chips of finish or fabric or actual samples. *Never* buy a chair without sitting in it first. Suppliers are listed from different parts of the country; you can often save significantly on shipping when you order in a geographical area that's nearby.

BIOTEC SYSTEMS is the line of modular, computer furniture that I have in my office. To get the name of your local representative or to receive a free copy of the BIOTEC Design Guide contact:
BIOTEC SYSTEMS
A Division of Hamilton Sorter Co., Inc.
PO Box 8
Fairfield, OH 45014

800/543-1605, in Ohio, 513/870-4400

Global Business Furniture is a mail-order catalog featuring a good selection of furniture and equipment.
Global
2318-17 E. Del Amo Blvd.
Compton, CA 90220
800/645-1232 (in California, 213/488-1087)

Media-Flex Workstations offer flexible furniture and storage modules for computerized work spaces.
Acme Visible Records, Inc.
1000 Allview Dr.
Crozet, VA 22932
800/368-2077 (in Virginia call collect, 804/823-4171)

National Business Furniture is a mail order catalog that offers a substantial selection of furniture at discount prices with a guarantee for six years (except for normal upholstery wear). They provide fast shipping on 10,000 different products.
National Business Furniture, Inc.
222 E. Michigan St.
Milwaukee, WI 53202-9956
800/558-1010 (in Wisconsin, 800/242-0030)

The WorkManager System is a new line of modular, computer furniture and accessories.
MicroComputer Accessories, Inc.
PO Box 66911
Los Angeles, CA 90066-0911
800/521-8270, in California, 213/301-9400

ACCESSORIES AND SUPPLIES

American Computer Supply is a mail order company that offers discounts on many items, usually same day shipping (with approved credit) and a 90-day guarantee. Call 800/527-0832 to get a sample catalog.
2828 Forest Lane
Dallas, TX 75234

Business & Institutional Furniture Co. mail order catalog includes the lowest prices on furniture (they'll meet or beat any price) and guarantees all products for six years. 800/558-8662
Located at:
PO Box 92069
Milwaukee, WI 53202

Comcor has a complete line of telephone products with a 30-day guarantee. 800/221-3085 (in New York, 212/689-9018).
Communications Corner
9 E. 37th St.
New York, NY 10016

Devoke Data Products is a mail-order catalog specializing in furniture, accessories and supplies for information processing with a 30-day guarantee and 24-hour shipment on supply items.
Call 408/980-1347.
PO Box 58051
Santa Clara, CA 95052-8051

Global Computer Supplies catalog offers computer supplies, accessories and furniture at a discount with a 30-day satisfaction guarantee, fast shipping and service. 800/8GLOBAL–800/845-6225 (in California, 213/603-2266)
Global Computer Supplies
2318 East Del Amo Blvd.
Compton, CA 90220

Inmac is a mail-order catalog featuring computer accessories, supplies and furniture with 14 sales and distribution centers nationwide. Priding itself on service, Inmac offers a 45-day trial period or your money back and a one-year unconditional guarantee (or more, depending on the product). The main number is 800/547-5444 (in California, 800/547-5447).
Inmac Corporate Office
2465 Augustine Dr.
Santa Clara, CA 95054

Misco Computer Supplies and Accessories carries a broad selection of quality products at very competitive prices. This easy-to-read mail-order catalog also includes furniture items.

Misco
One Misco Plaza
Holmdel, NJ 07733
800/631-2227 (in New Jersey, 201/946-3500)

Moore Computer Supplies & Forms Catalog includes an excellent selection of computer furniture and accessories as well as computer supplies. The catalog with its alphabetical index at the front is easy to use. Moore is a very service-oriented company. 800/323-6230
Moore Business Products Catalog Division
PO Box 20
Wheeling, IL 60090

PLAN-A-FLEX OFFICE DESIGNER by Stanley Tools is a kit that makes designing your office layout easy and fun. The kit comes with reusable peel-and-stick office and architectural symbols (e.g., desks, file cabinets, windows) that you press into place on a frosted film "GridBoard." Using the GridBoard, you can work directly over existing blueprints without obscuring them. The GridBoard lets you plan up to 18,000 square feet of space. Besides the GridBoard, the kit has four colorful symbol sheets and a design manual. PLAN-FLEX OFFICE DESIGNER kits are available at office supply stores, bookstores, selected specialty stores and catalogs. To get the name of your nearest dealer, call 800/648-7654.

BOOKS AND OTHER READING

9 to 5 Fact Sheets contain valuable information about good office design particularly for computer workers. Of particularly interest are: "The 9 to 5 Office Design Kit: How to Design the Work Area to Fit You," "9 to 5's Consumer Guide to Office Computers" and "Office Design for Video Display Terminals." Each fact sheet is $3 apiece or $15 for a complete set of eight fact sheets. **Do It At Your Desk** is a humorous book that helps computer users work out daily aches and pains through simple exercises at the desk. It also includes advice on choosing chairs and working at computer terminals. $2.95 To get the fact sheets and the book and to get a complete listing of other work-related books and reports contact:

9 to 5 National Association of Working Women
614 Superior Ave. NW
Cleveland, OH 44113
216/566-9308

Office At Home: Everything You need to Know to Work Efficiently and Happily From Home by Robert Scott (New York: Charles Scribner's Sons, 1985) provides useful tips on planning office space and selecting equipment, whether or not your office is in your home. Paperback, $9.95

The Office Book by Judy Graf Klein (New York: Facts on File, 1982) is a beautiful, coffee table book that provides full color photos of small and large office spaces. If aesthetics and good, clean design are important to you, this book will give you some good ideas. Hardback, $40

Office Furniture by Susan Szenasy (New York: Facts on File, 1985) is a useful guide to the many factors in choosing furniture: aesthetics, comfort, function, strength, size and versatility. Hardback, $19.95 and paperback, $12.95

Private and Executive Offices by Susan Szenasy (New York: Facts on File, 1985) is for people who have the luxury of a private office or at least have an important say in their office or company. This book shows how to make the most of personal office space and aesthetics and how to make an office reflect the profession and personal taste of its occupant. Hardback, $19.95, paperback, $12.95.

Sunset Home Offices & Workspaces (Menlo Park, California: Lane Publishing Co., 1986) is loaded with ideas, illustrations and full color photos to help you design and equip an efficient work area. The book includes a variety of innovative storage options and design solutions. There are also ideas on computerized work spaces. Paperback, $6.95

Working From Home: Everything You Need to Know About Living and Working Under the Same Roof by Paul and Sarah Edwards (Los Angeles: Jeremy P. Tarcher, Inc., 1985) has several excellent chapters on setting up and equipping a home office space. (Much of this information is useful even if your office isn't in your home.) Paperback, $11.95

THE TRAVELING OFFICE: HOW TO TRAVEL SMOOTHLY AND GET THINGS DONE

Quick Scan: If you're away from your office a good portion of the time, you need special time management techniques and office tools to handle work responsibilities. Discover how to master paperwork and the telephone from afar. Consider using the latest, high tech telecommunications options that are now available. Read about specific tips and tricks that on-the-go professionals use when they travel.

Whether you travel eight or eighty percent of the time for business, keeping up with all your responsibilities can be quite a challenge. As one executive admitted, keeping up is difficult even when you're *not* traveling. The tools, tips and techniques in this chapter could make the difference for you between travel exhaustion and exhilaration.

For many business people, traveling represents the opportunity to finally get some real work done without all the constant interruptions. Travel or commuting time can be a precious respite from the more demanding every day routine. For Public Relations Society of America Executive Vice President **Betsy Kovacs,** "The airplane is the best place to read, think and write because you're away from the telephone."

WORKING ON THE ROAD

Make special use of your travel time.

While on a plane, **Bill Butler**, president of BCG Consulting, likes to make use of "creative thinking time." He'll take a sheet of paper and jot down ideas in the form of mind maps (visual idea outlines) and decision trees (pros and cons) for two or three of his current projects.

Whenever **Mike Welch** of the Credit Union Executives Society travels, he brings along his portable dictaphone (the size of a pack of cigarettes) and some pre-stamped "Jiffy" envelopes. He mails back the tapes in the padded envelopes and he adds, "The *letters* are not waiting for my signature; what's waiting for me when I return is the *reply*."

For urgent dictation, Welch dials into his desk dictation machine, which is on 24 hours a day. And since his secretary is "super sharp," if a change has occurred since he dictated (e.g, a certain report already came in), she will automatically update and correct the final letter.

Welch will also dictate in the car. After a recent planning meeting for his association, he had dictated all the thank you notes and a staff report by the time he had returned to the office.

Welch also makes good use of his commuting time by listening to tapes every morning on his daily commute by car. He particularly enjoys listening to tapes put out by Newstrack, Inc., in Englewood, Colorado (303/778-1692). The "Newstrack Executive Tape Service" is a biweekly tape cassette series that summarizes newspapers and magazine articles. (Try listening to tapes such as Newstrack on a plane, too.)

Accomplish as much as you can in the allotted time by **consolidating activities** when you travel. Plan ahead all the meetings you want to have and the people you want to see in a particular location. Consolidate similar activities–for example, group together all your writing work. Because space is at a premium, you're almost forced to work in this linear way. It's harder to jump from one thing to another when you can't spread out all your "stuff." (And if you're one of those people who accomplishes more when you travel, perhaps you should incorporate this one-thing-at-a-time work style into your back-at-the-ranch office.)

HANDLING PAPERWORK ON THE ROAD

Set up a **portable system** to organize your paperwork and office supplies. As with everything else, there's no one right way to organize your paperwork. But having a regular system in place, with the right tools and routines for you, can guarantee a more productive trip.

Plan ahead. Do what Butler does. When you book your hotel reservation, make sure the room has the basic paperwork necessities: a flat writing surface with a light and a telephone. (Isn't it inconvenient when the telephone is on the night table when you have a lot of phoning to do?)

Select practical accessories to hold and transport paperwork and supplies. Butler carries an expandable, leather document case that has different colored folders. He also takes along a standard manilla folder to store materials collected during the trip. Butler carries a lightweight tote bag filled with reading material; when empty, the bag can be folded inside the document case. He also has a plastic folder that holds thank you notes, sympathy cards, get well cards, stamps, number 10 envelopes and letterhead.

Categorize different types of papers. Welch organizes his reading material for a trip into three categories. One category he calls "First Priority," which includes all of the material related to a meeting, such as the agenda and the registration list. Another category is "Fun Stuff" such as the daily paper, *USA Today* and the *Wall Street Journal*, which he says are good sources of conversation starters. A third category is "Business Reading," such as lengthy reports, industry newsletters and selected articles.

Derrick Crandall, president of the American Recreation Coalition, travels with a very heavy briefcase, which contains project files, his long-term projects list and a trip file that has a trip sheet on top and other related material underneath. To keep up with correspondence, he also carries three or four number 10 envelopes with 25-cent- and 45-cent-postage as well as one large envelope with three dollars of postage.

Kathryn Johnson, president of the Association of Western Hospitals, San Francisco, carries what she calls her "portable office," containing clear plastic folders, supplies, dictation tapes and an Express Mail envelope. If Johnson is away for more than three days, she always travels with an Express Mail envelope. She takes work with her, completes it on the plane and mails it back to her office in the envelope. She also mails back dictation tapes.

One association executive has mail sent to *him* on an extended trip. The San Francisco Convention and Visitors Bureau sends mail and reading material to Executive Director **George Kirkland** via Federal Express. Backup copies of written correspondence remain in the office. Kirkland says, "Nothing is more depressing than returning from a trip to a stack of papers. When I come back, rarely do I have anything on my desk."

Neither does Welch, but that's because his secretary files papers into his fifteen active projects folders in his credenza. When he returns, he checks these folders in order of their priority. At the very least, have your secretary–should you be lucky enough to have one–sort your papers into two colored folders, say, red for "urgent" and blue for "not urgent."

Take pertinent resource material with you in a concise, easy-to-carry format. **Duane Berger**, regional sales manager for Wheels, Inc., has created an alphabetical notebook system of his own which he takes with him when he travels. He says, "I'm not at my desk that often so I can't carry the whole file cabinet with me." So instead he carries a three-ring notebook with alphabetical tabs and reinforced paper sheets that contain summaries of clients and prospects, the latest meetings, the types of programs his company is offering.

Berger uses single word phrases, "buzz words" he calls them, so he can see information at a glance. Typical information Berger writes down would include people profile facts such as key contacts, spouse's name and special interests; buzz word summaries of problems and solutions which would instantly remind him of next actions to be taken. If a client calls when Berger is on the road, he is prepared to talk intelligently, armed with up-to-date information.

When he's in the office, he uses the book there, too, because it saves him the motion of filing.

A loose-leaf personal notebook organizer is an invaluable tool for carrying information you collect on a particular trip. Many organizers come with special expense envelopes that are great for keeping all your records and receipts together in one place. These envelopes make it easy to compile expense reports when you return from your trip.

Day Runner makes such expense envelopes to be used in their personal organizers. They also make a couple of wonderful items (shown in Figure 11-1) to help you keep up with correspondence on the go. **Message** pages are pressure sensitive, two-part pages for instant memos and replies. **Express-it** is a handy, self-mailer with a gummed edge that lets you drop someone a quick note.

Portable file boxes may work for you if your office is in your car trunk or you have many files to take with you on a business trip. File boxes come in all shapes and sizes and can accommodate legal and letter files, hanging file folders. Check your office supply catalog under "file boxes" or "storage files." As for the piles of papers that accumulate on any trip, organizing consultant **Barbara Hemphill**, who is author of *Taming the Paper Tiger*, offers several suggestions. She says the time to handle those papers is during the trip *before* you get home. Throw out what you can; sort the rest into file folders. (See Chapter 3 for file folders in your daily paperwork system, which can be adapted for your traveling office.)

One of Hemphill's folders has her secretary's name. She puts papers that her secretary will handle in this folder. Then she takes out her dictaphone and dictates instructions for each paper. This saves Hemphill time when she returns from her trip and gives her secretary some control over when she processes this paperwork.

If you're uncomfortable with dictating machines, you could use Post-its. Use different colored Post-its to distinguish paperwork with different priorities or to categorize different types of work.

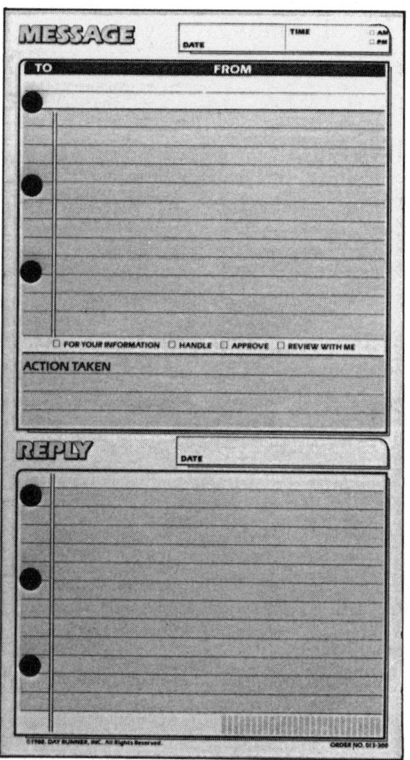

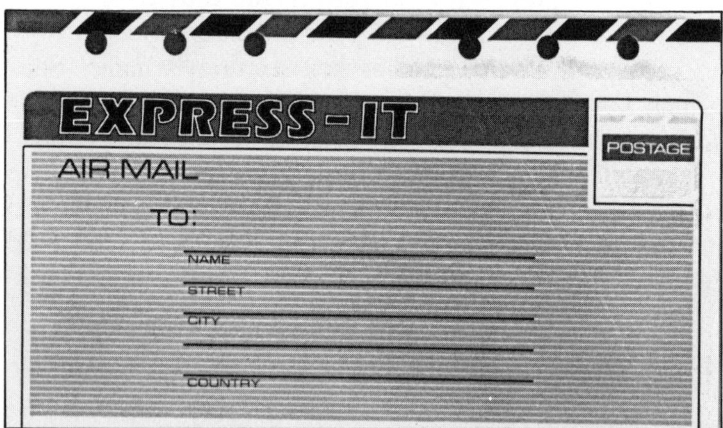

Figure 11-1. Day Runner Message and Express-it for easy, on-the-go communications

THE TRAVELING TELEPHONE

Today's high tech telecommunications make traveling and staying in touch easier than ever. The biggest problem is trying to decide which tools–or toys–to use.

I did some seminar work for one Fortune 100 firm that had a problem with too many telecommunications toys. Many employees had to check five or six systems several times a day just to make sure they received all their messages. Pity those employees who were less than positively organized and forgot to check their computer's electronic mail box or the computerized message center. The more tools and systems you have, the more likely it is something will slip through the cracks.

In addition, the company, through its strong emphasis on individualism, encouraged people to use communication channels that best fit them. This is a nice idea in theory, but when you have to remember how all of your colleagues like best to communicate and those colleagues are scattered across the country, your communications difficulties can easily multiply.

Rule Number One is use the right telecommunications tools for you and keep them simple but effective for your applications. Cost of the tools you select is a consideration but be sure you measure cost in terms of time and energy savings as well as actual dollars. Let's look at some of the most cost effective tools.

Telephone answering machines work great when you're out of your office. (Why is it you always seem to get more calls when you're away?) Of course, you will want to use a remote unit, preferably one where you can dial a code to retrieve messages versus carrying along a special beeper. There are also miniature answering machines, small enough to take with you and install in your hotel room. You'll probably need to bring a special double jack adapter and an alligator cord, which will accommodate your answering machine and the phone.

For telemarketing expert **George Walther**, author of **Phone Power**, a telephone answering machine is an essential tool on the road. Walther takes his machine with him and sets it up in hotel rooms. Walther says his hotel machine sure beats scrambled messages from busy hotel switchboards. Walther uses a small, compact model for travel–the **Code-a-Phone 3530**.

A **call director**, such as **ASAP 10** by Command Communications works with your answering machine. A call director is a device that plugs into your machine and dials your **pager**, which beeps as soon as you get a message.

Speaking of pagers, look for the numeric type, which provides a digital readout of the phone number of the person calling you. And if you need a cross between a pager and an answering machine, consider getting the **Motorola Spirit** tone and voice pager. According to **Barbara** and **Jim Suitor**, who manage the Holiday Hills Resort in Eddyville, Kentucky, this pager lets you call someone on the phone and leave a 15-second live, audible message.

A portable cellular telephone is state of the art and expensive but there are many other phones, some of which are not cellular, that may suffice. Consider a transportable car phone or a briefcase car phone. If you do decide to go for a cellular phone, telecommunications expert **Stuart Crump** says to look for these three features: hands-free speaker phone, memory and voice dialing.

Take advantage of other telephone time and money savers. Select a long distance telephone company and use its credit card when you travel. And if your call just can't wait until you're on the ground, use Airfone, which is on most major jets today.

KEEPING UP WITH CALLS WHILE AWAY

Kovacs says, "I stay flexible about which telephone I use–I don't have to be in a hotel room. If I'm waiting an hour in an airport, I'll make calls using my MCI card."

On a more philosophical note, Kovacs says that the telephone helps her "maintain the rhythm of life," no matter where she is. Besides telephoning for business, Kovacs will place "stay-in-touch" phone calls. "The telephone works from out of town. The other person doesn't really care where you are when you're calling to wish a happy birthday." She adds that personal telephoning also helps make travel less jolting.

Most business travelers will call in at least once a day for messages and try to return calls the same day. Derrick Crandall says,

"I'm a big believer in telephone services on the road." Crandall, with a staff of five, feels a greater need to stay in touch with his office so he calls in two or three times a day. He also calls the office's remote-controlled answering machine after business hours to leave or receive messages pertaining to staff.

Mike Welch, on the other hand, relies more heavily on his staff. He says, "If they need me, they'll call me–they know where I am." He was at a four-day conference this year and never needed to call in once.

SPECIAL TRAVEL TIPS

Let's face it: traveling is time consuming and energy draining, particularly when you're out several days at a time and you're crossing different time zones. All the more so if you tend toward disorganization. So part of maintaining an effective traveling office is learning to handle the logistics of travel.

TRAVEL PREPARATIONS

TAKING TIME TO PREPARE

You are only as organized as you are prepared. "I pack my suitcase, my briefcase and my mind for each trip," says Mike Welch. "I really think it through. Like great athletes who picture themselves leaping over the bar, I picture myself at the business meeting." In addition to packing all the pertinent meeting materials, Welch commits to memory all the important details concerning the agenda.

Wilford Butler advises, "Read any briefing papers or material pertaining to your trip *before* you leave. State Department research indicates information is not absorbed and retained as well when you're in travel mode."

SELECTING AIRLINE TRAVEL CLUBS AND PROGRAMS BASED ON YOUR GEOGRAPHICAL TRAVEL NEEDS

Business travelers are flying airlines such as American, TWA and United. Derrick Crandall, who is based in D.C., flies United almost exclusively and is part of their Mileage Plus Premier Executive program. He says you can get their "gold card" by flying 75,000 miles a year. And since he flies 150,000 miles a year, he is upgraded to first class about 50 percent of the time. Crandall says he has never paid more for a ticket to fly United but he is willing to be more flexible with his schedule in order to get the first class upgrade bonus. That bonus also enables him to board before the other passengers so he gets first crack at overhead storage.

Here's another way to get first crack at overhead storage, especially if you're a woman. When the airline announces "first class passengers and all those needing assistance may board now," I rush to the front of the line. No, I don't fly first class (yet) but I generally require an extra hand to help lift my garment bag up into the overhead storage. This isn't a 100 percent sure bet but it works most of the time when I'm flying alone.

TAKING RESPONSIBILITY FOR YOUR TRAVEL ARRANGEMENTS

Many business travelers believe that the trip logistics such as flight reservations and seat assignments are too important to delegate, particularly in this day and age of non-refundable or partially refundable airline tickets. You can't afford a mistake.

Bill Butler stays current on flight information by subscribing to the pocket-sized *OAG Pocket Flight Guide* (North American edition) and the *Airfare Discount Bulletin*. The bulletin is a directory of discount airfares for the business traveler. (The *Pocket Flight Guide* is available by subscription (12 issues a year) for $50 from Official Airline Guides, 2000 Clearwater Drive, Dept. M563, Oak Brook, IL 60521-9953; the *Airfare Discount Bulletin* is available by subscription for $150 per year from Airfare Discount Bulletin, Inc., PO Box 460, Riverside, CT 06878.)

Butler stays current, also, by following industry reports included in the *New York Times* travel section. He has learned, for example, that Atlanta often shows extra delays because of a big problem with early morning ground fog. On the other hand, Memphis, which has Federal Express' major terminal, is considered the "all weather airport." Butler points out Chicago is noted for lots of traffic so you need to allow extra time between connecting flights.

And as for flight times to avoid, Butler comments, "I look with a jaundiced eye at the first flight out which is often a very popular flight for business. I will usually avoid it because it's too crowded and hectic."

While you may not want the first flight out, do travel early in the day, if you can. You have more options if a flight is cancelled. Avoid connecting flights but if you must schedule them, leave enough time between them–at least double what the airline tells you. Also avoid traveling during holidays.

Be aware that there are hundreds of policies and procedures hidden away in airline rule books that detail such items as passenger check-in, boarding, overbooking, delayed flights, missed connections, reservations, lost tickets and damaged bags. A *Wall Street Journal* story reported that each airline has its own rules and that it's often difficult to get copies of the rule books–and in fact, many airline employees have never heard of the books.

To give you some idea of how airlines differ, consider how much variance exists among airlines regarding reporting periods for damaged bags. Pan Am has a 45-day deadline in which to report baggage, Delta a 21-day deadline and Continental a mere four hours!

To get a free copy of an airline's rules, contact their main headquarters office.

Leave nothing to chance. Butler advises, "Never leave home unless you have a confirmed, guaranteed reservation in hand." That goes for accommodations, too. Ideally, you should be *ticketed* for airline travel as well.

DON'T UNDERESTIMATE A GOOD TRAVEL AGENT

"I have an excellent travel agent," says Betsy Kovacs. "My agent finds flights that fit in my schedule with the least number of connections. I am price conscious but I won't settle for inconvenience."

We couldn't be luckier when it comes to convenience. We have a great travel agency located right next door to our office suite! Besides being convenient, **MacPherson Travel Services** has gone out of its way to follow-through on all the complex details connected with travel arrangements. Helpfulness and an exacting attention to detail are two criteria to keep in mind when selecting a good agent.

CHOOSING YOUR SEAT FOR COMFORT, CONVENIENCE AND ACCESSIBILITY

Many business travelers prefer aisle seats because they offer a little more leg room and are less confining. But not just any aisle seat will do. Crandall likes an aisle seat close to the boarding ramp since he carries on luggage rather than checking it in.

Welch's seat preference is a no-smoking, aisle seat. His preference is so strong that he jokes, "I'll sit on the wing rather than sit anywhere else."

Some people prefer the "bulkhead," which has seats with the most leg room—more leg room than aisle seats. The disadvantages are that you have no underseat storage and you'll have to move if you want to see the movie screen.

If you're safety conscious, you may prefer to take the advice of air safety engineer **Greg Jarrells**, a staff member of the Aviation Safety Institute in Worthington, Ohio. Jarrells recommends an aisle seat next to the rearmost overwing exit.

Jarrells also recommends reading the emergency card in the seat pocket to find out how to open the various door and window exits. Locate the four exits that are closest to your seat. Count the rows of seats to each exit; you might not be able to see the exit signs in an emergency but you could still feel and count the seats.

USING TRAVEL RESOURCE INFORMATION TO HELP YOU PLAN YOUR TRIP

Butler used to travel 50 to 60 percent of the time; he now travels 30 to 40 percent. With such a heavy travel schedule, it makes good sense to have fingertip travel information. Butler maintains files on major cities he visits frequently, such as New York and Washington, D.C., and he subscribes to *New York* and *Washingtonian* magazines.

Butler also keeps his own travel notebook, which is arranged by client and location. The notebook contains directions, places to stay, ground transportation, how long it takes to get to the airport at various times of day, the "leading food adventures to the locals," restaurants to avoid and hotel history, in particular his room preferences. (Nonsmokers may also want to request and note for future reference which hotel rooms and floors are smoke-free.)

CONSOLIDATING YOUR TRIP LOGISTICS

Organized travelers have a trip form they carry with them that lists their itinerary, transportation, lodging, key contacts and phone numbers. They also leave at least one copy of their trip sheet with a staff member. Butler has an expense report printed on the back of his form, which makes for a convenient system.

Welch uses a typewritten sheet that lists such things as the airlines and types of planes he'll be flying, seat assignments, who confirmed his reservations, rental car arrangements and who will pick him up. Along with this sheet, Welch also brings photocopies of airline guide pages he may need. He carries these items in his pockets, which have been specially organized for travel so that he doesn't have to look in a million places. Having a simple and dependable system, even when it comes to organizing your pockets, can make a big difference when traveling.

SELECTION OF CLOTHING AND LUGGAGE

Wear the right clothing. When you're flying, several layers of light-colored, well-fitting (but not tight) clothing are best according to Jarrells. Wool, a naturally flame retardant fabric, is better than most materials, especially synthetics and leather, which should be avoided. (A good way to test flammability is to snip off a small piece of fabric and set it afire. If it melts rather than chars, don't wear it.) Also avoid high-heeled shoes.

Kovacs buys clothing that doesn't wrinkle. She says, "If they are wrinkled on the rack, you know they will wrinkle on the road." She also wears (never packs) one all-purpose coat appropriate for a particular trip.

Butler simplifies his travel wardrobe. Butler packs black shoes and stockings, makes sure shirts go with all suits and relies on neckties to provide color.

When it comes to luggage, Butler checks two pieces of Ventura luggage–a large case (which will hold 3 suits) and an overnight case. He suggests buying luggage where the airlines send theirs to be repaired. "These places know what holds up and what doesn't."

Other than a briefcase, the only thing Butler likes to carry on board is a good attitude, "There are two things you can do if your suitcase goes south and you go north: get angry or plan for this eventuality. I'm always dressed in a suit when I travel."

You might also try taping a copy of your itinerary to the inside top of your suitcase or suit bag. Perhaps an airline will contact you and ship your baggage.

Many business travelers, myself included, prefer taking their luggage on board so as to avoid the hassles of lost, stolen or misdirected luggage. But the latest FAA (Federal Aviation Administration) guidelines may put a crimp in this practice.

The guidelines advise that passengers carry no more than two pieces of baggage. Here are three options from which to choose:

- an underseat piece that is 9-by-14-by-22 inches maximum
- an overhead bin item that is 10-by-14-by-36 maximum
- a cabin closet hanging piece that is 4-by-23-by-45.

Fortunately, personal items such as purses, coats, hats, umbrellas and cameras don't count as carry-on luggage; unfortunately, briefcases do.

Apparently, there may be some variation in how the guidelines are administered by different airlines depending on factors such as aircraft size and the number of passengers on a flight.

I always recommend carrying luggage on board. I never check luggage on my way to any destination, if I can help it; occasionally, coming back I will check luggage, depending on my own energy level or if I have a particularly heavy load.

I bring a heavy duty garment bag by Ventura which has loads of zippered pockets. Pockets are labeled with round colored key tags (you can get them in stationery stores). I have written the names of articles contained in each pocket on each tag. (Having all those pockets can be a blessing or a curse, depending on whether you stay consistent and always keep certain items in them.)

Some items stay in the garment bag all the time, in between trips. I have a cosmetic case that duplicates the cosmetics and toiletries I keep at home in my bathroom. Packing time can be cut in half when you have an extra toiletry kit that is ready when you are. The ideal time to replenish any supplies that are low is when you unpack at the end of each trip. Dental, medical, body care and makeup supplies in travel-sized containers are convenient. For extra protection, fill containers three-quarters full and secure them in self-sealing plastic bags. I keep four small, zip-lock bags in my cosmetic case for four different types of toiletries–dental, facial, hair and eye care.

I also keep an extra hair dryer and several brushes in the bag, too, as well a couple of large plastic bags and a bathing suit (I'm a native Californian).

I usually take my Janssport tote bag, which has four roomy pockets plus the main compartment. I keep the bag under the seat in front. The bag holds my cosmetic case, reading and work material and other items that I want to have accessible (or that fit better in this case than the garment bag). I also take my organizer (it has a shoulder strap). And I never go anywhere without my trusty luggage carrier. My model is sturdy enough, with its large, heavy-duty wheels to take stairs and curbs without missing a beat–or dropping my luggage. I put the luggage carrier in overhead storage, along with my garment bag. (If I'm lucky, I'll hang my garment bag in the closet.)

PACKING SYSTEMATICALLY

Kovacs starts by making a list that is divided into two parts: day and evening. She decides exactly what she is going to wear and which accessories will go with each outfit. She lays her accessories and clothes out on the bed before she packs them in her garment bag. (Her tote bag holds shoes and cosmetics.) She also has a permanent list of basics that she keeps in a pocket of her garment bag. Kovacs tries not to take too much but she also puts great emphasis on looking her best. When it comes to cosmetics and toiletries, Kovacs packs each item after she uses it the last time before the trip.

TRAVEL CHECKLISTS

It's always a good idea to maintain at least one travel checklist of items you always take on a trip. See Figure 11-2 for an example. In addition, you may want to keep sample packing lists for different types of trips that you will take again. If you have a computer, keep your lists there. Whether you prepare packing lists manually or on computer, group items by category. Some useful categories are: clothing, underwear, personal care, business materials and recreation.

THOSE EXTRA CONVENIENCES

You may want to include, for example, some of "Butler's batch of things to carry": the *OAG Pocket Flight Guide*, a small atlas, a name and address book, a list of restaurants in the major cities you'll be visiting, a digital alarm clock that keeps both current time and home-based time, a pocket calculator, extra shoelaces, a sewing kit and safety pins, aspirin, antacid tablets, foil-wrapped granola bars, a nasal decongestant in case you have to fly with a cold, cough drops, pleasure reading such as a John McDonald or Agatha Christie book and gifts wrapped with yarn instead of ribbon, which tends to become mashed in a suitcase. Here's some space to write in your own extra conveniences:

Figure 11-2. THE POSITIVELY ORGANIZED! TRAVELING OFFICE CHECKLIST

Here are some items to include in your traveling office. Check off the ones that you already have, circle the ones you want to get and add any others that would come in handy:

[] Briefcase
[] Attache case
[] Tote bag
[] Document case
[] Notebook-size:
[] Organizer
[] Calendar/appointment book
[] Telephone/address book
[] Paper-pads, loose sheets, personal or company stationery, business cards-underline any of these items or add what you'll need:

____

[] Writing tools-pens, pencils, markers:

____

[] Accessories: tape, scissors, stapler, clips, portable office kit

____

[] Equipment: pocket calculator, dictaphone, small tape player, portable computer

____

[] Labeled file folders, file pockets, expansion pockets, plastic folders

____

[] Stamps, return envelopes, Jiffy envelopes, Express/Federal Express envelopes

____

[] Work: schedule, agenda, files/info related to business trip, reading material, paperwork, project work

____

[] Travel materials: itinerary, tickets, legal documents- driver's license, passport, visa, certificate of registration (from U.S. Customs for items such as cameras and watches made in a foreign country); travelers checks, cash, credit cards

____

[] Any extra conveniences you can think of: ______________________________

____

HEALTH AND PRODUCTIVITY, HAND IN HAND

To maintain your rhythm and your effectiveness throughout your trip, recognize that as you travel you are subjecting yourself to different demanding environments. Part of staying organized on the road is preparing in advance for the adjustments you and your body may need to make and then following through while on the trip.

TAKING CARE OF YOUR BODY

Butler says avoid unnecessary travel. "Make sure you need to make the trip in the first place, that there is no other way you can possibly accomplish your goal. See if they can come to you. Traveling is mean to your body."

Butler suggests you avoid overeating and overdrinking. He also suggests drinking bottled water wherever you go. "Just the different chemicals in the water can have an adverse effect."

Don't forget to exercise. Kovacs suggests running or even jump roping. A jump rope is an easy item to pack, too.

Crandall keeps his body on Washington, D.C., time. He never resets his watch (unless he's on an extended trip for a few weeks, several time zones away). "I like to maintain East Coast mentality and body time," he says.

TAKING SPECIAL CARE OF YOUR BODY WHEN YOU FLY

Most airlines are cramped and uncomfortable but fortunately, there are steps you can take to help your body adjust.

Protect yourself against dehydration. When you're on board a jetliner you will experience dehydration of body and skin because of the cabin's low humidity. Dehydration leads to weariness.

Be sure to drink enough liquid–one expert recommends one glass of water every hour. Apple juice, cranberry juice or fruit punch are also good. Avoid tea, coffee, alcohol and soft drinks, all of which can have a diuretic effect.

Bring along lip balm and hand cream to combat cracked lips and dry skin, likely symptoms from exposure to cabin air. Don't forget a lubricant for your eyes, especially if you wear contact lenses.

Order your airline meals ahead of time, if possible. Most airlines will allow you to order special meals such as fruit and cheese or vegetarian plates; low-salt, low-fat, low-cholesterol fare; and special selections for frequent travelers. Ask each airline what kinds of meals are available one or two days before you fly. Or better yet, place your order at the time you book your reservation. Remember to avoid high-fat, salty foods, which cause body swelling and retention of fluid.

Keep your body limber and comfortable. There are four steps you can take.

First, wear comfortable shoes you can slip on and off. Remove them shortly after takeoff.

Second, to reduce swelling in feet and ankles, elevate your feet. (Body swelling and bloating occur because of an airplane's lower barometric pressure.) Elevating your feet even a few inches really helps; try placing your feet on the carry-on case you've stashed under the seat in front.

Third, take short exercise breaks. Frequency of breaks is more important than time duration. Once every one to two hours is ideal. Take walks around the cabin and do simple stretches at your seat. Hold each stretch for 30 to 60 seconds. (You might want to tell your neighbors beforehand what you're doing.) Fourth, help improve your posture by placing a pillow in the small of your back. The pillow provides extra support and helps you sit up straighter.

COMBINING BUSINESS WITH PLEASURE

Crandall has a real advantage because the members of the association he directs are actively involved in recreation. The good news is that Disney is one of his members. The bad news is when he has to tell his six-year-old, "You can't come."

Crandall, however, tries to fly three to five trips a year with his family–his wife and his two, young daughters. He looks for ways to combine business trips with family vacations.

PACING YOURSELF

"You have to really pace yourself when you travel," says Kovacs. "If you have to wait," she advises, "find a comfortable place, know you're there for the duration and roll with it." If there's a delay at the airport, Kovacs like to go to the airport restaurant to read, work or relax.

In fact, much of pacing yourself is just learning to relax. "Don't get too excited, don't rant and rave," says Welch. "A lot of people create a crisis to be a hero. Don't let anything get to the crisis stage. The whole secret boils down to communication–up, down, sideways. Don't take anything for granted."

What to do if, after all your planning, your airline cancels your flight? Avoid the mad rush to the reservation counter or through the airport terminal; simply use a pay phone to make your new reservation.

There are always options, according to Butler, even if you find yourself next to the little old lady from Des Moines who wants to talk your ear off. "I have a friend who speaks Spanish when she doesn't want to be disturbed. I'm tempted to learn a few words of something myself."

One final suggestion: Believe Murphy's Law next time you're on the road. Or as Butler says, "You have to anticipate that things won't be perfect but most of the time you can organize and prepare."

RESOURCE GUIDE

PERSONAL ACCESSORIES

Danish Bookbag is an oversize bag with a shoulder strap and a veritable labyrinth of roomy pockets.
Tools for Living
Dept. TDP03
400 S. Dean St.
Englewood, NJ 07631
800/228-5505 (800/624-9900 in Nebraska)

Design Tech's CarFinder is a system to help you quickly locate your car in a parking lot and if necessary, to activate your car lights and/or siren for protection. The tiny, hand held key ring activates the system which costs $100. Satisfaction guaranteed.
Dak Industries, Inc.
8200 Remmet Ave.
Canoga Park, CA 91304
800/DAK-0800 (order number), 800/888-9818 (technical information number), 800/888-7808 (other inquiries).

Dictaphone Travel Master LX is a portable recorder that is light, compact and fits in your hand. It functions as a voice-activated, hands-free dictation system. It also includes a digital clock, stopwatch in up or down timer modes, alarm, tape counter. You can start the recorder at any pre-set time to record or play.
Dictaphone Corp., a Pitney Bowes Company

Little Black Book is a software program that stores up to 400 names, telephone numbers and addresses along with up to three lines of notes for each entry. The program prints out a pocket-size personal phone book that fits into a handy black cover. Available from Cignet Technologies for $70, 800/621-4292 or 800/331-9113 (within California).

Personal Organizers, see Chapter 2

The Pocket Secretary is a credit card size database that stores and recalls approximately 400 names and telephone numbers, messages and appointments. It signals reminders with a programmable alarm clock and it's also a full function calculator. It's a tiny 8K computer that fits in your pocket, wallet, briefcase or purse. $44.90
American Express
800/528-8000

Sharp Dial Master Pocket Auto Phone Dialer stores and dials up to 200 phone numbers. It has a two-line display that shows name and number. Secret functions keep selected data confidential. The dialer is also a full-function calculator. This convenient pocket accessory comes with its own wallet case. Check local electronic stores or departments.

Traveling SideKick is a personal organizer software package that comes with a program diskette and a special organizer binder, which has sections for address book, phone directory, reference, finance, calendar, pending and storage pockets. Designed to be used with SideKick (see Chapter 8), this package is produced by Borland International, 4585 Scotts Valley Drive, Scotts Valley, CA 95066, 408/438-8400. $70.

PORTABLE OFFICE PRODUCTS

Fellowes Bankers Box R-Kive Organizer is a complete portable filing system made of corrugated fiberboard in woodgrain styling. It includes a cover and two handhold grips for easy carrying and it comes with 12 letter size hanging folders. $14.95 Available through office supply stores and catalogs.

Fellowes Neat Ideas Portable File and **Personal File** as shown in Figure 11-3 are great ways to transport paperwork and files. The

Portable File comes with 10 letter-size hanging files. Available through office supply stores and catalogs.

Figure 11-3. Fellowes Neat Ideas Portable File (left) and Personal File

File-N-Shuttle is a waterproof, dustproof and virtually damage-proof way to store and carry your files and supplies. It's great for car trunk "offices." A special stand with casters lets you roll your file to different areas of your office. The file has a clear, plastic lid that is hinged in the middle. File and stand, $59.95; file only, $39.95; stand only, $27.95.
Memindex, Inc.
149 Carter Street
Rochester, NY 14601
800/828-5885, in New York, 716/342-7890

File Pal II is a portable, stackable, high impact plastic file that holds 90 letter size or 70 legal size hanging file folders. It comes in five colors and it has a cover and a base. $19.95
Remarkable Products
245 Pegasus Avenue
Northvale, NJ 07647
201/784-0900

The **Memindex** catalog features two products for on-the-go offices, **The Commuter** ($69) and **The Portable Desk** ($39.95 to $89.95).

Both products fit easily into a briefcase and help you keep paperwork and office supplies organized and accessible. (See File-N-Shuttle for Memindex address.)

Oxford File-It Portable File Box (Figure 11-4) is a locking file box that includes a colored Pendaflex filing system–10 folders, 10 indexing tabs and one set of A-Z, household and blank headings. An expandable front makes files accessible even when the box is full. It's made of durable yet lightweight plastic with a flip-up handle and comes in six colors.

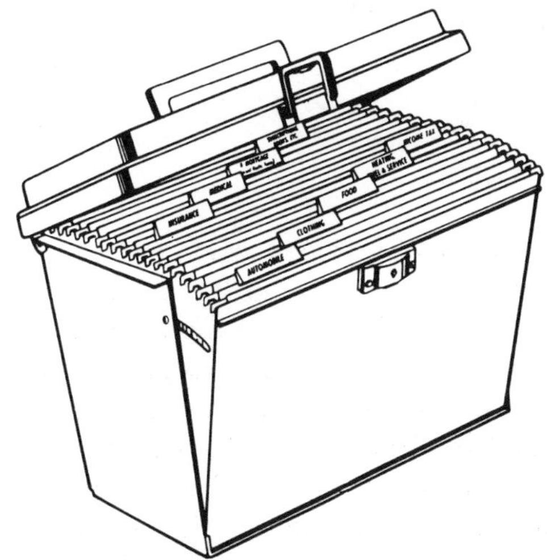

Figure 11-4. Oxford File-It Portable File Box

Oxford ToteFile is a compact, portable corrugated file that comes with a Pendaflex filing system–10 hanging folders in red, yellow or blue. The file box is white with a lid that matches the folder color. $14.89 Available through office supply stores and catalogs. See Figure 11-5.

Rolodex "Companion" is a portable file that comes with 500 Rolodex brand cards and is equipped with a retractable handle and sturdy latch. Available through office supply stores and catalogs.

Rubbermaid Design-a-Space portable office accessories in Figures 11-6 and 11-7 let you take your office with you. If you need to write while on the road, consider the **Storage Clipboard** with a durable

Figure 11-5. Oxford ToteFile

clip and pencil holder and a divided inside compartment that stores notebooks, paper, pens and pencils. The **Portable Desk** is lightweight, easy-to-carry with a large comfortable work surface. There are five divided compartments (two outside and three inside) that can hold a variety of paperwork and supplies. The **Large File**, the **Junior File** and the **Box Office File** are file/storage boxes that have ridges to accommodate hanging file folders. The Box Office File has a clear compartment in the lid to hold pens, pencils, calculator and other small office supplies. These Rubbermaid items are reasonably priced and are available in such stores as K-Mart and Target. For a store in your area, call Rubbermaid at 216/264-6464.

BOOKS

The Portable Office by Jefferson Bates and Stuart Crump, Jr. (Washington, D.C.: Acropolis Books Ltd., 1987). This book is loaded with information and resources on the latest technological tips and tools that are particularly useful for business travelers. Here's a useful guide to laptop computers, cellular telephones, electronic mail, on-line services, dictation machines, not to mention some great organization and travel tips. Hard cover, $16.95

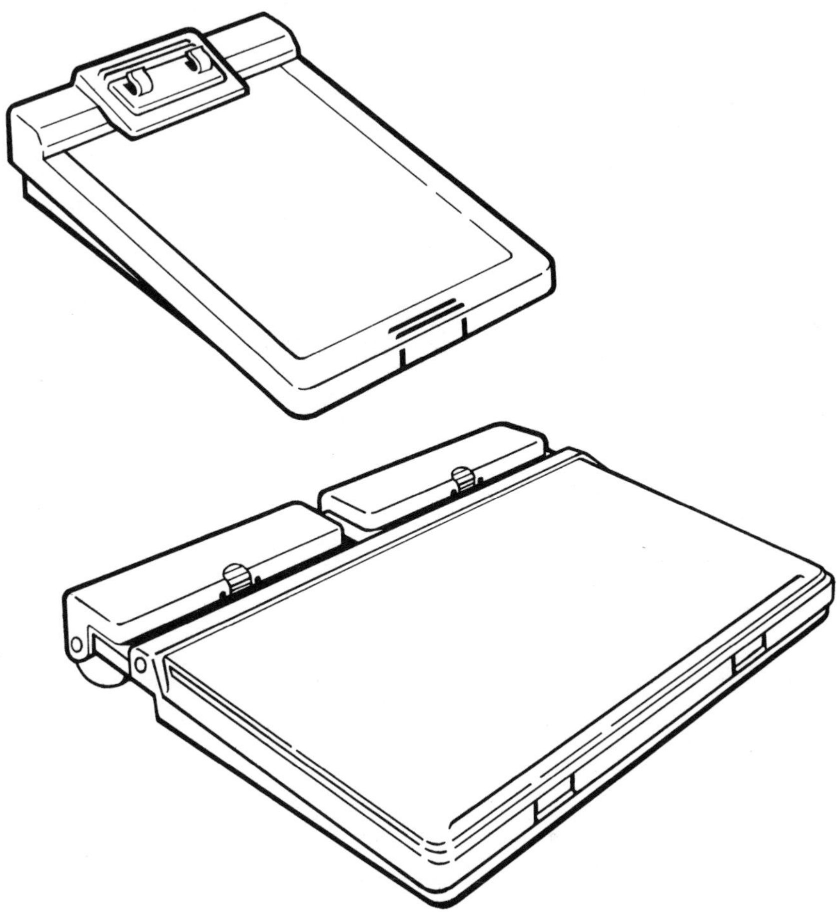

Figure 11-6. Rubbermaid Storage Clipboard and Portable Desk

Cellular Telephones: A Layman's Guide by Stuart Crump, Jr. (Blue Ridge Summit, PA: Tab Books Inc., 1985) Here's a useful book to get when you're ready to buy a cellular phone.

Executive Essentials: The One Guide to What Every Rising Business Person Should Know by Mitchell Posner (New York: Avon, 1982). This book has several excellent chapters on travel tips. Paper, $8.95

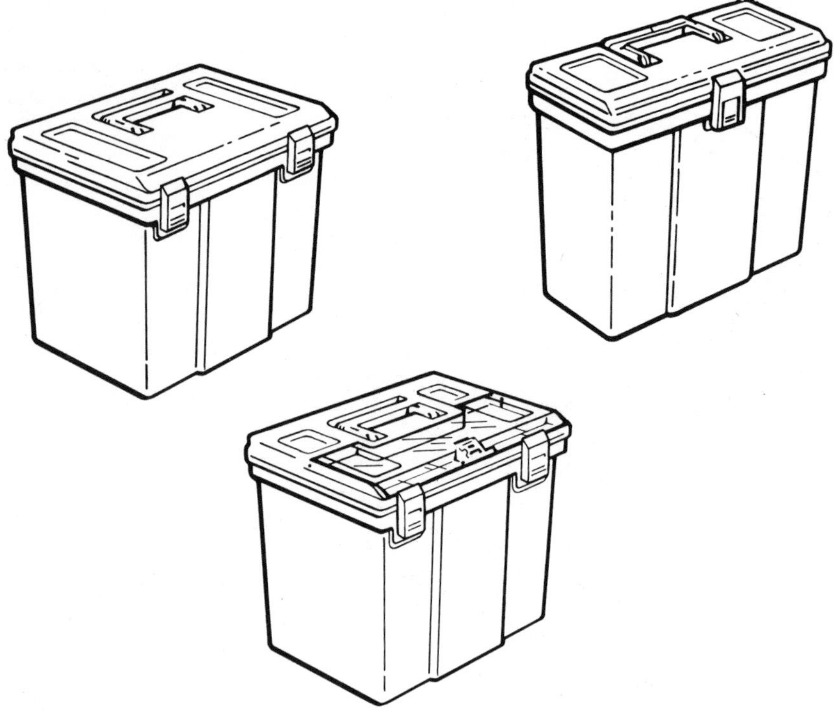

Figure 11-7. Rubbermaid Large File, Junior File and Box Office File

12 POSITIVELY ORGANIZED! IN ACTION

Quick Scan: This is the companion chapter to any other chapters you've read. It's the most important chapter because this is where you commit to action. Discover how to dramatically increase your own level of organization easily and quickly. Learn how to focus on your key areas for improvement in order to increase performance and achievement and become the best you can be.

If you want to be the best, it helps to be Positively Organized! But remember that's *Positively* Organized, not *perfectly* or *compulsively* organized.

I tell my clients, "**Be only as organized as you need to be.**" Don't become compulsive or guilty about organization. This is a tool to help you *prevent* stress, not add to it. Organization is not another thing to feel guilty about.

AN ACTION ORIENTATION

Now's the time to act. While organization is a process that evolves over time, you can boost this process by taking action and using this book as a springboard for action.

Where to Begin

Start small but think big. If you've read more than one chapter, go back to the table of contents and look at the titles of chapters that you've read. Which chapter will make the biggest difference to you in your career or life?

Now go back to that chapter and skim the headings and subheads as well as any underlines or notes you made. What jumps out? Find a small change you can make that will make a big difference. It might be changing a work habit or using a new system. Many clients find, for example, that setting aside five minutes a day to plan the next day is helpful. Some clients decide to set up and use a daily paperwork system.

Your Plan of Action

Dare to put your intentions in writing. When you write something down, you're giving a message to your subconscious. Besides reinforcing your subconscious, writing also helps you clarify your thinking so that you're better prepared to take action. Many, if not most people, though, are afraid that if they write something down, they'll forget about it. These people need to combine the act of writing with *reading* and *doing* what has been written. If you make a daily to-do list, for example, *read* it over several times during the day and *do* the listed activities.

I have my clients write a **plan of action** at the conclusion of a seminar or consultation. The plan can take a number of different formats–it can be a simple letter to yourself or a prepared form such as the one in Figure 12-1.

Figure 12-1. **PLAN OF ACTION**

Today's Date: ____________________

Organization Project or Activity:

____

Benefits or

Results:____

Ideas/Sketch/Brainstorm:

Action Steps	How long/often?	Calendared?

Rewards

____

Completion Date ________________________

Commit to yourself, commit to a deadline. The plan of action is basically a *written commitment to yourself.* Ideally, your first plan should focus on an organizational habit, tool, project or system that can be put into action in a *one- to four-week maximum block of time.* Create an experience of success. Don't overwhelm yourself with a six-month project where you may become discouraged or disinterested.

Be specific. Instead of the general "improving my time management skills," for your project, select something more specific, such as "I will take five minutes to plan and write tomorrow's to-do list at the end of each day." Instead of cleaning out all your file cabinets from the last 12 years, complete one file drawer in one week.

What's in it for you? Besides some hard work, you better be able to rattle off a whole list of benefits or results you hope to gain. Better yet, pick the *most important benefit*. Underline and star that benefit.

Plan step by step. If your project has more than two or three steps try "mind mapping" your steps before you put them in linear order. Mind mapping is a way to pour out your thoughts and ideas in a visual, picture outline. Once you can "see" your ideas, then you can determine their sequential relationship to one another. (See also Chapter 8 for a discussion of mind mapping.)

Make appointments with yourself. Once you've charted out your steps, schedule blocks of time to complete these steps. Schedule appointments with yourself and don't break them! Have calls screened (or turn on your answering machine), go off by yourself where no one can find you or pick a time when you won't be disturbed. Your plan of action should indicate how long steps will take–total time or time per day/week. Then write appointments in your calendar or planner based upon your plan of action projections.

Reward yourself! Make your plan of action more enjoyable by providing any or all of the three main types of rewards–tangible, psychological or experiential. Tangible rewards include physical things you give yourself–new clothes, a deluxe appointment book, a car phone. Psychological rewards are positive messages you tell yourself–stating positive affirmations and giving yourself little "pats on the back." Experiential rewards are a cross between tangible and psychological–getting a massage, taking a trip, dining out in a special restaurant are examples.

Getting others involved in your organization project can be a rewarding process in and of itself. Whether you engage a "buddy" who will offer positive reinforcement or you actually share the work with another, you will more likely increase your accountability and success rate as well as lighten your load. Encourage others to support you in your goals and do the same for them.

How to Change Habits

Getting more organized almost always involves habit changing behavior. But don't worry, it doesn't take a lifetime to change a habit. Actually it takes 21 to 30 days, provided you do the following:

1. Decide what new habit or behavior you intend to practice.
2. Write it down on paper. List *how, when* and *why* you're going to do it.
3. Share your new habit with someone else.
4. Reward yourself. Psychological affirmations before, during and after you practice a behavior can be particularly helpful.
5. Practice, practice, practice. You need to repeat the behavior, preferably every day, to create the habit.

Commitment to Be the Best

You will succeed with your plan of action and habit changes only if you are truly committed to being the best.

But what does being the best mean? For some, it's beating out the competition. For others, it's "doing your best"–being in competition with yourself.

How about being the best human being you can be? When all is said and done, isn't that what *really* counts?

Define it for yourself. After all, the way you live your life makes a statement about you–why not make the best statement?

According to Dr. David Viscott, author and radio psychiatrist, we each have at least one special gift to give the world. I agree that your gifts should extend beyond yourself in some way to make a better world. What are your gifts and how are you making the *best* of them?

Being Positively Organized! will help you *use* those gifts so you can indeed be the best.

ONLY THE BEGINNING: A NOTE FROM THE AUTHOR

Just a few more thoughts before we say good-bye.

I want to hear from you. Please write me in care of Adams-Hall Publishing with your results from this book as well as any comments or suggestions for future editions. You, too, could be in print!

Or be a part of my next book, which is on teamwork. Tell me what's working for *your* "team"–be it your company, non-profit group, office or family.

Upcoming editions of *Organized to be the Best!* will feature your contributions and keep you up to date on the latest organizational tools and techniques. You'll see how others are dealing with the challenges we all face. What's more, you'll be part of an ongoing process that's on the cutting edge of quality, performance and achievement.

You can also be a part of that process even more directly. Work with me through a personal consultation or a customized seminar program designed to produce positive results. I work with individuals, offices, companies and professional associations. Contact me in writing through the publisher:

Adams-Hall Publishing
PO Box 491002
Los Angeles, CA 90049

Or call me directly at 213/452-6332 at my Positively Organized! office.

One thing more. Remember organization is a tool. It's a means not an end. Never let it stand in the way of your humanity. Let it help you be the best in all you pursue and in all you are.

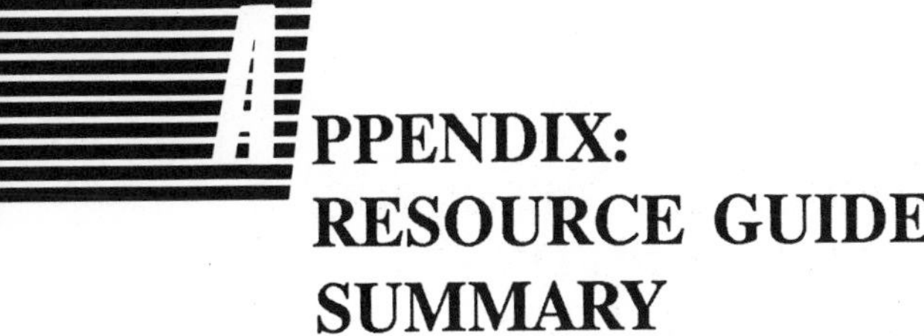

APPENDIX: RESOURCE GUIDE SUMMARY

What follows is a summary of all the main categories of products and resources listed in the chapter resource guides. For specific names, go directly to the resource guide or check the index.

CHAPTER 2 TIME MANAGEMENT: WHAT YOU REALLY NEED TO KNOW

Telephone Tools
Time Management Tools and Systems
Time/Self-Management Books and Tapes

CHAPTER 3 MASTERING YOUR DESK AND THE PAPER JUNGLE

Desk and Paper Management Accessories
Clips
Color Coding
Desk Accessories

Desk files
Other Organizers

CHAPTER 4 A PRICELESS RESOURCE: CAPITALIZING ON UP-TO-DATE FILES

Books and Booklets
Filing Supplies
Folders
Other Supplies

CHAPTER 5 POWERFUL COMPUTING: ORGANIZING YOUR IBM PERSONAL COMPUTER FILES

File Management Utility Programs
Menu Utility Programs
Multitasking Software Programs
Further Reading

CHAPTER 6 MAKING THE MOST OF YOUR MACINTOSH FILES

Desktop and File Management Desk Accessories and Utilities
Data Access/Data Recovery
Books, Catalogs, References

CHAPTER 7 THE BEST OF BOTH WORLDS: SPECIAL ORGANIZATION TIPS AND TOOLS FOR THE IBM AND THE MAC

IBM or IBM Compatible Products
Disk Backup and Storage Devices
Backup Utility Programs
Tape Backup Devices

Special Organizational Utility Programs
Hard Disk Maintenance Utilities
Data Recovery
Data Access

Macintosh Products
Disk Backup Devices
Backup Utility Programs
Tape Backup Device
Special Organizational Utility Programs
Data Access
Hard Disk Maintenance Utility

CHAPTER 8 DETAILS, DETAILS: GETTING THEM UNDER CONTROL

Work and Project Management
Tickler Systems
Manual
Computerized Ticklers & Time Management Programs
Forms, Checklists and Charts
Project Management Software
Other Work Management Tools

Resources and Records
Personal Computer Options--IBM
Database Software
Desktop Managers/Organizers and Personal Information Managers
Sales, Telemarketing Programs
Text-Based Programs
Reading Up On Software
Personal Computer Options--MAC
Client/Customer, Sales, Telemarketing Management
Databases, Desktop Organizers and Other Information Managers
Record Keeping Systems
Manual Record Keeping Systems
Record Keeping Software--IBM
Record Keeping Software--Mac
Other Record Keeping

CHAPTER 9 FOR COLLECTORS ONLY: HOW, WHEN AND WHAT TO SAVE

Art Work, Blueprints and Photographic Materials
Artist and Document Storage Files
For Flat Storage
For Rolled Storage
Photographic Storage--Slides and Prints

Files and Records

Literature organizers

CHAPTER 10 WORK SPACE BASICS ENHANCING YOUR PHYSICAL WORKING ENVIRONMENT

Furniture and Equipment
Accessories and Supplies
Books and Other Reading

CHAPTER 11 THE TRAVELING OFFICE: HOW TO TRAVEL SMOOTHLY AND GET THINGS DONE

Personal Accessories
Portable Office Products
Books

BIBLIOGRAPHY

CareerTracking: 26 Success Shortcuts to the Top by Jimmy Calano and Jeff Salzman (New York: Simon and Schuster, 1988). The authors have summarized the best of what they've read, heard, seen and experienced on the subject of career success. The book is easy to read, easy to use and will save you time on your way to the top and *at* the top, as well. Hardback, $15.95

Cellular Telephones: A Layman's Guide by Stuart Crump, Jr. (Blue Ridge Summit, PA: Tab Books Inc., 1985) Here's a useful book to get when you're ready to buy a cellular phone.

Executive Essentials: The One Guide to What Every Rising Business Person Should Know by Mitchell Posner (New York: Avon, 1982). This book has several excellent chapters on travel tips. Paper, $8.95

Feeling Good: The New Mood Therapy by David D. Burns, M.D. (New York: New American Library, 1980). If negativity, criticism, procrastination, perfectionism, mood swings or depression are frequent or even occasional companions, effective time management will be next to impossible. This is a breakthrough book that offers clinically tested, practical solutions presented in an inspiring, compassionate style. It's easy to read and use. Paperback, $4.95

Getting Organized: The Easy Way to Put Your Life in Order by Stephanie Winston (New York: Warner Books, 1978). Here's a great book to help you better manage personal areas of your life from financial planning to meal planning. Learn also to maximize storage space, organize your kitchen, run a household and even teach your child to organize. Paperback, $5.95

Getting Things Done by Edwin Bliss (New York: Bantam Books, 1976). Literally the ABCs of time management, Bliss takes time management and organization topics such as "Deadlines," "Goals" and "Priorities," puts them in alphabetical order and succinctly provides practical and entertaining gems of wisdom. Paperback, $3.50

Hard Disk Management for the Macintosh by Nancy Andrews (New York: Bantam Books, 1987) is easy to read and understand. The book comes with three utilities, LOCKIT, WHEREIS and BACKUP. $34.95, paper

Hard Disk Management in the PC and MS-DOS Environment by Thomas Sheldon (New York: Mc-Graw-Hill, 1987). This book expands upon the organizational areas covered in Chapter 5. You'll learn more about DOS commands, tree-structured directories, menus, batch files, data protection strategies and organizing a hard disk to suit your needs. Paperback, $24.95

How to Create Balance at Work, at Home, in Your Life by Bee Epstein, Ph.D. is a dynamic, six-cassette program for working women. Epstein herself is a model of balance and success. This is a great program to enhance your life. Available from Adams-Hall Publishing, PO Box 491002, Los Angeles, CA 90049. $49

How to File published by Esselte Pendaflex Corp., Clinton Rd., Garden City, NY 11530. A great little booklet with lots of photos, examples and information about filing tips, supplies and systems. 800/368-2077 or 516/741-3200. Paper. $4.95

How to Get Control of Your Time and Your Life by Alan Lakein (New York: Signet, 1973). This classic time management book is particularly useful in helping you sort out your life goals. Paperback, $2.50

How to Get Organized When You Don't Have the Time by Stephanie Culp (Cincinnati: Writer's Digest Books, 1986). Culp makes time management and getting organized *fun.* In her down-to-earth, humorous style, Culp cuts through with plenty of practical ideas to organize the time and space in your personal life. Paperback. $9.95

Inside OS-2 by Gordon Letwin (Bellevue: Microsoft Press, 1988). If you have IBM's PS-2 computer, you'll need to learn about the next generation of operating system software. OS-2 picks up where DOS leaves off. Because the author helped design OS-2 software, he'll help you understand it–from the inside out. Paperback, $19.95

MacGuide is a terrific quarterly guide/magazine that features reviews and listings of more than 3,000 Macintosh products. The guide is very well organized with helpful numerical ratings, thorough reviews, excellent feature articles. This is a user friendly publication that goes out of its way to help the reader.
$4.95 for one issue; $14.85 for a one year subscription (four issues)
MacGuide Magazine
818 17th Street, Suite 210
Denver, CO 80202
303/825-8166

The Macintosh Buyer's Guide is an excellent resource for learning about software and hardware for the Mac. $20, newsstand price for one year; $14, subscription price for new subscribers.
Redgate Communications Corp.
Attn: Circulation Dept.
660 Beachland Blvd.
Vero Beach, FL 32963-1794
800/262-3012

Macintosh Hard Disk Management by Charles Rubin and Bencion Calica (Indianapolis: Hayden Books, 1988) is superb. Rubin and Bencion write clearly and the book has many helpful techniques, illustrations, examples and resources. $19.95, paper

Macintosh Plus, Macintosh SE and **Macintosh II manuals** are filled with excellent illustrations, examples and shortcuts. Sure the Mac is friendly enough so you don't *have* to read the manual, but you'll

really benefit from doing so. At the very least, take a peek at the Contents pages and read selected chapters.
Apple Computer, Inc.
20525 Mariani Avenue
Cupertino, CA 95014
408/996-1010

MacUser is an excellent Macintosh monthly magazine that provides the latest in Macintosh software, peripherals and usage. This is a very practical, hands-on publication. $3.95 per newsstand copy; $19.97 for a one-year subscription (12 issues)
MacUser
PO Box 52461
Boulder, CO 80321-2461
415/378-5600

Macworld is a wonderful monthly magazine with top quality design and well-written columns and feature articles. $30 for a one-year subscription (12 issues)
PCW Communications, Inc.
501 Second St.
San Francisco, CA 94107
800/525-0643: in Colorado, 303/447-9330

MicroAge Quarterly is a quarterly magazine for business users of microcomputers. It focuses on problem-solving articles on office automation and computer applications oriented toward small and medium size businesses. For information contact:
MicroAge Computer Stores, Inc.
Box 1920
Tempe, AZ 85281
602/968-3168

Newstrack Executive Tape Service, Box 1178, Englewood, CO 80150, 303/778-1692 or 800/525-8389. Weekly tape cassette series that summarizes major newspaper and magazine articles related to business.

Nightingale-Conant business and motivational audiocassettes. An excellent selection of tape programs to get and keep you inspired to and from work. 800/323-5552.

9 to 5 Fact Sheets contain valuable information about good office design particularly for computer workers. Of particularly interest are: "The 9 to 5 Office Design Kit: How to Design the Work Area to Fit You," "9 to 5's Consumer Guide to Office Computers" and "Office Design for Video Display Terminals." Each fact sheet is $3 a piece or $15 for a complete set of eight fact sheets. **Do It At Your Desk** is a humorous book that helps computer users work out daily aches and pains through simple exercises at the desk. It also includes advice on choosing chairs and working at computer terminals. $2.95 To get the fact sheets and the book and to get a complete listing of other work-related books and reports contact:
9 to 5 National Association of Working Women
614 Superior Ave. NW
Cleveland, OH 44113
216/566-9308

Office At Home: Everything You need to Know to Work Efficiently and Happily From Home by Robert Scott (New York: Charles Scribner's Sons, 1985) provides useful tips on planning office space and selecting equipment, whether or not your office is in your home. Paperback, $9.95

The Office Book by Judy Graf Klein (New York: Facts on File, 1982) is a beautiful, coffee table book that provides full color photos of small and large office spaces. If aesthetics and good, clean design are important to you, this book will give you some good ideas. Hardback, $40

Office Furniture by Susan Szenasy (New York: Facts on File, 1985) is a useful guide to the many factors in choosing furniture: aesthetics, comfort, function, strength, size and versatility. Hardback, $19.95 and paperback, $12.95

Organize Yourself! by Ronni Eisenberg (New York: Macmillan Publishing Company, 1986). Eisenberg's book is an easy-to-read, easy-to-use guide to organizing your personal life. Paperback, $7.95

The Organized Executive: New Ways to Manage Time, Paper and People by Stephanie Winston (New York: Warner Books, 1985). Not just for the executive, this classic provides nuts 'n bolts techniques to streamline your work flow and office. Paperback, $7.95

PC Computing, America's Computing Magazine is a monthly magazine on personal computing aimed more at active PC users than experts. It provides shortcuts and secrets designed to increase productivity.
Ziff-Davis Publishing Co.
80 Blanchard Rd.
Burlington, MA 01803
617/221-0300

PC Magazine, The Independent Guide to IBM-standard Personal Computing, comes out every two weeks and features in-depth product reviews and industry trends. The "Editor's Choice" designation helps you quickly spot winning products and programs. A one-year subscription (22 issues) costs $39.97--for subscription information contact:
PC Magazine
PO Box 54093
Boulder, CO 80322
303/447-9330

PC World is a monthly that is well-designed and easy-to-read. There are plenty of reviews and features. $29.90 for one year.
PCW Communications, Inc.
501 Second St.
San Francisco, CA 94107
415/243-0500

Personal Computing, The Personal Systems Magazine, is a monthly magazine for professionals and managers who use personal computers as a tool in day-to-day business tasks. *Personal Computing* details hands-on computing tips and techniques, personal computing management strategies, product trends and manufacturer profiles and product analyses. $18 for one year.
VNU Business Publications, Inc.
Ten Holland Drive
Hasbrouck Heights, NJ 07604
800/423-1780, in Florida, 800/858-0095

Phone Power by George Walther (New York: Berkley Books, 1986). A great book to teach you just about everything when it comes to the telephone. Paperback, $3.50

The Portable Office by Jefferson Bates and Stuart Crump, Jr. (Washington, D.C.: Acropolis Books Ltd., 1987). This book is loaded with information and resources on the latest technological tips and tools that are particularly useful for business travelers. Here's a useful guide to laptop computers, cellular telephones, electronic mail, on-line services, dictation machines, not to mention some great organization and travel tips. Hard cover, $16.95

Private and Executive Offices by Susan Szenasy (New York: Facts on File, 1985) is for people who have the luxury of a private office or at least have an important say in their office or company. This book shows how to make the most of personal office space and aesthetics and how to make an office reflect the profession and personal taste of its occupant. Hardback, $19.95, paperback, $12.95.

The Psychology of Achievement by Brian Tracy is a six-cassette program that distills the key ingredients of high achievement. Brian Tracy presents proven, practical methods and techniques that high achievers regularly use in their lives and careers. Available from Brian Tracy Learning Systems, 462 Stevens Avenue, Suite 202, Solana Beach, CA 92075-2065, 800/542-4252 (outside California), 619/481-2977 (inside California). $55

Public Domain Software, Untapped Resources for the Business User, by Rusel DeMaria and George R. Fontaine, is a good book if you're all tapped out in terms of computer expenditures. In this book you'll discover hundreds of free or low-cost programs that rival the commercial programs. You will, however, need a modem to download these programs. $19.95
M&T Publishing Inc.
Redwood City, CA

Records Management Handbook with Retention Schedules. Fellowes Manufacturing Co. 1789 Norwood Ave., Itasca, IL 60143, 312/893-1600. While geared for large office filing systems, this booklet provides useful records retention/purging information applicable to smaller systems. Free.

Running MS-DOS: The Microsoft Guide to Getting the Most Out of the Standard Operating System for the IBM PC and 50 Other Personal Computers by Van Wolverton (Bellevue: Microsoft Press, 1988). This book is considered the definitive source on MS-DOS. It's highly readable, with excellent illustrations. The well-organized chapters, table of contents and descriptive index make this book a handy reference source, as well. Paperback, $19.95

Sacra Blue is the monthly newsletter/magazine for the Sacramento PC Users Group, Inc., one of the largest computer clubs in the U.S. To get a subscription, you pay $25 to join the group.
Sacramento PC Users Group, Inc.
Attn: Membership Director
PO Box 685
Citrus Heights, CA 95611-0685

Sunset Home Offices & Workspaces (Menlo Park, California: Lane Publishing Co., 1986) is loaded with ideas, illustrations and full color photos to help you design and equip an efficient work area. The book includes a variety of innovative storage options and design solutions. There are also ideas on computerized work spaces. Paperback, $6.95

The Superwoman Syndrome by Marjorie Hansen Shaevitz (New York: Warner Books, 1984). This wonderful book is for women who want more balance and control in their life. Paperback. $3.95.

Taming the Paper Tiger: Organizing the Paper in Your Life by Barbara Hemphill (New York: Dodd, Mead & Company, 1988). This is a delightful, easy-to-read guide with charming illustrations and many useful tips and techniques. Available through Barbara Hemphill Associates, 2000 Pennsylvania Ave., N.W., Ste. 171, Washington, D.C. 20006, 202/387-8007. Paperback, $9.95

What It Takes: Good News From 100 of America's Top Professional and Business Women by Lee Gardenswartz and Anita Rowe (New York: Doubleday, 1987). An inspiring work, this book shows how women at the top arrange their lives to achieve their goals and how you can assess your own aptitudes for success. Hardback, $16.95

Working From Home: Everything You Need to Know About Living and Working Under the Same Roof by Paul and Sarah Edwards (Los Angeles: Jeremy P. Tarcher, 1985). The Edwards put together a power-packed sourcebook that provides many time- and energy-saving shortcuts for the small entrepreneur or anyone who works at home. Paperback, $11.95

Working Smart: How to Accomplish More in Half the Time by Michael LeBoeuf (New York: Warner Books, 1980). This classic continues to sell strong and with good reason: this is a must-read book that hits the core of essential work habits you need to develop on the job. Paperback. $3.95.

INDEX

A

Abbot Office Systems, 17, 213, 231
Accessibility, 50-51, 285
Accountants, 71, 189, 229
Agenda, 220, 238
Airfare Discount Bulletin, 310
American Computer Supply, 296
Ampad quadrille/graph pads, 212
ArtFile, 237
Artists, 256-63
ASAP-10 Call Director, 40
Attorneys/legal, 71, 183, 185, 187, 227, 232, 244-45

B

Back-It, 167
Backup, computer, 160-170
    devices, 160, 163-70, 173-75
    macro, 160
    routine, 160-62
    types, 162-163
    utility programs, 164, 167-168
Baumgarten
    Arrow Klips, 60-61
    Plastiklips, 60-61
Benefits, 11, 37
Berger, Duane, 304-05
Bernoulli Box, 166, 173
Berra, Yogi, 5
Biotec furniture, 280-84, 295-96
Bliss, Edward, 14, 19, 45
Boards
    action board, 206-07
    magnetic, 206
    scheduling, 206
    visual control, 17, 205
    write-on-wipe-off, 17
Boorum (*See* Esselte Pendaflex)
Bravard, Greg, 222
Burns, David, 44
Business and Institutional Furniture Co., 297
Business Filevision, 243
Business Finance Forms, 109
Butler, Bill, 57, 255, 302-03, 309-13, 316, 318, 320

C

Caddylak Systems, 17, 23, 41, 231
  Activity/Task Worksheet, 189, 191
Calano, Jimmy, 44
Calendars, 38-39
Calica, Bencion, 140-41, 153
Cardfiler Plus, 215
Cardwear Hardware, 215-16, 245
Career Tracking, 44
C.A.T., 243
Cat-Mac, 150
Cellular Telephones: A Layman's Guide, 325
Charts (*See also* Project management, Work/Project Management), 188, 190, 201, 205-07, 231-33
  wall, 17, 205-7, 212-13
Checklists, 188, 190, 198-99, 317
C-Line, 62
Clips, 59-61
Clower, Beverly, 92, 95
CMS Software, 239
Code-A-Phone 3530, 40, 308
Collator (*See* Evans Collator)
Collectors, 250
Color Coding, 60-63, 91-92, 159, 206
Comcor, 297
Communitech, 41
Computer accessories, 289-90
Computer file maintenance (*See also* Backup, IBM personal computer files, Macintosh computer files) 156-160
  data access/recovery, 152-53, 171-73, 175
  directories, printed, 157, 159
  diskettes, quality, 159-60
  floppy organization, 158-160
  hard disk, 156, 158
  hard disk maintenance utilities, 170-71, 176
  optimize, 158
  organizational utilities, 170-73, 175-176
Concurrent DOS, 126
Congressional Toolkit, 237
Copyholders, 74, 77
Copy II, 173
CPA Tickler, 229
CPM, 201, 208-10
Crandall, Derrick, 96, 303-04, 309-10, 312, 318-19
Crawford Slip Method, 215, 218
Crump, Stuart, 308, 324-25
Cubit, 170
Cue Pager, 41
Culp, Stephanie, 45

D

Dac-Easy Base, 237
Danish Bookbag, 320
DataCare, 167
Day Runner, 17, 19, 29, 41, 231
  Cardfiler Plus, 215, 217
  Contacts form, 189, 192
  daily planning form, 29
  Express-it, 305-06
  Meeting form, 189, 192
  Message page, 305-06
Day-Timers, 16-17, 20-21, 24-25, 32-33, 41, 201, 208-10, 231
Delegation, 36-37
  reverse delegation, 37
  system and, 178
Design Tech's CarFinder, 320
Desk, 47-79
  accessibility, 50-51
  accessories, 61-79
  clearing a path, 49
  files, 64-70
  productivity and, 48
  work space/surface, 49, 50, 52
Deskview, 126
Devoke Data Products, 297
Dictaphone Travel Master LX, 320
Dictation (*See* Traveling)
Direct Access, 125
Discard, 87
Discipline, 27-28
Diskette Manager II, 123
Disk Express, 176
DiskFit, 174

Disk Optimizer, 170
DiskQuick, 150
Disk Ranger, 150
Disk Technician, 170
DiskTools Plus, 150
Disktop, 150
DOS2ools, 124
DoubleDOS, 126
DS Backup, 167

E

Edwards, Paul and Sarah, 46, 299
Eisenberg, Ronni, 45
Eldon, 62,
  Add-A-File, 64
  Catch'all/Mini Catch'll, 70
  Diagonal Files, 64, 66
  The Folder, 65, 67
  The Holder, 65, 68
  Hot Files and Pockets, 72-73
  Hot Rack, 69
  letter trays, Image 1500 and Reflection 2000, 75
  magazine files/holders, 286
  Stackable CRT Tray, 75
  Step-Up Step Rack, 64-65
  Stationery Tray, 70-71
  Versatilt, 71-72
Ergonomics, 283-85
Esselte Pendaflex
  Boorum Prizm Desktop File Organizer, 69-70
  Boorum Wireworks Catalog Rack, 74, 76
  Boorum Wireworks FileAll, 55
  Boorum Wireworks Sort-R-Rack, 55
  Boorum Wireworks Steprack, 64, 66
  magazine files/holders, 286
  Oxford Copyholders, 77
  Oxford DecoFile, 265-66
  Oxford DecoFlex, 56
  Oxford DecoRack, 74, 76
  Oxford desk file/sorter, 225
  Oxford File-It Portable File Box, 323
  Oxford Manila File Jackets, 103-04
  Oxford Tote-File, 323-24
  Pendaflex Colored Plastic Windows, 108
  Pendaflex Follow-up Tabs, 182-83, 226
  Pendaflex Hanging Box File, 100-01
  Pendaflex Hanging File Jacket, 100-101
  Pendaflex Hanging Folders, 98-99
  Pendaflex Hanging Partition Folders, 103
  Pendaflex Insertable Tabs, 108
  Pendaflex Interior Folders, 100-01
  Pendaflex Links and Stop Clamps, 108-09
  Pendaflex Printed Label Inserts, 108, 182
  Pendaflex Snap-On Tabs, 108
Epstein, Bee, 45
Eureka!, 152
Evans Collator, 71
Executive Essentials, 325
Executive Scan Card Organizer, 235
Expense Record, 221-23, 245

F

Fastback Mac, 174
Fastback Plus, 168
Feeling Good, 44
Fellowes
  Art-Folio, 256
  Bankers Boxes, 252, 264-65, 321
  Econo/Stor 40 Diskette Filing Tray, 159
  Literature Organizer, 267
  Literature Sorter, 267
  Magazine File, 265-66, 286
  Neat Ideas Active Files, 64, 67
  Neat Ideas Desk Top Sorter, 72, 74
  Neat Ideas Folder Files, 65, 68
  Neat Ideas Folder Holder, 65, 69
  Neat Ideas Personal File, 321-22
  Neat Ideas Portable File, 321-22
  Portable Storage Case, 256, 258
  Premier Line Mail/Literature Center, 267

Premier Line Visible Folder Files, 64, 67
Roll/Stor Files, 259, 262
Roll/Stor Stands, 259, 261
File Facility (Filefac), 171
FileMaker Plus, 243
File-N-Shuttle, 322
File Pal II, 322
Files, 81-110
accordion, 181
active and inactive, 83, 85-87, 94
computer, 111-176
desk, 64-70, 181-82, 225
expanding, 105, 107
key to, 83, 96
magazine, 265, 266, 286
step, 64-66
wall mount, 72
Filing, 81-110
file chart, 89-91
file index, 95
maintenance, 95-98
out guide, 95, 97
phobias, 82-83
supplies, 91, 98-110
system, creating a, 83-98
Filofax, 41-42
Fixed Disk Organizer (FIDO), 119
Folders
box bottom, 100
box file, 101
classification, 103
file jacket, 100-01, 103-04
file pocket, 103, 105
hanging file, 91, 98-100, 103
hanging partition, 103
interior, 91
materials, 107
partition, 103
reinforced, 101-02
wallet, expanding, 104-06
with fasteners, 102
Follow-up (*See* Tickler systems, Work/Project management)
For Comment, 235
Forms, 188-204, 231-233
FormsFile, 231-32
FormWorx, 232
Furniture and equipment, 280-91, 295-299
ergonomics, 283-85
modular furniture, 280-81

G

Gambrell, Don, 190
Gantt chart, 201, 207
Gardenswartz, Lee, 46
Genoa's Galaxy 3260, 168
Getting Organized, 45
Getting Things Done, 14, 45
Global Business Furniture, 296
Global Computer Supplies, 297
Goals, 2, 5-9, 19
decisions and, 52
goals work sheet, 7, 14
planning and, 19
priorities and, 14
targeting, 5-6
three questions, 6-7
written, 8
Gofer, 171
GrandView, 238
Guentner, Steve, 189

H

Habits, 3, 331
Hard Disk Backup, 174
Hard Disk Management in the PC and MS-DOS Environment, 128
Hard Disk Management for the Macintosh, 153
Harding, Alan, 269-70
Hemphill, Barbara, 46, 305
HFS Backup, 174
HFS Locator Plus, 152
Hierarchical File System (HFS), 129-35, 139-41
Hold Everything, 62
Holland, Nadia, 87
Homebase, 186, 229

How to Create Balance At Work, At Home, in Your Life, 45
How to File, 98
How to Get Control of Your Time and Your Life, 45
How to Get Organized When You Don't Have the Time, 45
HyperCard, 243
HyperEASY, 244

I

IBM personal computer files, 111-128
  AUTOEXEC.BAT, 122
  batch file, 121-22
  directories, tree-structured, 112-116
  DOS, 113-14, 120-123
  file management utilities, 123-34
  menu, 119, 125
  multitasking, 120, 125-26
  path name, 116
  PROMPT PG, 122
  root directory, 112-114
  subdirectories, 114-119
Idealiner, 244
Index cards, 88
Information management (*See also* Record keeping systems)
  Crawford Slip Method, 215, 218, 235
  databases, computerized, 218-19, 236-38, 243-45
  desktop managers/organizers, 219, 238, 243-45
  notebooks and accessories, 213-15
  personal information managers, 220-221, 243-45
  text-based programs, 220, 241-42
Inmac, 297
Inside MS-DOS, 127
IN.SIGHT, 172
Instant Business Forms Book, 232
Instaplan, 233
Insurance, 239
Intelligent Backup, 168
Independent Writers of So. Calif. (IWOSC), 201, 205
IZE, 241

J

Jarrells, Greg, 312-13
Johnson, Kathryn, 304

K

KeepTrack Plus, 124
Kirkland, George, 304
Klein, Calvin, 36
Klein, Judy Graf, 299
Kovacs, Betsy, 301-02, 308, 315, 319,

L

Labels
  file folder, 91-94
  protectors, 109
Labelon
  Cellugraf Plastic Signals, 63
  Graffco Nu-Vise Metal Signals, 63
  Owl Clips, 59
  Triumph Clamps, 60
Lakein, Alan, 45
Law Publications
  CaseGuard, 105
  Expense Record, 221-23, 245
  Tickler Record System, 183-85
  Time Record, 221-22, 245
Lawrence, Sharon, 253-54
LeBoeuf, Michael, 46
Lewis, Peter H., 159
Light Impressions, 263
  Nega*Guard System, 263-64
  PrintFile, 263-64
LIST, 172
Lists
  daily to-do, 19, 26-27
  master, 15-17
Little Black Book, 246, 321

M

Mace Utilities, 171
MacGuide, 153
Macintosh Buyer's Guide, 154
Macintosh computer files
  Apple menu, 142-43
  Control Panel, 142
  data access/recovery, 152-53

desk accessories, 142-43
desktop, 135, 137-38, 141-42
desktop and file management utilities, 150-52
Edit menu, 142, 144-45
Finder, 130-31, 140, 142-43
File menu, 142-44
Find File, 141-42
folders, 133-41
Font/DA Mover, 143
Hierarchical File System, 129-35, 139-41
names, 133-35
nested folders, 131-33,
organizing applications, 135-40
root directory, 131
Scrapbook, 142-43
Special menu, 142, 146-148
standard file dialog box, 131, 134
System files/folder, 130, 143
System Software Update, 130
View menu, 142, 145-49
window, disk, 131-32, 135-37, 139
Macintosh Hard Disk Management, 140-41, 153
Macintosh Plus, Macintosh SE and *Macintosh II* manuals, 153
MacInUse, 247
MacPherson Travel Services, 311
MacUser, 154
Macworld, 154
Magic Mirror, 172
Magid, Lawrence, 186
Magna Chart/Magna Visual, 212, 232
Market Master, 242
Maximizer, 239-40
Maynard's Maynstream 20, 169
McCormack, Mark, 9
Media-Flex Workstations, 296
Medical, 227, 232
Melton, Coleen, 255
Memindex, 42
The Commuter, 322-23
Desk Planning Guide, 42
File-N-Shuttle, 322
Memofile, 226
Pocket Planning Guide, 42
The Portable Desk, 322-23
Memogenda, 17, 27, 43
Memory Control Technology Corp., 160
Memory Lane, 172
Merge letter, 190, 200
Metro, 186, 229-30
Meyer-Poppe, 36, 225
MicroAge Quarterly, 127
Microsoft Project, 233
Mind map, 190, 200
Misco Computer Supplies and Accessories, 297-98
Moore Business Products, 290, 298
Moore Computer Supplies & Forms Catalog, 298
MORE, 244
Motorola Spirit, 308
Mountain Computer Drive Cards, 167
Mountain FileSafe Series 7120, 169
myDiskLabeler, 151

N

National Business Furniture, 296
National Satellite Pager, 41
Neumade Products Corp. slide cabinets, 263
Newstrack Executive Tape Service, 45, 302
New York Times, 159
Nightingale-Conant, 45
9 to 5, 298-99
Norton Commander, 124
Norton Utilities, 171
Notebooks, 213-15
anecdote, 214
business card, 214
prospect, 181
Nowak, Judy, 185
The #1 Personal Management System, 43

O

OAG Pocket Flight Guide, 310, 316
Office At Home, 299
The Office Book, 299

Office Furniture, 299
Ordesky, Maxine, 87
Organization, 1, 3,
  chart, 87-88
  personal organization system, 3, 9, 15, 39
Organize Yourself!, 45
Organizers
  drawer, 70
  literature, 72, 74, 265-67
  personal, 39-40, 41-43
Overdrive, 232
Oxford (*See* Esselte Pendaflex)

P

Paper/paperwork (*See also* Files, Desk)
  accessories, 59-79, 286-87
  CAYGO, 56
  daily paperwork system, 53-57
  decisions, 52-53, 56
  dump-it-on-desk syndrome, 58
  long-term, 58-59
  organizers, 55-56, 58-79, 246, 303-05
  time management tools and, 57
  traveling and, 303-06
Parkinson's Law, 26
Passport, 167
PC Computing, 127
PC-File:db, 237
PC Magazine, 127
PC Manager, 233-34
PC-MOS, 126
PC World, 127
Pendaflex (*See* Esselte Pendaflex)
Pentecost, Lloyd, 130
Perma Products
  Perma Pak, 264-65
  Vertical Roll Organizers, 259, 261
Personal computer files (*See* IBM computer files, Macintosh computer files, Computer file maintenance)
Personal Computing, 121, 127, 160
Personal Resource Systems, 17
  Personal Resource System, 22, 30-31, 43, 201-04
PERT chart, 201, 207-10
Phone Power, 35, 41, 307
Photographers, 263
Picture, whole, 15-17
  personal organization system, 15
PLAN-A-FLEX OFFICE DESIGNER, 274, 277, 298
Planmaster Information Control System, 235-36
Planner Pad, 43
Planning and prioritizing, 18-19, 26-27
  prime time, 18
Plantronics, 41, 288
Pocket Billing, 246
Pockets, 72
The Pocket Secretary, 321
Pop-Up DeskSet Plus, 186
The Portable Office, 324
Positively Organized, 1-2, 5, 10, 199, 327
Posner, Mitchell, 325
Post-its (*See* 3M)
Poynter, Dan, 214
PreCursor, 125
PrimeTime, 43, 187, 230
Priorities
  A, B, C priorities, 14, 19
  goals and, 14
Private and Executive Offices, 299
Procrastination, planned, 18
Pro-8 Client Timekeeping System, 247-48
Project Billing, 246
Project management
  charts, 201, 205-07, 212-13, 231-36
  planning forms, 17, 23-25, 188-89, 191, 201-04, 208-10, 212
  software, 207, 233-35
Proxemics, 278-79
The Psychology of Achievement, 28, 45-46
Public Domain Software, 242

Q

Q&A, 237-38
Q-DOSII, 124
QuickDEX, 244
QuickKeys and DialogKeys, 151

R

Reading, 57
Real estate, 232, 239-40
RecordHolderPlus, 244-45
Record keeping systems, 221-24, 245- 48
  Expense Record, 221-23, 245
  Safeguard bookkeeping system, 222, 224, 245
  Time Record, 221-22, 245
Records Management Handbook, 98
Redi-Tags, 61
Remarkable Products, 44, 233
  File Pal II, 322
  Re-Markable boards, 17, 26, 205-06, 233
Reminder System, 43, 187
The Reminder System Plus (Reminder Plus), 43, 188, 230
Riordan, Richard, 252
Robertson, Jeanne, 17
Rolodex, 288, 323
Rowe, Anita, 46
RPMS (Rep Profit Management System), 236, 240
Rubbermaid, 62, 286
  Design-a-Space portable office accessories, 323-26
  Quicksnap Vertical Filing System, 64
Rubin, Charles, 140-41, 153
Running MS-DOS, 121, 128

S

Sacra Blue, 128
Safco
  All Steel E-Z Stor Literature Organizer, 267
  Art Rack, 256, 257
  Corrugated Fiberboard Roll Files, 259, 261
  5-Drawer Corrugated Fiberboard Flat Files, 256, 258
  5-, 7-, and 10-Drawer Steel Flat Files, 258, 259
  Literature Organizer, 74
  Literature Shelf Trays, 72
  Mobile Roll Files, 259, 262
  Portable Art and Drawing Portfolio, 256, 257
  Tube-Stor KD Roll Files, 259, 262
  12-Drawer Budget Flat File, 256, 258
  Upright Roll Files, 259, 261
  Vertical Filing Systems, 258, 260
Safeguard
  bookkeeping system(s), 222, 224, 245-46
  General Reminder/Assignment System, 184, 225-26
SaleMaker, 240-41
Sales/telemarketing, 236, 239-41, 242
Salzman, Jeff, 44
San Diego State University memo, 190
Schlegel, Nancy, 254
Sentinel diskettes, 159
Shaevitz, Marjorie Hansen, 46
Sharp Dial Master Pocket Auto Phone Dialer, 321
The Sharper Image, 287
Sheet protectors, 214
Shoebox, 186, 230
Shoff, Dan, 130-31
Shopkeeper, 247
Sidekick, 245, 321
SideKick Plus, 238
Signals, 61, 63
Smart Alarms/Appointment Diary, 230- 31
SmartNotes, 241-42
SmartScrap & The Clipper, 151
Smead
  Chan-L-Slide Follow-Up Folder, 183
  Classification Folder, 104
  Desk File, 182, 225
  Flex-I-Vision Box Bottom Folder, 100
  Flex-I-Vision Hanging Folders, 98-99
  folders with fasteners, 102
  manila folder, 102
  Seal & View Label Protectors, 109
  steel frame for hanging file folders, 108
SoftBackup, 175
SoftwareCarousel, 126
Sonar, 153, 175
Sorters, desk, 181, 225
SpaceBase, 241
Space, work, 269-99

aesthetics, 291-92
air, 293-94
comfort and safety, 294
layout, 271-80
lighting, 294-95
location, 270-71
privacy, 295
SpinRite, 170
Splane, Rob, 190
Stanley Tools Plan-A-Flex Office Designer kit, 274, 277, 298
Stationery holders, 70-71
Sterling Step-Rack, 64-65
Suitcase, 143, 152
Suitor, Barbara and Jim, 308
Sunset Home Offices & Workspaces, 299
Superproject Plus, 234
The Superwoman Syndrome, 46
Surveys
accessibility, 51
quick survey, 10-12
work space location, 271
your files, 82
Swap, 172
Switcher Construction Kit, 152
SYCOM
label protectors, 109
That Reminds Me, 184, 227-28
Syncom Technologies diskettes, 159
Sysgen QIC-File, 169
Systems
delegation and, 178
details and, 178
filing, 83-98
personal organization, 3, 9
tools and habits, 9, 55
Szenasy, Susan, 299

T

Take Two, 168
Taming the Paper Tiger, 46, 305
Tecmar QIC-60H, 169
Tecmar QT-Mac40, 175
TeleMagic, 241
Telephone 29,
accessories, 287
action, 35
answering machine, 35, 40, 307
area and equipment, 34
communication, concise, 35
preparation and planning, 34
PTA, positive telephone attitude, 34
telephone team, 35
tools, 40-41
training, 35
traveling, 307-09
That Reminds Me, 184, 227-28
3M
Post-it Brand Correction and Cover-up Tape, 74-75, 79
Post-it Brand printed note pads, 74,78
Post-it Brand Removable File Folder Labels, 109-10
Post-it Brand Tape Flags, 61, 63
Post-its, 305
Scotch Brand Removable Magic Tape, 74-75, 79
Tickler Record System, 183-85, 229
Tickler systems, 178-89, 225-31
TIC-LA-DEX, 179-81, 229
Time Line, 234
Time management, 13-46
books and tapes, 44-46
challenges, 13
choices, 13
control, 13
decisions, 14
flexibility, 28
reading and, 57
tools and habits, using the right, 14
tools, best, 38, 40
tools and systems, 41-44
Time Manager, 187
Time Record, 221-22, 245
Timeslips III, 246-47
Tornado, 242
Tracy, Brian, 28, 45-46
Traveling
accessories, 320-21
checklists, 315-17

clothing and luggage, 313-15
dictation, 302
health and productivity, 317-20
portable office products, 321-26
preparations, 309-15
tips, 309-20
working and, 302-09
Trays
letter, 74-75
20th Century Plastics, 214, 246, 263
Tyler, Ben, 36

V

ViewPoint, 234
Viscott, David, 206-07, 331

W

Walther, George, 35, 307
Weiner, Allen, 35
Welch, Mike, 302-03, 309, 312-13, 319
Weniz, Marty, 187
What It Takes, 46
What They Don't Teach You at Harvard Business School, 9
WILLIAMS-SONOMA, 62
WilsonJones
desk file/sorter, 225
Color-Life Expanding Files, 105, 107
Color-Life Expanding Wallets, 106
ColorLife File Pockets, 105
Windows 386, 126
Winston, Stephanie, 44-45
Wolverton, Van, 121
Word Guide, 233
WordPerfect, 88, 161, 190, 236
Word processing, 88, 161, 190
Working From Home, 46, 299
Working Smart, 46
Work/Project Management, 233-48
forms, checklists, charts, 188-212, 231-33
project management software, 233-235
tickler systems, 178-188
The WorkManager System, 296

X

XTreePro, 125

Z

Zipagenda, 43
Zoo Keeper, 172
ZyINDEX Professional, 173